A Poem Containing History

A Poem Containing History

Textual Studies in *The Cantos*

EDITED BY LAWRENCE S. RAINEY

Ann Arbor
THE UNIVERSITY OF MICHIGAN PRESS

Previously unpublished material by Ezra Pound copyright © 1997 by
Mary de Rachewiltz and Omar Pound.
Copyright © by the University of Michigan 1997
All rights reserved
Published in the United States of America by
The University of Michigan Press
Manufactured in the United States of America
⊗ Printed on acid-free paper

2000   1999   1998   1997   4   3   2   1

A CIP catalog record for this book is available from the British Library.

Library of Congress Cataloging-in-Publication Data

A poem containing history : textual studies in The cantos / edited by
   Lawrence S. Rainey.
      p.   cm. — (Editorial theory and literary criticism)
   Includes bibliographical references.
   ISBN 0-472-10232-X
   1. Pound, Ezra, 1885–1972. Cantos—Criticism, Textual.
   I. Rainey, Lawrence S.   II. Series.
PS3531.082C2873   1996
811'.52—dc20   96-41212
                                                      CIP

Contents

Prospects

Preface

References to *The Cantos* of Ezra Pound are to the edition published by New Directions in New York, 1970 edition, eleventh printing, 1989, unless otherwise indicated. A specific canto is cited *in arabic numerals* (for the ease of readers who dislike the lengthy roman numerals more often used), in some cases followed by the page number within the canto. Thus a typical reference might be 8.54, for Canto 8, page 54. It should be noted that the "eleventh printing" is actually a new edition: it includes Cantos 72 and 73 for the first time within numerical sequence of all the cantos, and it deletes new lines that were added to the so-called tenth printing. The latter, published in 1986, was itself a new collected edition that (1) included Cantos 72 and 73 for the first time ever (placed as an appendix), incorporated a new fragment addressed to Olga Rudge, added new lines to "The Pisan Cantos," sported new illustrations on the title page and half title, and included a "Publisher's Note" explaining the illustrations.

Prior to assuming their "modern" form with *A Draft of XVI. Cantos* in 1925, thirteen of the first sixteen cantos were published in various versions, in some cases with different canto numbers. When these are under discussion, the canto number is given *in roman numerals*. The Malatesta Cantos, for example, were originally published in 1923 as Cantos IX–XII, but in their modern form are Cantos 8–11.

Ezra Pound's papers are conserved at the Beinecke Rare Book and Manuscript Library of Yale University in New Haven, Connecticut, where they are cataloged as YCAL Ms. 43 (i.e., Yale Collection of American Literature, Manuscript 43), sometimes popularly referred to as "the Ezra Pound archive." When authors are citing this collection in discussing unpublished letters or prepublication drafts and typescripts, no explicit reference is given in the text beyond a citation of the Box and Folder numbers, which appear in parentheses immediately following the quotation.

Another substantial collection of materials by Pound is held at the

Lilly Library of Indiana University in Bloomington, Indiana. The collection contains three groups of materials purchased at different dates, each having been cataloged as though it were a separate collection: Pound Manuscripts 1, Pound Manuscripts 2, and Pound Manuscripts 3. Reference is abbreviated to "Lilly Library, PM1," and so on for each group.

For the evolution of the text of *The Cantos,* two other collections are especially important. One consists of the files pertaining to Pound and *The Cantos* which are held at the New York office of New Directions Publishing Corporation, hereafter cited as New Directions files, New York. The other consists of analogous files in the possession of James Laughlin III, in Norfolk, Connecticut, hereafter cited as New Directions files, Norfolk. The authors and the editor wish to express their gratitude to Mr. Laughlin for his generosity in making these files accessible to interested scholars over the course of many years.

Several of the essays included in this volume were presented in an earlier form at the conference "A Poem Including History: *The Cantos* of Ezra Pound," held at the Whitney Humanities Center of Yale University, 27–28 October 1989. I am grateful to Professor Peter Brooks, who was then Director of the Center, for hosting the conference, and to the Office of the President of Yale University for help in defraying some of its costs. Above all I wish to express my genuine thanks to the conference speakers for their collaboration.

Acknowledgments

Grateful acknowledgment is given to New Directions Publishing Corporation and Faber & Faber Ltd. for permission to quote from the following copyrighted works of Ezra Pound.

A LUME SPENTO (Copyright © 1965 by Ezra Pound)
ABC OF READING (All rights reserved)
THE CANTOS (Copyright © 1934, 1937, 1940, 1948, 1956, 1959, 1962, 1963, 1966, and 1968 by Ezra Pound)
THE CLASSIC NOH THEATRE OF JAPAN (Copyright © 1959 by New Directions Publishing Corporation)
COLLECTED EARLY POEMS (Copyright © 1976 by the Trustees of the Ezra Pound Literary Property Trust)
CONFUCIUS: The Great Digest, The Unwobbling Pivot, The Analects (Copyright © 1947, 1950 by Ezra Pound)
CONFUCIUS TO CUMMINGS (Copyright © 1964 by New Directions)

Correspondence

EZRA POUND AND DOROTHY SHAKESPEAR (Copyright © 1976, 1984 by the Trustees of the Ezra Pound Literary Property Trust)
POUND/FORD (Copyright © 1971, 1972, 1973, 1982 by the Trustees of the Ezra Pound Literary Property Trust)
POUND/JOYCE (Copyright © 1967 by Ezra Pound)
POUND/LEWIS (Copyright © 1985 by the Trustees of the Ezra Pound Literary Property Trust)
POUND/THE LITTLE REVIEW (Copyright © 1988 by the Trustees of the Ezra Pound Literary Property Trust)

1

Introduction

Lawrence S. Rainey

Many critics have argued that *The Cantos* are the most important experiment of Anglo-American literary modernism, while poets such as Eliot, Williams, Olson, Zukofsky, Davie, and others have repeatedly paid it the tribute of homage and imitation. Even general readers have come to evince a consistent interest in the work, almost as if resolved not to be daunted by its notorious difficulties. Every year they purchase some two thousand copies, a remarkable figure for a volume of notable length and complexity, even if much of their interest stems from a vein of curiosity about Pound's life that has become diffused within the general culture. (A new biography is almost an annual event now, along with another volume of previously unpublished correspondence.)[1] As for specialized scholarship, it apparently knows no bounds, with one scholar reportedly having written an essay of eighty pages devoted to the elucidation of a single line from *The Cantos*. The prospects for the future, depending on one's viewpoint, are either bright or horrifying. Yet the intense attention that has been lavished on Pound in recent years has not significantly altered our critical understanding of his life's work. We still know remarkably little about *The Cantos*, and of all the major works of Anglo-American modernism, it remains the most enigmatic.

If *The Cantos* remain central to literary and cultural debate about the twentieth century, it is not because they offer delicate passages of modernist pastoral, however endearing those have proved to general readers and scholars alike. Pound could always turn out a line that invoked quite conventional, even banal notions of beauty—his nymphs and gods cavorting among the olive groves are surely to be classed among these—and in his mature years he seems to have tossed them off with abandon, even disdainfully, sprinkling them like faux bijous amid the thorny thickets of historical documents and endless lists of worthy emperors from China. But these sporadic gestures could never disguise the poem's abiding preoccupations with history, its massively overdetermined effort to trace a cultural genealogy of the twentieth century, to locate in the recesses of private and public memory the resources for a utopian transformation of Western culture. These aims remained central to the poem throughout most of Pound's career, and however inadvertently, they also contributed much to shaping its ultimate form. Perhaps no poet, and perhaps no poem, has ever been so firmly welded to the realm of secular time, to the present as history *in statu nascendi,* and certainly no poet has ever found the consequences of such engagement so terrifying or so terrible. "An epic," Pound would write in a work of critical prose that was meant to serve as a vade mecum to *The Cantos,* "is a poem including history";[2] but the idea that this formula might turn into its opposite, a history including a poem, was one whose force Pound came to appreciate only when it was far too late, when the rickety edifice of fascist culture to which he had pledged himself had collapsed in ruins around him. What had once been contemporary events were now part of a past that was permanently irremediable, unredeemable: had the same fate engulfed his life's work? The question is explored repeatedly in the essays that follow.

Such claims may seem to conflate the poet's life and his art in ways that violate the separation of the two that was achieved by New Criticism and reinforced through the systemic paradigms of deconstruction, especially as articulated in its American form. It was a premise that Pound himself did not share. Placing a photograph of himself by Arnold Genthe as the frontispiece opposite the title page of *The Cantos,* he tacitly encouraged an iconic identification of author and book, life and work. That identification, in turn, can be read as a minor but telling variant of what Peter Bürger has defined as the principal impetus behind the project of the historical avant-garde, the impulse to reunite the domains of everyday life and art.[3] While Bürger's thesis obviously oversimplifies a historical development that was infinitely more complex, and while the interpretive sanctions issued by Pound (or any other author) are only a starting point to be integrated into an array of hermeneutic stratagems, their coincidence points to a feature essential to assessment of *The Cantos:* "it is an objective and reticent autobiography," remarked T. S. Eliot in 1919.[4]

When the earliest version of Cantos 1–3 was published in the autumn of 1917, Pound was not yet thirty-two years old; it would be fifty-five years later and several days after Pound's death when a "final" fragment of eight lines would be published that, in a slightly altered form, would stand as the poem's conclusion for the next thirteen years (from 1973 to 1986).[5] Since then a new "ending" has appeared in the final pages of *The Cantos*, and it is likely that still others will appear in the future. Yet the uncertainty that has surrounded the poem's ending has been only a single episode in a publishing odyssey that defies the imagination. To give a highly schematic account, a single canto or small group of cantos (two to four) was typically issued first in a magazine or journal, then integrated into a larger grouping of ten to twenty cantos, which was issued as an independent book. The scale of this program was immense: ultimately it embraced more than twenty-five journals located in seven different countries on three continents, while collected volumes were issued by publishing firms in Paris, London, New York, and Milan, each following distinctive editorial styles and conventions, each reaching out to a discrete audience. Consider only a few of the different readerships that were addressed at various times: mainstream readers of contemporary poetry during the late 1910s and early 1920s (in *Poetry* magazine and the *Dial*), wealthy collectors of rare books during the middle and late 1920s (the three deluxe and limited editions of 1925, 1928, and 1930), followers of Social Credit theory during the 1930s (in journals such as *Prosperity* and *New Democracy*), adherents of the Fascist Republic of Salò in 1945 (*La Marina Repubblicana*), a burgeoning audience of new students influenced by the New Criticism in the late 1940s and 1950s (the collected editions from 1948 through 1973), and even the readers of the *New Yorker*, that bastion of light journalism, in 1968. No reader, in actual practice, ever belonged to all these audiences, and in fact no reader other than Pound could ever have traced all the parts of *The Cantos* as they were progressively published. This complexity finds its reflex in a stark but simple fact: no library in the world, including the library that houses Pound's own papers, holds all the journals and volumes in which *The Cantos* were gradually issued.

The protracted publication history of *The Cantos* poses dilemmas that extend beyond the issue of which text should be considered "correct," or which might best reflect the intentions of its author, and ultimately they are inseparable from larger questions about how we understand the meanings of cultural works. One way to think of them is epitomized in the familiar image of the hermeneutic circle, the reciprocal relation of parts to wholes. Each time that a new canto or grouping of cantos appeared in print, it was offered as part of a whole that would eventually be realized. Canto 24, for example, would mean one thing if the total number of cantos were twenty-five: it would be the penultimate canto, presaging the climax to follow and glancing retrospectively at what had preceded. But as Canto 24 became part of a work that consisted now of fifty cantos, now a hundred, its meaning continued to shift by virtue of its changing place within an order that was always emerging, always in flux. The place and meaning of Canto 24 were now vested in a realm of historical and secular contingency, given over to human and social change.

Still, such neutral and essentially formal terms (parts, wholes) cannot adequately account for the relations epitomized in the successive publication of various cantos and groups of cantos, precisely because the parts that made up the whole were issued in specific sociomaterial forms, as individual cantos and particular collections of them were addressed to heterogeneous and incompatible audiences. The parts and the wholes, in other words, were never just neutral formal components, but always emplotted in specific social and institutional codes of meaning, in the contradictory network of usages that had constituted them historically. Canto 73 is a classic example. It was originally published in *La Marina Repubblicana* (15 February 1945), a newspaper for Italian sailors that was edited by Ubaldo degli Uberti, the undersecretary of the navy for the Social Republic of Italy (the puppet regime created by Nazi Germany after Mussolini's fall from power in the summer of 1943). Pound had first met degli Uberti in 1934, when they began to exchange letters as a result of Pound's efforts to explain the workings of fascism to Anglo-Americans. During the war years, when Pound was often in Rome, they became close friends, united by their mutual involvement in propaganda activities and their common cultural interests. When degli Uberti learned that Pound wished to publish a new installment of his life's work at a time when paper was in short supply, he offered the pages of the newspaper under his control. The outcome has been a source of ongoing debate.[6]

The story told in Canto 73 is relatively simple. The spirit of Cavalcanti meets the ghost of a young woman who has recently died, and he asks her to recount her death. She has deliberately led a platoon of Canadian infantry to a beach on the Adriatic coastline, where, a day earlier, her brother had planted some land mines. As a result of the explosion, she has been killed, together with all the soldiers. Cavalcanti then praises her heroism:

Glory of the fatherland!
       Glory! It is glorious
To die for the fatherland
         in Romagna!

[Six lines omitted.]

What a beautiful winter!
      In the north the fatherland is being reborn,
But what a young girl!
    Such good young girls,
        Such good lads,
           Who wear the black uniform [of fascism]!
                    (Canto 73)

As has recently been shown, the story that Pound recounts is a tawdry fabrication issued by propaganda authorities in the *Corriere della Sera* in occupied Milan.[7] Its call for "heroic" and suicidal resistance, in its original newspaper appearance in *La Marina Repubblicana,* is enclosed in a box that appears below a photograph (see fig. 1) of young Italian troops who are being inspected by their commander before being sent to the front. The men stand stiffly at attention in an orderly file before a row of menacing machine guns. The juxtaposition of the photograph and the text below turns the orderly lines of the poem below into analogues of the soldiers and machine guns; the lines of verse become weapons waiting to go into action, or soldiers offering their service for the climactic defense of the Fascist regime. Yet this version of Canto 73 was wholly unknown to almost all readers of *The Cantos.* Both Cantos 72 and 73 were omitted from every collected edition of *The Cantos* from 1948 to 1986.[8] Moreover, even when the two cantos were published separately in a deluxe and limited edition (130 copies) in 1983, they were integrated into an entirely different set of social and bibliographic codes. Now they were rarities to be prized by collectors, speculators in the rare-book market, and specialized libraries; the new volume was issued with pure white covers, its title printed in an elegant design with reversed embossing. What had once been weapons of war were now precious objets d'art, diamonds nestled in the white silk of a jewelry box.

    All this suggests the extraordinary range of purposes that were imbricated in each serial publication and each collection of cantos, ranging from

S..A..F.
MARINA

Italia chiama: va!

Donne d'Italia, un giorno una regina offrì il piccolo cerchio d'oro, pegno del suo regal amore, come supremo simbolo di dedizione e fede alla Patria in guerra, perchè nei nel sequissimo l'esempio. Poi, purtroppo, essa tradì la sua, la nostra fede!

Oggi è l'umile sposa di un soldato che non tradì nè tradirà giammai, che si offre alla Patria dolorante e ultipesa.

Vorrei che tutte le mamme di questo lembo libero di nostra terra, come falange forte ed invincibile, giurasse con me, sulla bandiera, per l'onore dell'Italia con nel cuore una viva fiamma di fede nella rivendicazione e nella vittoria. E non per impugnare la spada, che non si addice alla sublime missione della donna, ma per poter insieme compiere l'ascesa faticosa dei nostri morti sciutitianti al sole, raccogliendi ancora della voce sacra dei nostri morti, fermarci ad ogni calvario, ad ogni grutta, compiere la grande opera di redenzione, gridando

«al dissueti orecchi
ai pigri cuori, agli animi giacenti
Italia Italia! ».

Pater insieme seguire i nostri soldati, questo pugno d'eroi forti ed arditi salvati da Dio dalla marca crescente di fango e di vergogna agitata dai tradimento, perchè Essi un giorno non lontano nel loro sacrificio possano ridonare in ipente nostro al suo antico onore alla sua millenaria potenza, fatta di poesia, arte e lavoro.

Poterli seguire nella battaglia e nel riposo, con un sorriso e una parola di conforto onde essi possano ancora e sempre trovare la forza e il coraggio di combattere e di morire per la Patria.

E una guardare sprezzanti e con ciglio di rimprovero, o mamme, questa squbbra di fanciulle coraggiose, che sdegnando ogni basso e pettegola critica, sta impettita e in divisa di guerra, contando ai Canti le canzoni della Patria e che domani forse, cantando e sorridendo così potrà morire, ma seguitate col palpito più sincero del vostro cuore con la vostra preghiera e la vostra simpatia!

Dal Golgota la Madre Divina e il Divin Figliuolo ci mostrano attraverso i secoli, che col dolore e col sangue si conquista la gloria: ogni mestre giuro, badia in fronte il mio figliuolo e dico: Italia chiama, va!

Sandra Tucci

L'ALLEGRA BRIGATA

Siamo tutte in piedi!

C'è un appello per noi nel giornale *Italia Repubblicana*, e questo appello è della Commissaria dei Servizi Ausiliari Femminili. Veramente le sue parole sarebbero per le donne triestine e giuliane, ma noi donne di tutta Italia, che portiamo nell'animo tutto l'onore di Patria accumulatosi attraverso i nostri antenati in secoli di lotte e di vittorie, rispondiamo egualmente alle parole di Gemma de Calò, e non potendo chiedere l'onore della divisa, perchè già la indossiamo, intensifichiamo per essa l'ardore dei nostri sentimenti, il fervore delle opere nostre, visto che in ciò non esiste ne un massimo, nè una perfezione assoluta, visto che ogni eroismo supera i precedenti, ogni sacrificio nè richiama per necessità infiniti altri.

Abbiamo già fatto la nostra professione di fede, rinunciando a tutto ciò che è frivolo, pur mantenendo ben viva nel nostro animo e nelle opere nostre quella squisita femminilità che è sempre stata l'arma più bella e più efficace nelle deboli mani della donna. Abbiamo avuto la nostra la rivendicando l'onore di fregiarci dell'ancoretta, di affiancarci a questi arditi marinai d'ogni tempo, di essere le Ausiliarie della rinascente Marina, che vittima barbaramente colpita dal tradimento, ha proprio per questo maggior bisogno del sangue nuovo e ardente, di uomini pur costruire, di donne per educare.

I nostri occhi sentono il bisogno di posarsi ancora su quell'azzurro lembo di mare che è il vetusto solino, il nostro cuore sente il desiderio prepotente di difendere ed oltranza questo emblema che a della di alcuno dovrebbe essere mai mainato per mancanza di prore, la nostra forza morale l'aiuterà a risorgere perchè se entoli più bello e reco di nuove glorie il giorno in cui altri lamiere si riuniranno a formare nuovi ponti di comando da dove partiranno gli ordini a dirigere il traffico del Mediterraneo.

Noi, che abbiamo risposto soltanto all'appello del nostro cuore e del nostro amore di Patria, salutiamo quelle che oggi si decideranno a rompere finalmente le catene della vita placida e dell'attondismo, sicure di trovare in esse il nostro entusiasmo e la nostra decisione di vittoria. Cosa importa se oggi si soffre? Questa è la vita vera, perchè qua c'è l'onore.

Noi abbiamo avuto un moto di delusione, un lampo di alzan nello sguardo quando ci hanno detto che la nostra vita sarebbe momentaneamente svolta qua, in un ufficio, tra carta e inchiostro e abbiamo sinceramente invidiato la sorte di coloro che partivano con incarichi più periculosi ma più soddisfacenti, più consoni al moto di riscossa del nostro animo, all'impulso che ci ha spinto in queste fila. E il sacrificio di fare il nostro dovere contro le più forti aspirazioni di ognuna di noi è più dolce oggi che ne abbiamo compreso l'utilità. Lavoriamo e sbbellimmo, pronte a scattare al primo cenno, pronte a dare il cambio là dove si lotta con la morte per contendere a l'essa il maggior numero possibile di vittime, dove si può far sorridere la vita porgendo ad un soldato stanco il suo rancio e una parola dolce e animosa, dove si difende la vita costruendo e lavorando per dare al combattente armi e vveri, indumenti e assistenza morale. Siamo tutte in piedi, col pensiero fisso ad una meta e l'intelligenza vigile per raggiungerla, e per nessuna di noi saranno certamente i veri manoanisi!

... e dolente per sempre colui che da lungi, dal labbro d'altrui come uomo straniero che udrà, che ai suoi figli narrando un giorno dovrà dir sospirando: Io non c'era, che la santa, vittrice bandiera salutava quel dì non avrò!

Nicla Fiori

Il Comandante Borghese ispeziona un Reparto della Decima Mas pronto ad entrare in linea

(Luce · Scavo)

CANTO LXXIII : Cavalcanti - Corrispondenza Repubblicana

di Ezra Pound

E poi dormii
E svegliandomi nell'aer pazzo
Vidi e sentii,
E quel ch'io vidi mi pareva andar a cavallo
E sentii:
«A me non fa gioia
Che la mia stirpe muoia
infangata dalla vergogna
Governala dalla carogna
e spergiurata
Roosevelt, Churchill ed Eden
bastardi ed ebroucci
Lurchi e bugiardi tutti
e il popolo' spremuto in tutto
ed idiota!
Morto che fui a Sarzana
aspetto la diana
della riscossa.
Sono quel Guido che amasti
pel mio spirito altiero
E la chiarezza del mio intendimento.
De la Ciprigna sfera
Conobbi il fulgore
già cavalcante
(mai postiglione)
Per le vie del Borgo
detto altramente
La città dolente
(Firenze)
sempre divisa.
Gente stizzosa e leggiadra
che razza di schiavi!
Passai per Arimino
ed incontrai
uno spirito gagliardo
Che cantava come incantato
di gioia;
Era una contadinella
Un po' tozza ma bella
ch'aveva a braccio due tedeschi
E cantava,
cantava sempre
senz'aver bisogno
d'andar in cielo.
Aveva condotto i canadesi
su un campo di mine.
Dove era il Tempio
della bella Ixotta
Camminavano in quattro o in cinque
e io ero ghiotto
d'amore ancora,
malgrado i miei anni.
Così sono le ragazze
nella Romagna.

Veniam canadesi
a espugnar i todeschi!
A rosinar quel che rimaneva
della città di Rimini!
Domandano la strada
per la Via Emilia
a una ragazza,
una ragazza stupenda:
— Bé! Bé! soldati!
Quest'è la strada.
— Andiamo, andiamo
a Via Emilia!
Con loro proseguiva
i buchi per le mine,
là verso il mare.
Verso il mare la ragazza,
un po' tozza ma bella,
condusse la truppa.
Che brava pupa! che brava pupetta!
Le davo un vezzo
per puro amore,
che eroina!
Sfidava la morte,
Conquistò la sorte
peregrina.
Tozza un po' ma non troppo,
raggiunse lo scopo.
Che splendore!
All'inferno 'l nemico,
furon venti morti.
Morta la ragazza
fra quella canaglia.
Salvi i prigionieri.
Gagliardo lo spirito
della pupetta
Cantava, cantava
incantata di gioia,
Or ora per la strada
che va verso 'l mare.
Gloria della patria!
Gloria! gloria
Morir per la patria
nella Romagna!
Morti non morti son,
Io tornato son
dal terzo cielo
per veder la Romagna,
Per veder le montagne
la riscossa.
Che bell'inverno!
Nel settentrion rinasce la patria,
Ma che ragazze!
che ragazze,
che ragazzi,
portan il nero!

Pound's need to make money (as in the deluxe editions of the 1920s and later), to his impulse to proclaim his imaginary solidarity with Italy in the closing months of the war (as in Cantos 72 and 73), to a desire on the part of his publisher to secure copyright (as in *Drafts and Fragments*). Even this skeletal listing is misleading, insofar as it suggests that each publication event was dominated by a single goal. In reality, each was composed of numerous pertinent contexts and driven by conflicting imperatives: literary and stylistic, philosophical and ideological, financial and practical. Each also offered an occasion for establishing continuity with previous events, or for announcing change and transformation, or even for rereading earlier parts of *The Cantos*. Cantos 72 and 73, to cite a now familiar example, involve a radical rereading of the earlier Malatesta Cantos that fully assimilates them to Pound's crude confession of loyalty to the decaying Fascist regime, even though fascism had been little more than a curiosity for Pound when he had begun composing the Malatesta Cantos in June 1922.

If the material record of *The Cantos'* publication is overwhelming, as is also the complex of ideological and imperatives that informed it, the same is true for the numerous prepublication manuscripts, typescripts, and other documents that Pound gathered during the course of composing his long poem. Consider a single group of four cantos that he wrote over a span of eleven months in 1922 and 1923. For these Pound wrote more than sixty different drafts and draft fragments. Together with numerous reading notes and aides-mémoir, they comprise some seven hundred pages of documents. To accumulate these materials Pound visited thirteen different cities during the course of a three-month tour in Italy, at each city stopping in the local library or archive to consult historical documents from the fifteenth century. To assess his drafts, therefore, we must assess his notes, but to assess his notes we must identify the original document from which he was working. To be sure, these four cantos required an unusually large amount of work and should not be taken as a norm. Yet even a rough calculation (one might multiply the figures given above by thirty in order to estimate for 120 cantos) suggests a quantity of prepublication materials that is more than overwhelming, while the density of historical referencing and cross-referencing that it implies would require an annotational apparatus that defies imagination.

We know very little about all these prepublication documents. A plan to reproduce them in facsimile was proposed some years ago but has not gone forward. Nor is it clear that a facsimile edition, in itself, would greatly advance our knowledge. Unless the materials were dated (a laborious process) and placed in a coherent order that facilitated cross-referencing, the facsimile would be largely meaningless, however carefully reproduced. And yet without a systematic study of the prepublication documents, it is unimaginable that we could have a critical edition of *The Cantos,* or even an annotated variorum. These "technical" exigencies, in turn, are inseparable from a series of questions about institutional contexts: research funding, publication support, potential audiences, and so on. A critical edition of *The Cantos* is not very likely for the present or the immediate future, and for some time beyond as well. All of which raises a question about the essays that follow.

The essays gathered here are not preliminary steps toward a critical edition of *The Cantos.* They do not survey the manuscript materials for any single group of cantos, and they speculate only occasionally about editorial problems that would have to be confronted in a critical edition. They will prove disappointing to those who believe that textual scholarship consists solely of efforts to identify the correct or best reading of a given line, phrase, or work, for in only one case is a question of that sort even broached. They do, however, share a number of other features, which, though not systematically represented in any one essay, overlap with one another enough that we can legitimately identify salient points of intersection. All of them, for example, focus less on the text as a linguistic code or the author as the source of a unique and permanent truth that has been lodged within the work, and more on the conditions that shaped the work's production and transmission, on the historical usages that many agents (including the author) have made of the work-to-be as it crossed their paths. Pound inevitably occupies a prominent role in these discussions, some of which are overtly biographical in orientation, but his role is significantly altered: he is less an omniscient author, more a fallible reader and student, at times a consumer and interpreter of his own drafts, at times an entrepreneur and a publicist, or even a bewildered spectator who is relegated to the sidelines as major decisions about the published form of his work proceed with his limited participation. His activities are less Olympian, more conditioned by contingencies and occasions. And the very multiplicity of his roles, their complex and interactive character, tends to dissolve the fundamental opposition between creation and consumption, production and reception. Instead, the process of transmission looms large, shaping the materials that he locates, molding the uses that he makes of them, and inflecting his later attempts to reappropriate his own writings from earlier years. There are, in these essays, no pure ideas or forms that have an intrinsic significance apart from their appropriation by subjects, and Pound is only one subject among the many who are actively engaged in appropriating and misappropriating the very ideas and forms that he has helped to engender. The text, in other words, is confronted here in the contradictory network of utilizations, including Pound's own, that have constituted it historically.

One consequence of this approach might be characterized as a common tendency to impossibilize (it is an ungainly neologism, but a useful one here) interpretation, whether editorial or critical. Ronald Bush's essay on *The Pisan Cantos* and Peter Stoicheff's on *Drafts and Fragments* make only too clear the sheer impossibility of a definitive representation of the works that they consider. Instead, the essays invite us to contemplate an immense constellation of writings that are always in progress, always subject to revision, and always interacting with a host of agents, be it readers or publishers, booksellers or editors, naval undersecretaries or aspiring poets hoping to "freak something into print." That provisional character is apparent in the essays themselves. All of them tacitly invite revision in the light of new archival materials or reconceptualizations of our extant knowledge. None tries to present a definitive or final judgment about *The Cantos*. Our knowledge and our understanding are changing too rapidly at present to succumb to the easy allure of abstract coherence that has been gained at the cost of all connection with the reality purportedly being assessed. There is about these essays a refreshing note of modesty, and if one sometimes feels it has been achieved at the cost of neglecting important theoretical questions, one may also suspect that keeping closer to the ground may enable us to travel much further, at least at this point in time. Do the essays constitute a new movement, a new current within criticism? No one who lives at the end of the twentieth century can believe in such questions any more. Postmodernism, it is increasingly charged, may be little more than another example of the media's insatiable appetite for novelty; to abet it with further declarations of newness would be pointless.

The volume begins with two essays that offer synthetic surveys of Pound's engagement with philology and the material forms of his work. The first is Hugh Kenner's overview of the role that philology has played in shaping not just *The Cantos*, but Pound's approach to composition. Pound, after all, was a student of "Romance Philology" at the University of Pennsylvania, and the period of his intellectual training coincided with the last great flowering of the philological tradition, epitomized by the publication of the Oxford *New English Dictionary on Historical Principles* (1884–1928) or Emil Levy's eight-volume supplement to Raynouard's *Lexique Roman* (1885–1910). Modern philology is distinguished by two traits: its methodological emphasis on the individual word as its primary analytical unit; and its ongoing discovery of the oral/aural traditions informing poetry, from the Homeric epic to the Provençal lyric. What informed philology, in other words, was an unresolved tension between its method and its object of attention, between meaning and melody, *mortz el son,* a tension that one can also discern in Pound's approach to his poem. As Kenner remarks, "Part of his mind was at home with Emil Levy's assumptions [the semantics of individual words], but part of it with Homer's [the melodics of larger units]." The conflict shaped not only his compositional practice, but also his seemingly ad hoc approach to corrections suggested by scholars. Tracing the origins of seven significant variants in Pound's works, Kenner recounts the later efforts of scholars to suggest and often to effect changes in Pound's text, and he describes a series of corrections that Pound entered into Kenner's own copy of the 1948 collected edition. He urges that the best edition of *The Cantos* would be an annotated variorum, and by way of example he calls attention to Pound's decision to retain an apparently "superfluous quotation mark" in one passage, a decision that "acknowledges a chain of transmission" that produced it. Pound, in other words, was deeply aware that transmission (*motz*) was crucial in the constitution of his own work, an awareness that stood in tension with his no less fervent aspiration to unmediated experience of "the thing itself" (*el son*). The result was a productive contradiction that is central to *The Cantos,* one that is repeatedly explored in the essays to follow.

Jerome McGann begins with sample pages taken from the first four editions of *The Cantos* (1925, 1928, 1930, and 1933), charting the changes that mark the transition from the early artisanal and hand-processed editions to the industrialized and standardized text that we have received since 1933. The differences among these pose a serious challenge for any critical edition of *The Cantos* and show how deeply interpretive and editorial theory are intertwined. Yet all four editions also show how firmly Pound was committed to the notion that poetry should "be brought forth . . . in every feature of the media available to the scriptural imagination," while the 1925 and 1928 editions in particular set forth "an elaborate act of cultural allusion" to early modern bookmaking, when printing "had not yet become an engine of cultural alienation." McGann calls attention to

Pound's lifelong responsiveness "to the semiotic potential that lay in the physical aspects of book and text production," whether in the early "In a Station of the Metro," the middle *Hugh Selwyn Mauberley,* or the later use of Chinese characters in the cantos of the 1930s. Repeatedly he uses signs in ways that alter the perspective of the larger linguistic and textual horizon in which they are set. *The Cantos,* in this view, dramatize the degree to which the meaning of works is embodied in the bibliographic as well as the linguistic level, remaining profoundly interwoven with, even inseparable from, the dynamics of transmission by which they have been produced and received.

Immediately following McGann's essay is my own. Its immediate subject is two lines of poetry that Pound wrote in 1923, lines that are puzzling because they contain several words that are indecipherable, seemingly belonging to no recognizable language. Paradoxically, and yet appropriately, the two lines turn out to be about interpretation, and specifically about how one should interpret an event that is seemingly random and yet fraught with significance. In effect they articulate a hermeneutics of understanding that is paradigmatic for *The Cantos,* one that is repeatedly internalized and restaged within the poem, but that is also inseparable from Pound's earliest experiences with fascism. The essay then traces, for the first time, Pound's encounters with Fascist Party members and sympathizers in March 1923, chronicling a series of previously undisclosed events and offering a revisionary account of Pound's initial attraction to fascism. Far from developing in response to the global economic crisis after 1929, his interest stemmed, new documents show, from a complex of issues involving cultural patronage, efficiency, and violence. Already by the second half of 1923, Pound was attempting to contact Mussolini, offering his services as a cultural consultant for the new regime and requesting Mussolini to write an essay for the *Transatlantic Review.* The events of March 1923 marked a turning point in Pound's life, and understanding them enables us to resolve the problematic "identity" of the indecipherable two lines, themselves a dramatization of a crisis of identity that stands at the heart of *The Cantos.*

The essays by McGann and Rainey on the earlier cantos are followed by two others treating the so-called Middle Cantos, or those that appeared between 1933 and 1940. Tim Redman examines Cantos 31 to 41, first collected in the volume entitled *Eleven New Cantos* in 1934. The new cantos mark Pound's "momentous conversion" to fascism and the Social Credit theories of Silvio Gesell, a conversion registered in the careful structural movement that begins with Thomas Jefferson and culminates in the figure of Mussolini. After briefly surveying their form and principal themes, Redman identifies the exact sources from which several passages in a single canto were taken, usefully showing how acquaintance with them can alter our understanding of Pound's intentions in several senses: pinpointing the motivations behind his choice of specific subjects, appreciating his often witty variations on themes furnished by his sources, or assaying the genuine obscurity caused by Pound's ruthless condensation. More important, the insights gleaned from this procedure make clear that a dense intertextuality was a feature fundamental to *The Cantos,* a work that aspired to effects that were in advance of its time and that have become practicable only recently with the advent of hypertext. For Redman, hypertext is both a model and a metaphor for a kind of poetics that presses at the boundaries of a fundamental tension between centrifugal and centripetal forces, between the freedom of endless association and the imperative of structure. This tension need not be resolved, either in hypertext or the "protohypertext" that is *The Cantos.* Instead of resolution, a responsive reader discovers "a new kind of poetic coherence and complexity of astonishing beauty."

Ira Nadel also considers a section of the Middle Cantos, in this case Cantos 52–71, which were issued in January 1940 (five months after the outbreak of World War II). Nadel focuses on the Chinese Cantos (52–61) and the substantial apparatus of commentary and annotation that accompanied them: a table of contents with summaries for each canto, a prefatory explanatory note, as well as Chinese ideograms and dates placed in the margins to help a reader follow the narrative. Further commentary was included on the dust jacket of the Faber and Faber edition, while a fifteen-page brochure containing "Notes on the Cantos" and "Notes on the Versification of the Cantos" served as a chaperon to the first five hundred copies of the New Directions edition. And even this congeries of parerga was significantly less than James Laughlin, Pound's American publisher, had originally requested. At one point Pound also planned to include a map of China, which, though ultimately not printed, testifies to his ongoing interest throughout *The Cantos* in "visualizing history"—or using "nonverbal, pictorial elements"—which "clarifies and extends the meanings of language," a usage that obviously recalls Pound's concerns with Fenellosa's theory of the Chinese written character.

The essays on the Middle Cantos are followed by two on the later cantos, those that were published between 1948, when *The Pisan Cantos* were issued, and Pound's death in 1972. Ronald Bush's essay focuses on the composition of *The Pisan Cantos* during the dramatic period that ran from January to late October 1945. The story has three distinct moments. While publishing most of Cantos 72 and 73 in *La Marina Repubblicana* in January and February 1945, Pound began a series of drafts in Italian that registered glimpses of a visionary encounter with Cunizza, the sister of Ezzelino da Romano who was courted by the troubadour Sordello and passed the waning years of her life in Florence in the house of Guido Cavalcanti—a figure, in other words, for the powers of erotic lyricism that had once found voice in Provençal poetry, powers subsequently transmitted to Dante and later revived at the court of Sigismondo Malatesta in Rimini. The early drafts explore motifs evoked by diaphanous women speaking in paradisal landscapes. But when Pound was arrested and confined in an outdoor cell in May 1945, then released into the infirmary in June, he began a second stage of composition that continued the otherworldly and aestheticizing mood of his previous drafts but also introduced a very different note derived partly from quotidian experience, as indicated by the use of diary-like entries, and partly from Pound's "premeditated exercise of remembering," his effort to combat the forgetfulness that had overcome him during his collapse when confined outdoors. It is this latter vein, dominated by generosity in remembrance, that constitutes the core of Pound's poetic achievement in these cantos. But there was to be yet a third phase of composition in October 1945, when Pound began Canto 84, the last of the Pisan sequence. Now he added a polemical defense of his fascist politics, one that included a new beginning for the entire sequence (the famous passage on Mussolini in Canto 74) and substantial additions to the ten cantos he had already composed. The result changed not just the framing of the sequence, but the resonance of passages that had remained unaltered. Yet in Bush's view, the visionary, the elegiac, and the ideological motifs coexist in a productive tension, a tension that he argues is central to the work not just of Pound, but of the entire modernist tradition, in which an attraction to organicism and aestheticism is always counterbalanced by a skeptical vein of resistance to them.

Peter Stoicheff also offers a complex reconstruction of composition and publication, this time of *Drafts and Fragments,* the last portion of *The Cantos* to be published in Pound's lifetime. Stoicheff shows how the 1968 volume was conceived wholly in response to a pirated edition that had been issued a year earlier by Ed Sanders, who had fortuitously obtained a typescript copy of Pound's drafts at just the moment when he was looking for anything he could "instantly freak into print." The collection's title and the sequence and choice of materials were largely the work of others. But because of their position at, or near, the end of the long poem, they were soon endowed with special bearing for critical interpretation, a burden of significance at odds with the contingencies of their composition and publication genetics. Moreover, when *Drafts and Fragments* was included in the 1972 edition of all the cantos that had been issued to date, it now sported a new Canto 120 that stood as the poem's ending from then until 1986. All or most of the new canto's lines may derive from Pound, but it is beyond doubt that the order in which they have been transmitted was that of another hand. This complex and fractured history raises a series of questions. On the one hand, any interpretation of the poem's final sections must be grounded in awareness of their historical dynamics and composite authority, a social authority in which Pound's intentions are contiguous with those of editors, readers, and even the logic of his own poem as it had unfolded to that point. For as Stoicheff also shows, the fragmentation of authority at the level of publication was also a reflex of a process that had already occurred at the level of composition, as Pound discovered that the dynamics of his poem "had eluded his control, that the poem had ceased to remain compliant, and had instead become adversarial." The poem's deep commitment to historical understanding had rendered all but impossible, and yet utterly indispensable, the political and social paradise for which *The Cantos* had always searched. Faced with a compositional task that was beset by insoluble paradox and compromise, Pound increasingly relinquished his authority over the process of publication, to become part of a more complex process in which readers and editors played a preponderant role.

The concluding section contains two essays and a "statement" that sketch out the prospects for a variorum or critical edition of *The Cantos*. The first, by Richard Taylor, surveys various editions in which *The Cantos* have appeared: a bewildering melange of collected and selected editions as well as periodical publications and piracies running up to the advent of *Drafts & Fragments*. He also presents a panoramic view of the questions that preoccupied Pound's admirers during the 1950s and 1960s when they proffered suggestions for emendations or posed questions for clarification, hoping to spur him toward a definitive edition, a prospect that ended in 1965 when James Laughlin met with Pound in Venice and showed him a copy of *The Cantos* containing hundreds of possible corrections for his approval: "He would stare at the page where the correction was marked for a long time, without answering, and then just start turning pages aimlessly." At the end of their conversation, Laughlin has said in a private interview, Pound closed the volume and said: "Why don't you just take *The Cantos* and burn them once and for all?" The conflicting imperatives encoded in Pound's own attitude toward the text, Taylor argues, make a variorum, rather than a critical edition, "the ideal vehicle for a serious reader of *The Cantos*." In effect he outlines the principles that have guided him in collecting information toward a variorum edition, a project now under way for fifteen years and the most advanced of several that have recently been discussed, a trial version of it having been issued in 1991.[9]

The second essay, by Mary de Rachewiltz, explores a variety of questions raised by her long experience of translating *The Cantos* into Italian for a dual-language text that was issued by Mondadori in 1985. De Rachewiltz treats several related points: the rationale behind a number of specific decisions that she made when preparing her own edition; a plea to incorporate a sense of magnanimity into the philological enterprise; a correction to the increasingly widespread but mistaken impression that Pound was careless when correcting proofs; and a personal account of Pound's mental and physical exhaustion after 1959. But its central argument is to urge that *The Cantos* be assigned a more central place in American literary culture, recognized "as America's epic." The poem's "sacrificial function" and "'economic' virtue" are a function of the way in which "America grew inside" of both the poet and his poem, and in the current global scene the poem is a point of resistance against "the monumental arms racket and obfuscation of history and culture."

The concluding piece is a one-page public statement issued by New Directions Publishing Corporation in 1989, reprinted here in its entirety.[10] It announces the firm's opposition to a critical edition of *The Cantos,* a viewpoint that will have practical repercussions for many years to come. For New Directions, and in particular its founder and owner James Laughlin, continues to exercise a customary right—it is neither a contractual or legal one, it should be noted—of first refusal regarding any proposal to publish or republish materials by Pound. As a result, a critical edition of *The Cantos* will not be published during the lifetime of Mr. Laughlin, and probably not for some years afterward.

Paradoxically, the lack of any prospects for the realization of a critical edition may be less an impediment, more a spur toward further textual studies of *The Cantos*. Textual study has traditionally thrived when confronted with problems that are seemingly insuperable, as the scholarly traditions of Homer and Shakespeare abundantly attest. It is when received paradigms no longer function that new formulations are devised that enable scholars to reconsider the materials already at their disposal. None of the essays in this volume attempts a global theoretical survey of the textual tradition informing *The Cantos*, but taken together they catalog the kinds of questions one would need to confront in doing so, just as they suggest how much we still have to learn about *The Cantos*, at almost every imaginable level: prepublication manuscripts, biographical backgrounds, genetic development, and publishing history. Viewed not as individual essays, but as a collective work, they present a challenging effort to reconceptualize the project of *The Cantos* and to explore the implications of that reconceptualization for critical interpretation.

NOTES

1. On the publication of Pound's correspondence since 1981, see Lawrence Rainey, "The Letters and the Spirit: Pound's Correspondence and the Concept of Modernism," *Text* 8 (1993): 365–96.
2. Ezra Pound, *ABC of Reading* (New York: New Directions, 1960; 1st edition, 1934), 46.
3. Peter Bürger, *Theory of the Avant-Garde*, trans. Michael Shaw (Minneapolis: University of Minnesota Press, 1984; 1st German ed. 1974).
4. T. S. Eliot, "Ezra Pound," *To-Day* 4, no. 19 (September 1918): 7.
5. The first publication of material from *The Cantos* is in *Poetry* 10, no. 3 (June 1917): 113–21. The notorious "Canto 120" appeared in the *New York Times Book Review*, 26 November 1972, 42. The same eight lines, in the same order, had been printed three years earlier under the byline "The Fox" in *Anonym* (Buffalo, N.Y.) 4 (1969): 1. For a detailed history of the various poems that came to make up *Drafts and Fragments*, see Peter Stoicheff, *The Hall of Mirrors:* Drafts & Fragments *and the end of Ezra Pound's* Cantos (Ann Arbor: University of Michigan Press, 1995).
6. See Barbara Eastman, "The Gap in *The Cantos:* 72 and 73," *Paideuma* 8, (1979): 415–27; Massimo Bacigalupo, "Poet at War: Pound's Suppressed Italian Cantos," *South Atlantic Quarterly* 83 (1984): 69–79; and Robert Casillo, "Fascists of the Final Hour: Pound's Italian *Cantos*," in *Fascism, Aesthetics, and Culture*, Richard J. Golsan (Hanover, N.H.: University Press of New England, 1992), 98–127, which includes a translation.
7. See Lawrence Rainey, *Ezra Pound and the Monument of Culture: Text, His-*

tory, and the Malatesta Cantos (Chicago: University of Chicago Press, 1991), 214–17, 243–47.

8. A mimeographed edition of Cantos 72–73 was published in 1973, consisting of twenty-five copies, three deposited for copyright in Canadian and U.S. libraries, one given to Pound's bibliographer, and the other twenty-one distributed privately. On this edition, see Donald Gallup, *Ezra Pound: A Bibliography,* rev. ed. (Charlottesville: University Press of Virginia, 1983), A94. On the deluxe edition of 1983, see Lawrence Rainey, *"The Cantos" of Ezra Pound: A Poem Including History* (New Haven: Beinecke Rare Book and Manuscript Library, 1989), xxx. See also Ira Nadel in *Paideuma* 30:15–17. Cantos 72–73 were incorporated into the "tenth printing" of the so-called third edition of *The Cantos* (1973), which is dated 1986, though copies were not actually distributed until 1987.

9. Richard Taylor, *Variorum Edition of "Three Cantos": A Prototype* (Bayreuth, Germany: Boomerang Press–Norbert AAS, 1991).

10. The statement was read by a representative of New Directions Publishing Corporation at "A Poem Including History: *The Cantos* of Ezra Pound," a conference held at the Whitney Humanities Center of Yale University, 27–28 October 1989.

Retrospects

2

Notes on Amateur Emendations

Hugh Kenner

I was once assigned to introduce a Robert Lowell reading. And what, I asked Lowell, might he like me to say about him? His jocular response was, "Compare me to Homer!" I did what I could. (I didn't mention Horace's *bonus dormitat Homerus:* even Homer sometimes nods.)

But if there was ever a modern poet it would seem pertinent to compare to Homer, it wasn't Cal Lowell, it was Ezra Pound. For the nature of the Poundian and the Homeric texts is oddly similar. Pound composed orally/aurally. From both the Disciplinary Training Center (DTC) and Schloss Brunnenburg we have accounts of the odd inarticulate chant he'd utter as he worked, shaping the sound of a line, the sound of a passage, groping after words that could mime that shape. So acoustic was his memory, when he wrote a note for my benefit about the *Li Ki*—Book of Rites—that underlies Canto 51, his ear prompted "Rites" but his hand wrote "Rights." Also, he'd alter his texts long after they'd been printed, with inconsistencies that drive editors to despair. There are deep analogies with what we've been taught to regard as the "oral-formulaic" poetry of Homer. (A Homer with a typewriter? That is tenable.)

Much of the peculiar texture of Pound's work stems from his situation in history. His time at university came near the end of one of the West's great collaborative enterprises, the era of historical philology during which, for two generations at least, some of the best minds in England, Germany, and France bent their energies to reclaiming publishable texts from manuscripts: from the scribblings of scribes who'd *heard* in their heads what they were copying, then set that down phonetically, indifferent to orthodoxies of spelling or word division. And the work of reclamation never seemed quite done. Editions once published, a new generation of scholars would take on cleanup tasks. Thus Emil Levy, as we learn from Canto 20, puzzled six months over the nonword "Noigandres" in Canello's 1883 edition of Arnaut Daniel, until he realized that it could come apart into two dictionary items, "d'enoi gandres": wards off ennui.

The presence of that anecdote in the *Cantos* ought to have aroused more attention than it has. The 1911 visit to Levy will have resembled, for the young Pound, an audience with Bohr for a young 1930s scientist. Printed texts, Pound's teachers had impressed upon him, are signals devoted craft combs out of static. As Fred Robinson has shown, Pound dabbled in the craft himself, second-guessing, with the aid of endnotes and lexicons, the text of "The Seafarer" as he had received it. Only if you take a printed text for divine revelation are you apt to dismiss him as an ignorant blunderer. (Robinson judges some of Pound's emendations unlikely, but others highly plausible.) For, with the "Seafarer" bard as with Homer, editors must attempt a puzzle to which there are no final answers; they can't pretend to reconstruct what the poet wanted, since the poet couldn't have begun to imagine a printed edition, least of all the finality of the way it displays permutations of eighty-odd signs.

Dictionary items—"words"—are simply letter sequences separated by spaces; the reason Frenchmen are reputed to "talk so fast" is that book-taught visitors listen for word divisions and seldom hear any. The isolate *word* is a by-product of writing. So, of course, is the ideogram, Pound's enthusiasm for which in the 1930s synchronizes with his fondness for citing Confucius on firm definitions. The dictionary he was using, that of Morrison (1815–22), followed Chinese custom in indexing characters by their visible "radicals" and their stroke counts; not till the St. Elizabeths period, when he got hold of the Mathews dictionary, which indexes by sound, was he paying much attention to Chinese pronunciation. The two dictionaries illustrate, neatly, a deep division in his mind. He cared, we know, for the integrity of words. But he tended to start composition with cadences, unpunctuated tunes. So part of his mind was at home with Emil Levy's assumptions, but part of it with Homer's. He never enjoyed Joyce's comfort with the idea that a writer's job is encoding instructions for printers. Hence problems with his own texts, problems even he wasn't able to solve.

Oxford's great *New English Dictionary on Historical Principles* insisted, as any dictionary must, on "words." The first part of its first edition was published in 1884, the year before Ezra Pound was born. The final fascicle is dated April 1928, by which time Pound was halfway through his forty-third year. The Early English Text Society existed, in part, to get manuscript texts into print so the NED could cite them. (One such text was *Agenbite of Inwit,* a title that caught the attention of Stephen Dedalus.) Canello's *Arnaut Daniel* was a comparable enterprise, as was Levy's eight-volume supplement to Raynouard's *Lexique Roman.* It cannot be emphasized too often that when Bill Shepard at Hamilton College put young Pound onto Provençal, and Hugo Rennart at the University of Pennsylvania reinforced the addiction, they brought him into touch with the leading edge of scholarship, which was mediating between *motz el son*—speech fitted to a tune—and sequences of written words you can look up.

So a single word (as Homer might not have understood) may become its fundamental unit of attention. *Epi oinopi ponton,* upon the (something) sea: and what does *oinopi* say? Well, (1) we establish *oinopi* as an independent unit of attention; (2) we devise, for dictionary purposes, an unrecorded nominative form, *oinops;* (3) we decide that *oinops* is indeed Greek (for, yes, alien words did survive into Greek; visitors to Athens are shown a Mount Lykabettos, not a Greek name, something inherited); (4) we affirm that the first syllable has to do with *oinos,* wine, the second with *ops,* face, look, appearance; (5) we permit Professor Passau, in Germany, to decide that the comparison is one of color; (6) we accept his notion that the wine in question is red, not white; finally, (7) with Liddell and Scott, we assent to Passau's *Weindunkel* in defining *oinops* as "wine-dark." Perhaps the best-known of all Greek definitions, that's the outcome of building a card house of guesses on a "word" that exists in the nominative form in no Greek text.

And in doing so we disregard the awkward fact that Sophocles uses the word of a human forearm. In Canto 97 Pound has "the gloss, probably, not the colour," alongside the Homeric phrase *oinos aithiops.* Yes, perhaps a glossy forearm shone with sweat; or Homer wasn't adducing color but sheen. . . . All we can say for certain of *wine-dark* is that it stems not from Homer's world but from Passau's. Readers of *Henry V* are perhaps happier; pondering "'a babbl'd of green fields,'" they can wonder whether Theobald's eighteenth-century guess does perhaps resurrect an obliterated fancy of Shakespeare's, whose printer left us merely "a table of greenfields."

Perhaps we can guess what Homer meant to say ("the gloss, probably, not the colour": the glistening sea?). But perhaps Homer didn't know what he was saying? Perhaps he parroted something inherited, formulaic.

Is it even conceivable that his famed ox-eyed goddess—the Greek word says "ox-faced"—had migrated from Egypt, where divinities sport bovine heads? In that case, "ox-eyed" was a desperate nineteenth-century expedient, still enshrined in lexicons.

Yet, to get started, students must trust lexicons. And we're all students always; there's no finality. So Pound called a *Lustra* poem "Imerro" (in Greek letters), which means "I yearn" in the usage of the folk of Sappho's island, who dropped their aitches and wouldn't have said "Himmero" like Athenians. That spelling—meant to send readers' minds to Sappho—persisted through three printings of *Lustra*. Then, for the 1926 *Personae*, a definitive edition of his poems other than the cantos-in-progress, Pound thought to recheck the word in what he'd no reason to distrust, the concise edition of the Liddell and Scott Greek lexicon. And there a misprint (!) incited him to change his smooth-breathing sign to a rough, thus making the title "Himmero." (Alas; Sappho's dialect vanishes, and so does she. Rejoice; they're restored in the most recent *Personae* printings.) Note that, though his first title shows him following the classroom rule—Lesbian dialect marked by absence of rough breathings—he assumed the dictionary folk knew what they were doing. For Pound did tend to assume that real specialists knew. (And I prize a letter from Oxford University Press, acknowledging that the concise lexicon, just there, indeed went wrong. One tiny character, of maybe two million, had happened to get reversed about 1871. I've not been able to check the latest printing.)

Pound's unconscious affinity for the crux deserves notice. Thus Bion's lament for Adonis: in Canto 47 we read:

> But in the pale night the small lamps float seaward
> Τυ Διώνα
> TU DIONA

Και Μοιραι' Ἄδονιν
KAI MORAI' ADONIN
The sea is streaked red with Adonis.

Annotators will tell you the Greek's an ungodly botch. What they won't tell you is that they've been checking against a "corrected" text, editorial guesswork so shaky the Bude editors have thrown up their hands and reverted to the manuscript reading, which is exactly what Pound took from a blessedly naive eighteenth-century edition he'd bought in Venice.

Or look at Canto 39, where we find phrases from the Clark-Ernestus Latin version of the *Odyssey* Pound mentions in his "Notes on Some

Translators of Homer." In the canto, here are men in the power of Circe, and here's "nec ivi in harum," which is exactly what the 1804 printing of Clark and Ernestus offers. But "harum" makes no sense; it's a demonstrative pronoun, genitive plural. What makes sense is what we find in the second Clark-Emestus printing: "in haram": into the pigsty. But Pound had the first printing and trusted what he assumed was the authors' learning. Question: Emend? Or preserve the record of an error encountered, copied? ("Periplum, not as land looks on a map / but as sea bord seen by men sailing.")

So what's an editor to do? An editor with a lust for cleaning things up ("'Rihaku'? Pooh. Li Po") had best be wary. Leslie Fiedler drew laughs at a 1985 conference by affirming, with heavy irony, that poor Pound even believed there'd been a Chinese poet called Ri ha ku; the chairperson ruled correction out of order. It's easy, though, to be sure that Pound knew Li Po's Chinese name when *Cathay* was published: the April 1915 *Poetry* contains his note on "Li Po, usually considered the greatest poet of China." So in attributing the poems to "Rihaku" he was doing in *Cathay* what he'd regularly do in the *Cantos:* recording the chain of transmission. Li Po had come to Kensington from Mori and Ariga via Fenollosa, in whose notebooks the proper names have their Japanese forms. Likewise, Chinese names in the "Chinese Cantos" (52–61) get French transliterations because the source is a French Jesuit's book. The spellings say, these names came to Europe in the eighteenth century, via France. Some of the same names in later cantos get differently spelled, to acknowledge later sources.

A somewhat analogous case: the American (Farrar and Rinehart) text of *A Draft of XXX Cantos,* the plates of which were later taken over by New Directions, was set from Nancy Cunard's 1930 Hours Press Edition. The British text (Faber) seems to have been set from a revised typescript; it was advertised as offering "Mr. Pound's latest revisions." The most notable discrepancy between the two occurs near the end of Canto 13, where the American text goes,

And Kung said "Wan ruled with moderation,
   In his day the state was well kept,
And even I can remember
A day when the historians left blanks in their writings,
I mean for things they didn't know,
But that time seems to be passing."

A day when the historians left blanks in their writings,
But that time seems to be passing."

The Faber text omits the last two lines. Well, the repeated closing quotation mark signals something amiss; sure enough, the Hours Press printer did manage to duplicate two lines exactly, and the American typesetter made a scrupulous copy. Back in 1956, proposing to anthologize this canto, I wrote Pound: what about that repeat? His reply: "Repeat in 13 sanctioned by time and the author, or rather first by the author, who never objects to the typesetter making improvements."

What that doesn't address is what to do about the superfluous quotation mark at the end of the sixth line cited. In my anthology (*The Art of Poetry* [Rinehart, 1959]) I deleted it. Three decades later I'd have been less confident. Like "Rihaku" for "Li Po," that little symbol acknowledges a chain of transmission. Had Pound purposely left it in place, a silent tip of the hat to a lucky typesetting accident? (But then, since he liked the "repeat," why didn't he have it inserted into the Faber edition? *Bonus dormitat Homerus.*)[1]

But nothing checks a mania for uniformity, notably on the part of well-wishers driven to help a presumably flurried Pound. For many years New Directions' printing-house technology did keep *Personae* and the *Cantos* reasonably immune to tinkering. The "plates" that stayed in storage between reprintings could be altered only by drilling out old words, soldering in new ones, a job for a nimble and expensive blacksmith. Even changes the author wanted made got resisted as too costly. But, late in the 1960s, photo-offset obsolesced those tons of plates. Nothing easier now than to paste new words onto a proof sheet, rephotograph, Presto! And the floodgates opened, and the changes flooded in, printing after printing after printing. Why not? Let's get it *right!* We owe it to Ezra . . .

Barbara Eastman's *Ezra Pound's Cantos: The Story of the Text* chronicles what ensued. The Faber text stayed fairly stable; absence of college adoptions meant fewer reprints; also, at Faber, they inclined to make a surly retreat behind that hoariest of cop-outs, "The author read the proofs." (As if Ezra, not seeing, but hearing what *ought* to have been on the page, hadn't been the worst of proofreaders; it was Dorothy, *visuel,* who caught most of the first-printing errors that were caught.)

Well, in 1970 New Directions issued Cantos 1–117: the whole poem for the first time in one volume, including the terminal *Drafts and Fragments.* For the first time, too, the pages were numbered consecutively throughout; New Directions had at last jettisoned plates and gone to photo-offset and was no longer shackled by the pagination of the original eight volumes. Also, New Directions was free to make corrections cheaply, and it made 138 in the first seventy-four cantos. A new printing in 1971 added 92 more, mostly from Canto 75 onward. And now let us look closely.

There's a class of errors that clearly came from a printer, and these we may correct with clear conscience. Upside-down ideograms: several of those were caught. They happened because ideograms were photoengraved, like pictures, leaving a makeup man to insert a lead-faced wooden block into a page, with no clue which way up it ought to go. Wrong Greek letters? Well, Υ and γ look enough alike to an innocent compositor to have prompted the unpronounceable "Hgperionidas" (for "Hyperionidas"). Fix it. And "The veil held close to his side"? Though compositors tend to reach for familiar words, what the troubadour held was a viel, a stringed instrument. Fix that too.

But what about this? Canto 4:

> And So-Gioku, saying:
> "This wind, sire, is the king's wind,
>   This wind is wind of the palace,
> Shaking imperial water-jets."
>   And Ran-ti, opening his collar . . .

Well, in 1970 "So-Gioku" became "Sung Yü" in somebody's marking of a source copy but stayed put in print, while "Ranti" became "Hsiang," apparently on the Rihaku/Li Po principle. The energumen here was Eva Hesse's care for scholastic consistency.[2] The source, she said, will have been Sung Yü's "The Man-wind and the Woman-wind." No. It will have been something of Fenollosa's. And "Ran-ti" was what Pound heard, as often as he repolished the lines.

But wait, there's more. In 1950 Pound penciled into my copy of the 1948 printing a sequence of corrections that's never been followed. "Hymen, Io Hymenaee!" became Ὕμεν Ὕμεναι Ἰο. (That was never touched, though he said he wanted the Greek because he'd learned the source wasn't Catullus but Aristophanes.) "A scarlet flower" became "One scarlet flower" (that's been changed). He crossed out the "And" before "So-Gioku," changed the "And" before "Ran-ti" to "That," the "opening" to "opened," but let both names stand. Also he deleted "sire" before "wind." A few of these changes revert to the Faber version. The gestalt isn't present intact in any printing.

The author's final intention? It could vary from month to month, as he sounded lines and re-sounded them. Forget that chimera. Try three editorial principles:

1. What's amiss that's uncontrovertibly a printer's misdeed can be safely corrected.
2. Never mind encyclopedia "accuracy," e.g., Japanese words replaced by Chinese forms. When Pound was composing—by sound—he heard, for example, Japanese sounds.
3. For the rest, record printed variants and insert a note.

That is a formula for a variorum, the only thinkable edition that can be reasonably faithful both to textual givens and to what the poet aimed at, besieged as he was, decade after decade, by melodic patterns versus semantic ones, and by afterthoughts.

An afterthought: the author's final intention? When Pound rethought the *Homage to Sextus Propertius* for the 1926 *Personae,* his most interesting innovation is typographic. Strophe answers antistrophe, voices from the right margin replying to those from the left:

> Bringing the Grecian orgies into Italy,
> > and the dance into Italy.
> Who hath brought you so subtle a measure,
> > in what hall have you heard it;
> What foot beat out your time-bar,
> > what water has mellowed your whistles?

Likewise:

> There are enough women in hell,
> > quite enough beautiful women,
> Iope, and Tyro, and Pasiphae, and the formal girls of Achaia,
> And out of Troad, and from the Campania,
> Death has his tooth in the lot,
> > Avernus lusts for the lot of them,
> Beauty is not eternal, no man has perenniel fortune,
> Slow foot, or swift foot, death delays but for a season.

It's unique in *Personae,* that rulered symmetry left and right. It must have cost numerous instructions to Liveright's printer. And in the 1990 revised edition of *Personae* there's some fuss about "later orthographic changes later authorized by Pound that appeared in the eclectic text edited by J. P. Sullivan." But indents begin at seemingly random intervals, and the right-margin symmetry is gone. It seems to have been supposed that "the author's final intention" (1926, with 1964 emendations) began and ended with the spelling of words. But, that time, his 1926 intention seems to have included the look of the page. Moral: leave everything alone that you conscientiously can. And of such is the kingdom of editing.

NOTES

1. Analogy: for the fifth episode of *Ulysses* Joyce set out to devise a typewritten mash note, fumbles and all. On the fourth set of proofs he changed a "write" to a "wrote": "if you do not wrote." That mimes a finger slipping one key rightward, something he may have spotted on an actual typescript, and he took care to certify the "error" by having Bloom make a deadpan allusion a few lines down: "Wonder did she wrote it herself." The sixty-year history of publishers' efforts to get *that* exactly right would fill a longish paragraph.
2. Barbara Eastman, here as elsewhere, credits me with input I'm innocent of. She attributes far too much to "Eva Hesse's [1964] meeting with Kenner."

The Early Years

3

Pound's *Cantos:* A Poem Including Bibliography

Jerome McGann

Anyone thinking to edit Pound's poetry, and in particular the poetry of the *Cantos,* cannot avoid a number of specialized and even pedantic inquiries of great importance. "Of great importance" technically and in themselves, because they involve practical difficulties in text and book production. But also "of great importance" because such technical matters conceal some of the most fundamental questions that the student of textuality has to confront. The bibliographical problems of the *Cantos* are simutaneously hermeneutical. They go to the very heart of the work's meaning.

The issues are so many and complex that I shall not attempt to survey them all here, let alone give detailed investigations. I shall not have much to say about the sociological and institutional problems of editing Pound's texts, for example, nor about the question of textual annotations. I shall also have little to say about the linguistic difficulties that the editor (and the reader) of Pound's *Cantos* must grapple with. My principal concern will be to look at the bibliographical codes embedded in Pound's texts: the layout of the page, the spatial relations of the scripts (including letters, words, lines, and any other inscribed materials)—in general, the physical manifold that makes up an edition—any edition—of the *Cantos.* This subject necessarily includes issues of paper, ink, binding, covers, and endpapers. I shall pass with small comment all these matters as well, however—somewhat reluctantly, since critics and readers of literature are generally unaware of the crucial part these factors play in the installment of what we like to call "the meaning of the text." Even among that band of angels who are alive to the hermeneutic significance of, for example, paper, ink, page size, leading, and so forth, critical dialects for exploring these subjects are not in general use.

Those caveats understood, let me begin with a series of texts. The illustration in figure 1 represents one page from the first book installment of the *Cantos* project, *A Draft of XVI. Cantos* (1925). It was published by Willlam Bird at the Three Mountains Press in Paris. (The second book installment, published by John Rodker in London, was *A Draft of the Cantos 17–27* (1928), and its format is in the same decorative mode as the 1925 book.) It was printed in two colors (red and black).

Only a few of Pound's current readers are aware that Pound arranged and carefully oversaw the production of these two initial books of *Cantos*. Most readers encounter the texts of the opening cantos in a much modified format (For example, see fig. 2.) This is the first page of Canto 13 as it was printed in *A Draft of XXX Cantos* published in 1933 by Farrar and Rinehart. The disappearance of two-color printing and of the elaborate ornamental materials is only the most dramatic sign of a set of wholesale alterations in page layout, typeface, ink, and paper. We have moved from a decorated and hand-processed work toward one that bears all the insignia of what Walter Benjamin called "the age of mechanical reproduction." Our received texts of the *Cantos*—that is to say, those that come to us through New Directions or Faber and Faber—follow the highly standardized bibliographical codes of the 1933 edition.

The descent from texts of 1925 and 1928—which culminate Pound's appropriation of his Pre-Raphaelite inheritance—to the industrial text of 1933 was not immediate. In 1930 Pound published his first complete edition of *A Draft of XXX Cantos* with the Hours Press in Paris. The opening page of Canto 13 in the 1930 edition appears as shown in figure 3. In this 1930 text we are still in the world of fine printing, as this book's decorative capitals—all designed by Pound's wife, incidentally— show. The 1930 capitals possess a distinctive (clearly "vorticist") style that mediates between the self-consciously antiqued physicalness of the 1925 and 1928 texts and capitals, and the more transparent trade-edition texts of 1933 and thereafter.

The (uniform) title covering both the 1930 and the 1933 texts would eventually come to designate what we now rightly think of as the "first installment" of the *Cantos*. A single structure of thirty cantos replaced the earlier two-part structure that had come out as the *Draft of XVI. Cantos* and the *Draft of the Cantos 17–27*. The incorporation of these first two parts into a single (and slightly larger) unit was perhaps foreshadowed by the unusual bibliographical coding shared by these two early decorated books. This matter is important, of course, because the *Cantos* (somewhat

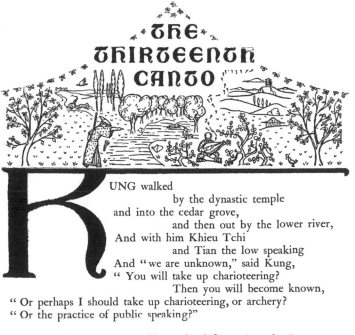

THE THIRTEENTH CANTO

KUNG walked
            by the dynastic temple
and into the cedar grove,
         and then out by the lower river,
And with him Khieu Tchi
         and Tian the low speaking
And "we are unknown," said Kung,
  " You will take up charioteering?
        Then you will become known,
" Or perhaps I should take up charioteering, or archery?
" Or the practice of public speaking?"

And Tseu-lou said, "I would put the defences in order,"

And Khieu said, "If I were lord of a province
I would put it in better order than this is."
And Tchi said, "I would prefer a small mountain temple,
" With order in the observances,
        with a suitable performance of the ritual,"
And Tian said, with his hand on the strings of his lute
The low sounds continuing
        after his hand left the strings,
And the sound went up like smoke, under the leaves,
And he looked after the sound:
      " The old swimming hole,
" And the boys flopping off the planks,
" Or sitting in the underbrush playing mandolins."
        And Kung smiled upon all of them equally.
And Thseng-sie desired to know:
      " Which had answered correctly?"
And Kung said, " They have all answered correctly,
" That is to say, each in his nature."

Fig. 1. Ezra Pound, *A Draft of XVI. Cantos* (Paris: Three Mountains Press, 1925), p. 50. The Yale Collection of American Literature, Beinecke Rare Book and Manuscript Library, Yale University.

K   XIII

    ung walked
        by the dynastic temple
and into the cedar grove,
        and then out by the lower river,
And with him Khieu Tchi
        and Tian the low speaking
And 'we are unknown,' said Kung,
'You will take up charioteering?
        'Then you will become known,
'Or perhaps I should take up charioteering, or archery?
'Or the practice of public speaking?'
And Tseu-lou said, 'I would put the defences in order,'
And Khieu said, 'If I were lord of a province
I would put it in better order than this is.'
And Tchi said, 'I should prefer a small mountain temple,
'With order in the observances,
        with a suitable performance of the ritual,'
And Tian said, with his hand on the strings of his lute
The low sounds continuing
        after his hand left the strings,
And the sound went up like smoke, under the leaves,
And he looked after the sound:
        'The old swimming hole,
'And the boys flopping off the planks,
'Or sitting in the underbrush playing mandolins.'
        And Kung smiled upon all of them equally.
And Thseng-sie desired to know:
        'Which had answered correctly?'
And Kung said, 'They have all answered correctly,
'That is to say, each in his nature.'
And Kung raised his cane against Yuan Jang,

Fig. 2.   Ezra Pound, *A Draft of XXX Cantos* (New York: Farrar and Rine-
hart, 1933), p. 62; the two-color printing and the ornamental materials
(see fig. 1) have disappeared in this publication of the now standardized,
industrial *Cantos*.

仸子

KUNG walked
        by the dynastic temple
and into the cedar grove,
            and then out by the lower river,
And with him Khieu Tchi
            and Tian the low speaking
And " we are unknown, " said Kung,
    " You will take up charioteering?
            Then you will become known,
" Or perhaps I should take up charioteering, or archery?
" Or the practice of public speaking? "
And Tseu-lou said, " I would put the defences in order, "
And Khieu said, " If I were lord of a province
I would put it in better order than this is. "
And Tchi said, " I would prefer a small mountain temple,
" With order in the observances,
            with a suitable performance of the ritual, "
And Tian said, with his hand on the strings of his lute
The low sounds continuing
            after his hand left the strings,
And the sound went up like smoke, under the leaves,
And he looked after the sound :
            " The old swimming hole,
" And the boys flopping off the planks,
" Or sitting in the underbrush playing mandolins. "
                And Kung smiled upon all of them equally.
And Thseng-sie desired to know :
            " Which had answered correctly? "
And Kung said, " They have all answered correctly,
" That is to say, each in his nature. "
And Kung raised his cane against Yuan Jang,
            Yuan Jang being his elder,
For Yuan Jang sat by the roadside pretending to
            be receiving wisdom.

. 57

Fig. 3. Ezra Pound, *A Draft of XXX Cantos* (Paris: The Hours Press, 1930), p. 57; a volume that is "still in the world of fine printing."

like *Don Juan,* but not at all like *The Prelude*) is a work comprised of—organized as—a series of distinct sequences whose distinctness was initially defined by the event of publication. An edition of the *Cantos* will want to preserve the integrity of those separate parts—which are, after all, devices for organizing the reading experience. New Directions and Faber and Faber have always preserved the distinctions by printing the first thirty cantos as a single unit.[1]

But what about the decorated layout of the 1925 and 1928 texts, or for that matter the fine printing of the 1930 Hours Press text? It is true that, by the time the work descended to the trade edition of 1933, the "first installment" of *Cantos* had abandoned what an anthropologist might call its "thick" original textuality. Should an edition of the *Cantos* restore the decorative texts of 1925, 1928, and 1930 to that unit of the *Cantos* we now call "A Draft of XXX Cantos"?

American textual scholarship has operated for about forty years under the following commandment: "Thou shalt not mix literary criticism and editorial practice." This commandment was reaffirmed only a few years ago by one of its chief proponents, the distinguished and immensely influential scholar Fredson Bowers. In a recent issue of *Text,* the annual publication of the Society for Textual Scholarship, the commandment is issued yet again by several parties, including Bowers in his 1985 presidential address to the Society. In this case, however, the pronouncement is made in a context—the context of the particular issue of *Text*—where the authority of the reissued commandment is being, at the same time, questioned, attacked, or simply ignored.[2]

I bring up this matter of textual and editorial theory because the case of the *Cantos* illustrates in the most dramatic ways the difficulty, if not the impossibility, of separating textual/editorial work from critical/interpretive work. A decision about how to treat the physical presentation of Cantos 1–30 in an edition will drastically affect how the work is read and understood.

Furthermore, when we attempt to arrive at such a decision, we will not be able to avoid literary-critical and interpretive analysis and argumentation. No matter how technical the discourse of bibliography and textual criticism becomes, it is ultimately a humane and not a technological pursuit, as A. E. Housman once so eloquently argued.[3] What Housman left unsaid, however, and what needs to be clearly understood today, is that the symbiosis of editorial and interpretive work functions best when the more materially oriented textual and bibliographical studies return the favor of interpretation's gifts to editors and editing.

We can see what is involved here if we consider for a moment the titles of the first three book installments of the *Cantos:* that is to say, the titles of the 1925, 1928, and 1930 texts. I am particularly interested in Pound's representation of the *number* of the cantos being issued. These are, in one simple sense, sixteen, eleven, and thirty cantos respectively. But notice the way Pound's text represents these numerical facts. I leave aside altogether the frequently remarked word "Draft," which is extremely important of course, in order to call attention to the "XXX" of the 1930 text. Whether or not Pound added three cantos to the 1925/1928 unit in order to secure an arbitrary wordplay on the year of publication—something no one has suggested, so far as I am aware, even though such a textual/historical rhyme works very nicely in the event—the typographical form of the number is remarkable (even if it too has thus far gone *un*remarked).

The title of *A Draft of XXX Cantos* presents the concept of thirty neither in an English script nor even in Arabic numerals, but in roman signs: XXX. This small detail is a visual cue calling attention to the linguistic importance of the material form of every script. That Pound was aware of the significance of the material form that signs assume (or are given) hardly needs emphasizing. Indeed, the different forms that Pound gives to numerical units in the titles of the 1925 and 1928 texts—roman and Arabic respectively—partly attract our notice by the differential they make with each other.[4]

The forms *thirty, 30,* and *XXX,* while equivalent at one level, at various other levels diverge into very different horizons of meaning. These differences would have remained invisible, however, had Pound chosen to represent the numerical value of these early books of cantos in the form of the common English script. Having been represented in print as "XXX" and not *thirty* (or even *30*), the work draws the reader's eye to the physique of the texts. Pound's use of roman and Arabic numerals in these titles has the paradoxical effect of heightening our awareness of the peculiarity of the word *thirty* and makes of that word—which does not even put in an appearance here—an index of the sleep into which, in Pound's view, our common English scripts—which is to say the users of those scripts—have fallen. "XXX" is Pound's equivalent of Thoreau's call to wake his neighbors up: in this case, to wake them up to the reality and truth of language.

One of Pound's greatest contributions to poetry lies concealed in his attentiveness to the smallest details of his texts' bibliographical codes. Along with Mallarmé, Apollinaire, and many other modernist innovators, Pound felt that the renewal of the resources of poetry in an age of advanced mechanical reproduction required the artist to bring all aspects of textual production under the aegis of imagination.[5] Nothing was to be taken for granted; the poetry would be brought forth not simply at the linguistic level, but in every feature of the media available to the scriptural imagination.

More than any other of the early modernists, however, Pound was also keenly aware of the large sociohistorical horizon within which the codes of textual production necessarily existed. The scale of his textual vision appears with great clarity in the ornamental features of those early books of 1925, 1928, and 1930. We begin to see this by looking at the decorative initials that Dorothy Pound executed for the 1930 Hours Press edition. These vorticist initials comprise a bibliographical allusion to Pound's own earlier efforts to "gather the limbs of Osiris."[6] Pound's vorticism was one of the early forms that his modernist program took;[7] before 1912 his work was still closely tied to the protomodernist innovations of those important late-nineteenth-century movements, Pre-Raphaelitism and aestheticism.

The decorative materials in the 1925 and 1928 books also comprise an elaborate act of cultural allusion. In this case Pound's text is (as it were) thinking back through a signal event in book production, the founding of the Kelmscott Press by William Morris in May 1891. That month Morris issued his own prose romance *The Story of the Glittering Plain,* which was followed in October by his *Poems by the Way.* Like Pound's 1925 and 1928 texts, these books are distinguished by elaborate ornamental materials, including decorative capitals and two-color printing in red and black.[8] (See fig. 4.)

To understand the full context of what was involved in Pound's act of bibliographical homage and allusion, we should recall the immediate historical background of the founding of Morris's Kelmscott Press.[9] The invention of chromolithography in 1816 was of course decisive, but its impact on decorative book production took some time to develop. The key textual events took place between 1849, when Henry Noel Humphreys completed *The Illuminated Books of the Middle Ages,* and 1861, when Emily Faithfull's Victoria Press brought out its first work, the decorated collection of stories titled *Victoria Regia,* with an introduction by Adelaide

And can I die now that thou biddest live?
What joy this space 'twixt birth and death can
give.
Can we depart, who are so happy here?

A GARDEN BY THE SEA.

I KNOW a little
gardenclose,
Set thick with lily and
red rose,
Where I would wander if I might
From dewy morn to
dewy night,
And have one with me
wandering.

And though within it no birds sing,
And though no pillared house is there,
And though the appleboughs are bare
Of fruit and blossom, would to God
Her feet upon the green grass trod,
And I beheld them as before.

There comes a murmur from the shore,
And in the close two fair streams are,
Drawn from the purple hills afar,
Drawn down unto the restless sea:
Dark hills whose heathbloom feeds no bee,

69   f 3

Fig. 4. William Morris, *Poems by the Way* (London: Kelmscott Press, 1891), p. 69; the kind of book to which Pound pays homage in the early editions of *The Cantos*.

Ann Proctor. Proctor founded the Society for the Promotion of Employment for Women in 1860 as a result of hearing Ruskin lecture and of reading his work, and the Victoria Press—with its company of women compositors—was established under the aegis of the society.[10]

During the 1850s some of the key events were the appearance of Ruskin's *Stones of Venice* and the publication of several manuals teaching decorative book design and manuscript illumination. The Victoria Press emerged at a moment when the interest in decorative printing had become quite strong. Most of the work dealt directly with medieval and religious materials, but secular avenues also began to open up, as the printing of *Victoria Regia* itself shows. In 1857 Humphreys published his decorated *Sentiments and Similes of William Shakespeare,* and Edward Moxon produced his *Illustrated Edition* of the selected poems of Tennyson. This last project drew upon the work of some of the leading young artists of the period, including D. G. Rossetti.

The interest in decorative-book production thus fed directly into the work of the two key figures of the Pre-Raphaelite movement, Morris and D. G. Rossetti. In 1862 Rossetti designed the gold-stamped covers and supplied the material for his sister's decorated title page to *Goblin Market and other Poems,* and in 1870 Rossetti's own collection of poetry was produced with handsome endpapers designed by himself and beautifully ornamented covers. Morris's *Love Is Enough* followed in 1872 in an edition produced with similar decorative features, and he made plans to reissue it with printing ornaments of his own design. These plans, however, had to be abandoned for lack of appropriate typefaces.

All of this activity forms the context in which the idea of the Kelmscott Press was eventually born. Behind it lay a consciousness that the passing of the fifteenth century marked an epochal European event. Pre-Raphaelitism does not merely involve a gesture back to certain medieval styles of art, but to a period when craft-based production was a general feature of European life. The books coming out of the Kelmscott Press were meant to recall that historical moment when a newly discovered tool of mechanical reproduction—the printing press—had not yet become an engine of cultural alienation.

As we know, Kelmscott Press would have an immediate and immense influence on book production in England. During the thirty years after its founding, a whole series of presses sprang up that specialized in fine and decorative printing. However, like the Chiswick Press earlier, which produced manuals of illumination, books of heraldry, and so forth, these presses did not customarily print works of contemporary literature.[11] To the extent that they dealt in books with a relatively broad cultural interest, they issued decorative reprintings of older and often well-known works—classical texts that would recall Aldus Manutius and the other heroes of the printing revolution, or crucial medieval authors like Dante and Villon.

So far as Pound's work is concerned, then, the Victorian decorated book was most important for its medieval preoccupations. Many Victorian decorated books were produced that did not take their inspiration from an imaginative turn back to the Middle Ages, but it is the tradition that did make that turn that made its impact upon Pound. And the key figure in that tradition was of course William Morris.[12]

The Kelmscott Press Chaucer is a good example of this effort to make historicized aesthetic arguments via elaborate bibliographical means. But unlike the Chiswick Press earlier or most of the later printing houses that sprang up under its inspiration, Kelmscott Press began by publishing contemporary work, and it never abandoned that imagination of its mission. This is also important to remember, in relation to Pound's 1925 and 1928 *Cantos* books, because the historicist argument embedded in the Kelmscott *Story of the Glittering Plain* and the 1925 and 1928 editions of early cantos is emphasized by the contemporaneity of the work being printed.

The physique of Pound's 1925 and 1928 editions is thus not simply an allusion to Morris, Pre-Raphaelitism, and the recent history of decorative printing.[13] It is equally an allusion, *through them,* to the Renaissance revolution in printing initiated in the fifteenth and sixteenth centuries. In this respect Pound's elaborate bibliographical coding rhymes with topics he raises and pursues at the work's linguistic levels—most dramatically, perhaps, in the famous allusion to the sixteenth-century printing house of Christian Wechel at the end of the first canto.

Pound's use of the physique of the book in his 1925 and 1928 editions of the early cantos thus goes far beyond the bibliographical experiments of Mallarmé, Apollinaire, the vorticists, the imagists, and the futurists. In all the latter cases no programmatic effort is made to set these experiments in a world-historical scale. But this is exactly what Pound is trying to do, and his effort turns the *Cantos,* properly understood, into an epic project—grounded in that horizon of cultural self-understanding that has dominated the twentieth-century: Language. Pound's *Cantos* is an epic of language, with language conceived as a widely dispersed and world-historical set of different social, institutional, and material events.

The ambition of a project like the *Cantos* forced Pound to pay the closest attention to the semiotic potential that lay in the physical aspects of book and text production. We observe this attentiveness throughout his career—although after World War II his involvement with the printing processes of his works was largely confined to the editions put out by the Milanese firm of Scheiwiller. His typescripts—the setting copy for all his work, early and late—carefully compose the spatial relations of their characters and as such represent "directions for printing," as it were. In random comparisons I have made for the later cantos, the printed texts faithfully reproduce the spatial relations of the words and lines that appear in the typescripts.

Pound was alive, from the beginning of his career, to these semiotics. One of his most famous poems—the imagist manifesto "In a Station of the Metro"—has been reprinted and commented upon many times, but because scholars have seldom gone back to the original printing of the poem, the extreme performativity of that early text has not been remarked.[14]

The poem was first printed in Harriet Monroe's new magazine *Poetry* along with eleven other short poems by Pound. Of these eleven poems, ten appear in standard typographical form—but not "In a Station of the Metro." This, the last of the series printed, appears in the following unusual typographical format:[15]

In a Station of the Metro

The apparition   of these faces   in the crowd   :
Petals   on a wet, black   bough

The arrangement of the text's signs distinctly recalls Pound's typewriting habits—especially in the extended spacing before the final punctuation marks. Pound regularly left this kind of spacing before various marks of punctuation in his typescripts. The point to be emphasized, however, is that he did not *regularly* carry this habit over to the printed texts.

Pound himself (not Harriet Monroe) was almost certainly responsible for the performative typography of "In a Station of the Metro." In any case, we know he took an active part in the physical presentation of many of his later texts. The case of *Hugh Selwyn Mauberley* is especially interesting. This book was published by John Rodker's Ovid Press in 1920. Rodker was an important figure on the scene of modernism as both a writer and a producer of some key modernist books, including Eliot's *Ara Vos Prec* (also published in 1920) as well as the second installment of Pound's *Cantos* (Cantos 17–27).

An extant set of corrected proof sheets of *Hugh Selwyn Mauberley* displays Pound's recurrent directions to the printer about minor details of the text's physical presentation. Next to the half title Pound writes "? higher in page," and the motto page has two of his notes: "T[op] of margin shd always be narrower than bottom. even excessively so." and next to the motto: "set higher in page." On page 10 (the opening page of section 2, "The Age Demanded") Pound circles the printer's handwritten *10* at the top and pulls it to the bottom with the note: "numerals at bottom of page." Once again Pound adds a note for the placement of the page's block of type: "Set Higher."[16]

Perhaps the most startling typographical intervention was made in Pound's manipulation of the book's decorated capitals, made by the artist Edward Wadsworth, one of which was to appear at the beginning of each new section. In the published book, however, there is one deviation from the pattern: the initial letter on page 16 (the "Brennbaum" section) is an italic capital, not a decorated capital. (See fig. 5.) The letter is the letter *T* (the "Brennbaum" section opens with the line "The skylike limpid eyes").

Let me begin by stating in simple declarative terms the significance of that italic capital, so far as Pound was concerned. It constituted a bibliographical allusion to what Pound called the practices of "old printers" who, when they ran out of decorated initials, would use "plain caps or italics" instead. The italic capital was a deliberate moment of modernist constructivism in the text—a moment that, by breaking from the pattern of the decorated capitals, called attention to the book's self-conscious imitation of decorated book production. A good part of the satire in the poem operates through the bibliographical code consciously deployed at the typographical level of the work. The physique of *Hugh Selwyn Mauberley* raises up an image of an artistic practice that would triumph over all that "The Age Demanded." The fact that this work, this book, is itself a part of what "The Age Demanded" only underscores the extremity of Pound's satiric idealism.

How shall I persuade you that this reading of the italic capital on page 16 is not simply my personal interpretive fantasia? The answer is, by laying out the scholarly evidence. The extant proofs of the book are now in the Rodker collection of the Humanities Research Center, University of Texas. They are a composite set, with two pages from an earlier proof (i.e.,

16

BRENNBAUM.

*T*HE sky-like limpid eyes,
    The circular infant's face,
    The stiffness from spats to collar
Never relaxing into grace ;

The heavy memories of Horeb, Sinai and the forty years,
Showed only when the daylight fell
Level across the face
Of Brennbaum " The Impeccable ".

Fig. 5. Ezra Pound, *Hugh Selwyn Mauberley* (London: Ovid Press, 1920),
p. 16. An italic capital, rather than an ornamental one, is deliberately being
deployed by Pound.

received pp. 21 and 22 containing the sections "Envoi (1919)" and
"1920 (Mauberly)").

    Collation of this composite proof with the first edition shows that at
least one more proof of the text must have been made. This fact is appar-
ent not least of all from the decorated capital in the proof. In a number of
cases these do not correspond to the letter called for by the text, and in
each of these instances Pound crosses out the wrong capital and indicates
the proper letter (for example, an pp. 12 and 13, where the printer had put
decorated capitals *F* and *L* respectively) .

    In order to print *Hugh Selwyn Mauberley* according to the design pro-
gram evidently decided upon, the printer needed five decorated *T*s. He
needed one for the first letter of each of the following sections of the
poem: sections 3, 4, 5, "Brennbaum," and "1920 (Mauberly)," corre-
sponding to pages 11, 12, 13, 16, and 22 respectively. However, during
his initial course of typesetting the printer seems to have had access only to
two decorated *T*s. He used one to set the type on the separate earlier proof
of pages 21 and 22, while on the other set of coherent proofs—the main
body of the extant material, which includes pages 11, 12, 13, and 16—he
only puts a decorated *T* on page 11.

In correcting the proofs Pound noted the three instances where the printer put the wrong decorated capital (i.e., on pp. 12, 13, and 16). So, for example, the decorated initial on page 12, which is wrongly an *F,* is corrected by Pound, and at this point he adds the significant note in the margin: "use plain caps or italics as in H. S. Mauberly," that is, as in the italic half-title. "The old printers did this when fancy caps ran out."[17] Similarly, the decorated initials in the proof for pages 13 and 16 are not *T*s; Pound indicates the proper letter in each case, and on page 13 has this note: "Supply of *T*s ran out."

But if Rodker's printer did not have his five decorated *T*s when he was actually setting the type at the first two proof stages, he must have had access to the five at the final stage of printing. When the book appeared, four of the five *T*s were decorated capitals, the fifth being the italic capital that is the central subject of this discussion. It is important that the italic capital in this case should appear on page 16, because in that position one becomes aware of the character's arbitrary placement. That is to say, in the final printed text the single undecorated *T* does not come as the last in the sequence of initial *T*s (the last is on p. 22; see fig. 6), but as the next to last, on page 16.

One might conclude, from this bibliographical anomaly, that Rodker's printer finally and in *fact* had only four decorated *T* initials, and that the undecorated *T* appears on page 16 because *in the final printing sequence* page 16 was the last to be corrected. Page 22, that is to say, already had its decorated *T,* as we can tell from the extant (early) proof of pages 21 and 22. This theory of the text might be supported from Pound's marginal note next to his page 13 correction of the decorated *T:* "Supply of *T*s ran out."

When Pound wrote that note, however, the proofs he was correcting suggested that the "Supply of *T*s" had run out with the setting of page 11, not the setting of page 13. However, the note probably does not mean to indicate that Pound thought the "Supply of *T*s" had run out after page 13. Rather, it must be a general note, indicating his belief—after having had to correct two successive decorated capitals (on pp. 12 and 13)—that Rodker's printer had only two decorated *T*s.

But we know from the final printed text of *Hugh Selwyn Mauberley* that the printer had—in the end at any rate—access to at least four decorated *T*s. Furthermore, we know from other evidence that the printer could have put decorated *T*s for all five of the initials on pages 11, 12, 13, 16, and 22. We know this because the Ovid Press edition of Eliot's *Ara*

1920

(MAUBERLEY)

I.

URNED from the "eau-forte
Par Jaquemart "
To the strait head
Of Messalina :

" His true Penelope
Was Flaubert ",
And his tool
The engraver's

Firmness,
Not the full smile,
His art, but an art
In profile ;

Colourless
Pier Francesca,
Pisanello lacking the skill
To forge Achaia.

Fig. 6.   Ezra Pound, *Hugh Selwyn Mauberley* (London: Ovid Press, 1920), p. 22, with an ornamental capital *T*.

Vos Prec prints each poem with the same set of decorated initials designed by Edward Wadsworth, and in this book six ornamental *T*s are needed. All are present in the printed text.

Evidently Pound assumed at first that there were only two decorated *T*s in Rodker's shop, and he worked from that assumption to fashion from the typography a meaningful symbolic moment.

> PRINTER'S DEVIL. Really? To me Eliot's book only shows that no one is playing poetical games with its typography. Of course it's obvious that Pound is making allusions to the "old printers." But all this talk of multiple decorated *T*s is too elaborate surely. Rodker didn't need all that many if—as must have been the case, given the size of Rodker's operation—the pages were printed off and left standing. The needed *T*s could be moved from forme to forme. So Pound "assumed . . . that there were only two decorated *T*s"? On the contrary: he knew there were only two. He was there, after all.

Tiny as it is, that moment's differential does more to call attention to the work's general bibliographical codes than perhaps any other features of the text.

More than that, however, the bibliographical moment only functions because of the general historical allusion it entails. *Hugh Selwyn Mauberley* is a satire on the tawdry world of cultured London immediately after World War I. The 1920 Ovid Press edition, by the symbology of its carefully crafted printing, means to comment on the debasement of art and imagination in the contemporary and commercial world of England; and it means to develop its commentary by aligning itself with what it sees as other, less debased cultures. Pound's poetic sequence is well aware of the limits and ineffectualities of Pre-Raphaelite aestheticism—including the inheritance of the decorated book that the Pre-Raphaelites passed on. Nevertheless, his work is also aware of the faith that the Pre-Raphaelite tradition had kept with those earlier European cultural traditions that Pound saw as less debased and less commercially driven. The italic *T* on page 16 is not merely Pound's allusion to certain "old printers," it is the index of a massive act of reverential recollection being executed in *Hugh Selwyn Mauberley*.

Implicit in the foregoing is the idea that language has many translinguistic communicative resources. Like so many of his contemporaries, Pound *as a writer* repeatedly imagines the page and the book the way a painter or a book designer would imagine it. This bibliographical imagination can be traced back through Pound's vorticism to the Pre-Raphaelites and—their point of modern departure—to William Blake.

At its most extreme form, this habit of perception can turn a page of text into a "wall of words"—which is the way one good contemporary reader of Blake has described the effect of many of the pages of his illuminated epics:[18] for example, the page from *Jerusalem* in figure 7. This text is very difficult to read. In fact, much of its force derives from the play our eyes and mind are driven to engage with each other, the contest of their shifting claims to authority over our reading experience. This text is breaking down the ordinary distinction readers and scholars make between, on one hand, "the [verbal] text," and, on the other, "the [visual] ornamentation." Like Coleridge when he received in a dream the full text of "Kubla Khan," Blake seems the producer of poetical works "in which all the images rose up before him as *things,* with a parallel production of the correspondent expressions." Words as images, words as things.

In this respect, it is difficult to avoid the similarity of Blake's work to the books Morris turned out from his Kelmscott Press. We can see the connection, for example, when the distinguished historian of the book, Douglas McMurtrie, alludes to certain criticisms that have been raised against Morris's work:

> The criticism levelled by competent critics against the Kelmscott books holds that the fundamental purpose of books is to be read and that the Morris books are neither legible in their type matter nor convenient for handling in their format. They contend that they are, first, exercises in decorative design and only secondarily, books intended for reading; that even if one endeavors to read them, the mind is distracted from the sense of the author by spots or masses of decoration so insistent in area and color as to completely overshadow the text.[19]

"Even the most enthusiastic admirers of William Morris must admit that there is much of truth in these criticisms," McMurtrie adds—to which one would perhaps want to reply, "True, but hardly true enough." For such criticisms miss one of the chief points that Blake and Morris are making about the translinguistic features of language. Because language is always materialized and embodied in one way or another, these material phenomena (they have an acoustic dimension as well) assume independent

17

His Spectre divides & Los in fury compells it to divide:
To labour in the fire. in the water. in the earth. in the air,
To follow the Daughters of Albion as the hound follows the scent
Of the wild inhabitant of the forest, to drive them from his own:
To make a way for the Children of Los to come from the Furnaces
But Los himself against Albions Sons his fury bends. for he
Dare not approach the Daughters openly lest he be consumed
In the fires of their beauty & perfection & be Vegetated beneath
Their Looms. in a Generation of death & resurrection to forgetfulness
They woo Los continually to subdue his strength: he continually
Shews them his Spectre: sending him abroad over the four points of heaven
In the fierce desires of beauty & in the tortures of repulse: He is
The Spectre of the Living pursuing the Emanations of the Dead.
Shuddring they flee: they hide in the Druid Temples in cold chastity:
Subdued by the Spectre of the Living & terrified by undisguisd desire.

For Los said: Tho my Spectre is divided: as I am a Living Man
I must compell him to obey me wholly: that Enitharmon may not
Be lost: & lest he should devour Enitharmon: Ah me!
Piteous image of my soft desires, & loves: O Enitharmon:
I will compell my Spectre to obey: I will restore to thee thy Children.
No one bruises or starves himself to make himself fit for labours

Tormented with sweet desire for these beauties of Albion
They would never love my power if they did not seek to destroy
Enitharmon: Vala would never have sought & loved Albion
If she had not sought to destroy Jerusalem: such is that false
And Generating Love: a pretence of love to destroy love:
Cruel hipocrisy unlike the lovely delusions of Beulah:
And cruel forms, unlike the merciful forms of Beulahs Night

They know not why they love nor wherefore they sicken & die
Calling that Holy Love: which is Envy Revenge & Cruelty Of Man:
Which separated the stars from the mountains: the mountains from
And left Man a little grovelling Root, outside of Himself
Negations are not Contraries: Contraries mutually Exist:
But Negations Exist Not: Exceptions & Objections & Unbeliefs
Exist not: nor shall they ever be Organized for ever & ever:
If thou separate from me, thou art a Negation: a meer
Reasoning & Derogation from me, an Objecting & cruel Spite
And Malice & Envy: but my Emanation, Alas! will become
My Contrary: O thou Negation I will continually compell
Thee to be invisible to any but whom I please, & when
And where & how I please, and never never shalt thou be Organized
But as a distorted & reversed Reflexion in the Darkness
And in the Non Entity: nor shall that which is above
Ever descend into thee: but thou shalt be a Non Entity for ever
And if any enter into thee, thou shalt be an Unquenchable Fire
And he shall be a never dying Worm, mutually tormented by
Those that thou tormentest, a Hell & Despair for ever & ever.

So Los in secret with himself communed & Enitharmon heard
In her darkness & was comforted: yet still she divided away
In gnawing pain from Los's bosom in the deadly Night:
First as a red Globe of blood trembling beneath his bosom
Suspended over her he hung: he infolded her in his garments
Of wool: he hid her from the Spectre, in shame & confusion of
Face; in terrors & pains of Hell & Eternal Death, the
Trembling Globe shot forth Self living & Los howld over it:
Feeding it with his groans & tears day & night without ceasing:
And the Spectrous Darkness from his back divided in temptations.
And in grinding agonies in threats: stiflings: & direful strugglings

Go thou to Skofeld: ask him if he is Bath or if he is Canterbury
Tell him to be no more dubious: demand explicit words
Tell him: I will dash him into shivers, where & at what time
I please: tell Hand & Skofeld they are my ministers of evil
To those I hate: for I can hate also as well as they:

Fig. 7.   William Blake, *Jerusalem*.

signifying functions. Poets like Blake, Morris, and Pound are bent upon the exploitation of the entirety of language's signifying mechanisms.

Pound's *Cantos* never neglect or abandon this signifying dimension of language. Nevertheless, his texts—like those of the Cuala Press, which so influenced his mind on these matters—definitely attempt to preserve the clear readability of the text.[20] He does not treat his pages as paintings or full-scale visual designs, which both Blake and Morris most certainly do.[21] Furthermore, after 1930 Pound no longer exploited the phanopoeic textual resources passed on to him through Pre-Raphaelitism: with one significant exception, all the parts of the *Cantos* published after 1930 are commercially produced.[22] (That exception, which I shall return to in a moment, involves the notorious "forbidden cantos," which were printed in Italy but not placed in sequence as Cantos 72–73 until 1989.)

If, after 1930, Pound leaves behind that highly decorative approach to the *Cantos* so spectacularly displayed in the 1925 and 1928 books, he does not by any means abandon his commitments to bibliographical coding for his work. Pound's Pre-Raphaelite cantos—and I do think Cantos 1–27 ought to be called that—signal important historical meanings, both in the development of European poetry at large, and in the more immediate context of Pound's (and modernism's) evolution. Pound's Pre-Raphaelite cantos are the equivalent of what Yeats did a few years later when he placed his "free verse" text of Pater's *Mona Lisa* at the outset of his *Oxford Book of Modern Verse*.

In the recession of the conventions of decorative-book production from the post-1930 *Cantos* we continue to see Pound exploiting the bibliographical resources of commercial-press printing. These effects appear most spectacularly whenever Pound introduces Chinese characters into a textual field dominated by Western scripts—for instance, in the pages shown in figure 8. If pages like this are being imagined as texts to be read, they are also being treated as visual constructions of printed characters. Looking and reading converge as reciprocal functions.

The effect, moreover, controls the signifying process at the macro as well as the micro level. Perhaps one's first impression, in seeing pages like this, is to register the gestalt of the figuration—the page treated as a *composition,* with that term to be taken simultaneously as a typographer and as a painter would use it. But such effects of general page design are controlled by the way the text forces a reader to pay attention to the smallest detail.

In pages like these, for instance, the Chinese characters appear before

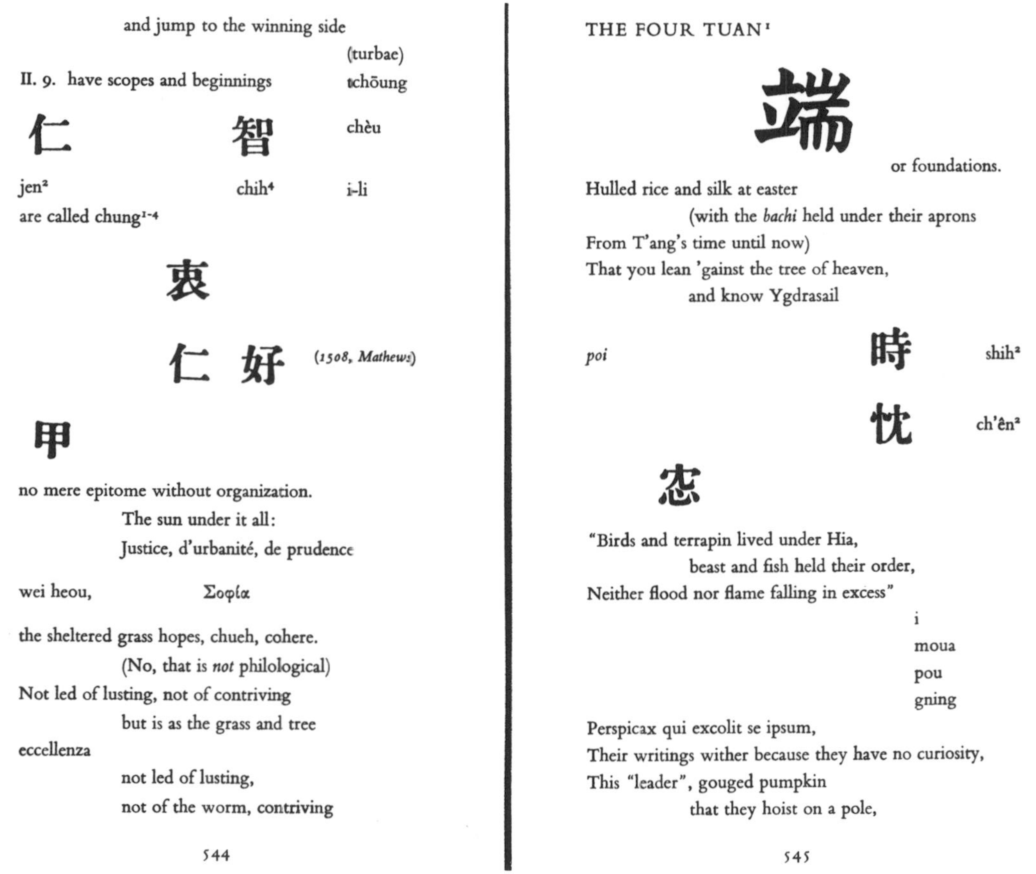

and jump to the winning side

(turbae)

II. 9. have scopes and beginnings   tchōung

chēu

仁 智 衷   chih⁴   i-li

jen²

are called chung¹⁻⁴

甲 仁 奸   (1508, Mathews)

no mere epitome without organization.
    The sun under it all:

wei heou,   Justice, d'urbanité, de prudence

Σοφία

the sheltered grass hopes, chueh, cohere.
    (No, that is *not* philological)

Not led of lusting, not of contriving
    but is as the grass and tree

eccellenza

    not led of lusting,
    not of the worm, contriving

544

THE FOUR TUAN'

蹴   or foundations.

Hulled rice and silk at easter
    (with the *bachi* held under their aprons
From T'ang's time until now)
That you lean 'gainst the tree of heaven,
    and know Ygdrasail

時   shih²

仁 忧   ch'ēn²

poi

恋

"Birds and terrapin lived under Hia,
    beast and fish held their order,
Neither flood nor flame falling in excess"

i

moua

pou

gning

Perspicax qui excolit se ipsum,
Their writings wither because they have no curiosity,
This "leader", gouged pumpkin
    that they hoist on a pole,

545

Fig. 8. Ezra Pound, *The Cantos of Ezra Pound* (New York: New Directions, 11th printing, 1989), pp. 544–45, with Chinese characters introduced into a field of Western scripts.

our eyes with all their unique ideographic force. They work this way because the characters are so unfamiliar to us. We have to remember, in reflecting on texts like this, that Pound's poem is written for a Euro-American audience and that its rhetoric depends upon certain assumptions Pound makes about the language(s) that have descended to (and *in*to) that audience in its historical emergence. If Pound's Chinese characters invoke the entire apparatus of Pound's Fenellosan approach to such materials, that conceptual framework only serves to focus our attention on the immediate text's smallest particularities. English and other Euro-American languages are the large field into which Pound has introduced his Chinese characters, but it is the latter that throw the details of that larger field into an entirely new perspective. To put it as simply as possible: the Chinese characters are an index of the kind of attention all scripted forms demand, even—and perhaps most crucially—those forms that are most familiar to us, such as the forms of our own languages. The *ming* ideogram on page 539, for example, is explicitly presented as the sign of an essential feature of signs in general: that they preserve "distinctions in clarity," and that every sign, even the smallest character of a language, must be attended to for the "distinctions" it draws. (See fig. 9.) In this case, the *ming* character is a composite of two base characters that signify (respectively) "moon" and "sun" as sources light. In the composite character the two are brought together as a single *figura* meaning "intelligence," but this more abstract meaning is (as it were) dramatized in the ideogram itself, where the two base characters are joined but also distinguished.

The small superscripts attached to the English transliterations of the Chinese ideograms—for instance, the superscript *2* attached to *ming* on page 539—are a good index of the presence of such distinctions at the phonic level of the Chinese language. Western translators of Chinese evolved a convention of four superscripts, numbered 1, 2, 3, 4, to designate different possible phonic values that a particular word might have. These four numbers represent Western translators' drawing necessary distinctions of tonal value for different words; for in Chinese, the same written character is not absolutely self-identical, since it may stand for very different words (or perhaps we should say here, things) depending upon the tone in which it is uttered.[23]

But the words and characters of every language are never self-identical or transparent. One of the great objects of the *Cantos* is to reeducate Western readers in the use of their own inherited languages, in the understanding of how language works in general, and how materially and his-

and my old great aunt did likewise
with that too large hotel
but at least she saw damn all Europe
    and rode on that mule in Tangiers
        and in general had a run for her money

like Natalie
      " perhaps more than was in it "

    Under white clouds, cielo di Pisa
out of all this beauty something must come,

O moon my pin-up,
          chronometer
Wei, Chi and Pi-kan
Yin had these three men full of humanitas (manhood)
      or jên^2
Xaire Alessandro
      Xaire Fernando, e il Capo,
Pierre, Vidkun,
    Henriot
and as to gradations
who went out of industrials into Government
  when the slump was in the offing
as against whom, prepense, got OUT of Imperial Chemicals
in 1938
so as not to be nourished by blood-bath?

quand vos venetz al som de l'escalina
        ἦθος gradations
These are distinctions in clarity

ming^2 明   these are distinctions

539

Fig. 9. Ezra Pound, *The Cantos of Ezra Pound* (New York: New Directions, 11th printing, 1989), p. 539, with careful attention given to the *Ming* character toward the bottom.

torically grounded are its meanings. Pound's use of Chinese characters dramatizes the presence of sharp distinctions in fields that might otherwise appear smooth and uniform. There are *differences* that have to be attended to, at the top of page 780, in the way Pound repeats the Greek word "kalliastragalos." There is upper case and there is lower case; there is English script and there is Greek script; there is even the placement of the repeated word at the center of the page, as well as the (perhaps fortuitous, but nevertheless equally significant) appearance of the repeated word at the *top* of the page in the received New Directions text.[24]

In this entire context, the problem of editing the *Cantos* becomes at one and the same time a problem of interpreting the work. This happens because the poem will not allow an editor to proceed on the assumption that final distinctions can be drawn, for example, between substantives and accidentals, between "the text" and its ornaments—between the work of the poet, on one hand, and the work of the compositor, the printer, even the bibliographer on the other. There is not first a text and then the meaning of a text. The transmission history of poetical work is as much a part of the poetry as is the "original" work of the author.

The relevance of the transmissive medium is particularly apparent when we consider the "forbidden cantos," the two sections (Cantos 72–73) that belong immediately before the Pisan Cantos. These two parts were kept out of the New Directions and Faber collected cantos until the tenth printing in 1986. At that point they are placed in the text out of sequence—near the end of the book, as a kind of appendix to the "Drafts and Fragments" section.

The textual history of these two cantos is eloquent, a material sign in itself of why these texts have been called the forbidden cantos. They were written in 1944 and first published in 1945 in two succeeding issues of *La Marina Repubblicana* (15 Jan. and 1 Feb.), a propaganda organ of Mussolini's Salò regime. They comprise an extended act of homage to Italy's disintegrating Fascist government. The physical text of this first printing, which was recently on display at the Beinecke Library's Pound exhibition, is of the utmost importance: it demonstrates with great force the way a verbal text and its printing medium can be made to interact and comment on each other.

When the new installment of Pound's *Cantos* came to be printed, however, Cantos 72–73 were absent: the new group included only Cantos 74–84, and they appeared in print under the title *The Pisan Cantos*. The two fascist cantos were "forbidden" an entrance into the ongoing text, their subject matter being, in the immediate postwar context, both forbidding and forbidden. It is not clear to me whether Pound himself withheld Cantos 72–73 in 1948, or whether he was persuaded to do so by others. In any event, a new edition (with an augmented Canto 72) was printed for copyright purposes in 1973—probably just twenty-five were printed. Then, in 1983, the two cantos were printed complete by Vanni Scheiwiller, in Milan, with an introduction by Mary de Rachewiltz.

I narrate this printing history because each part of the history contains a proleptic explanation of the later parts. The 1986 New Directions text differs only in the most trivial ways from the 1983 text *so far as the linguistic level of the text is concerned;* and whereas the texts of Canto 72 printed after 1945 are longer than that of the initial printing, the linguistic material, once it appears in print, preserves a noticeable stability. Nevertheless, the physical presentation of these two cantos is patently relevant to their "meaning." Cantos 72–73 are forbidden cantos, for example, not by "author's intentions" but by historical and social circumstances, and those circumstantialities are preserved in the bibliographical codes through which the "forbidden cantos" have been transmitted to us.

The most recent phase of this textual history was inaugurated in 1989, when New Directions issued its eleventh printing of the *Cantos*. In this new format Cantos 72–73 are moved once again, this time to a position just before the Pisan Cantos, where their numeration would indicate they ought to be placed. Perhaps they have at last come to rest. In any case, their wanderings comprise an important feature of their meaning and their textual history, and any scholarly edition of the entire work will have to highlight such matters.

Pound's *Cantos* dramatize, on an epic scale, a related pair of important truths about poetry and all written texts: that the meaning of works committed into language is carried at the bibliographical as well as the linguistic level, and that the transmission of such works is as much a part of their meaning as anything else we can distinguish about them. Transmission is an elementary kind of translation, a reenactment (and often one kind of completion) of the poetical act the artist sets in motion. That Pound understood these matters is clear from his deep involvement with the material transmissions of his work, as we have seen.

I should not conclude this discussion, however, without recalling Dante Gabriel Rossetti; for Rossetti, like Morris, was one of the first to speak in this particular modernist tongue, though he did so—also like Morris—in a distinctly Victorian dialect. Rossetti's involvement with the decorative-book tradition was not so deep as Morris's, of course, but it was—as I have already noted—significant. Besides, Rossetti's book of translations, *The Early Italian Poets* (1862), was one of modernism's seminal (if forgotten) points of reference and departure, not least of all for Pound.

But Rossetti's connection to Pound also comes through Rossetti's important series of "Sonnets for Pictures," which distinctly forecast the modernist attempt to break away from one hundred years of symbolist thinking about art and language, with its implicit (or even explicit) ideological distinction between poetry and the meaning of poetry. The "Sonnets for Pictures" represent Rossetti's understanding that the work of art (poem or painting) and its meaning are not two, but one thing. Meaning in art does not require an attendant hermeneutical operation to be revealed. Far from being an absent or precious secret, art's meaning is present and manifest. It is the act and eventuality of the work itself.

The function of criticism, in such circumstances, is an enabling one—to facilitate as immediate and direct an experience of the work as possible. Blake called it cleansing the doors of perception. In Rossetti it appears as an explicit critique of the hermeneutical and symbolist program. His "Sonnets for Pictures" aspire to the condition of pictorial concreteness: words as characterological figures, words as images in need of no further interpretation. It is phanopoeia and ideography in a Victorian mode:

> This is that blessed Mary, pre-elect
> God's Virgin.
>
> ("Mary's Girlhood")

> Here meet together the prefiguring day
> And day prefigured.
>
> ("The Passover in the Holy Family")[25]

The method is clear from the way Rossetti uses terms like "preelect" and "prefiguring." These are interpretation's words, but Rossetti's poetry offers them to us as if they stood on the same plane of meaning as the visual figures he also presents:

> John binds the shoes
> He deemed himself not worthy to unloose;
> And Mary culls the bitter herbs ordained.
>
> ("The Passover in the Holy Family")

In such texts meaning becomes another concrete detail, for the poetry is working to transform symbols back into an original concreteness. Rossetti's sonnet "Mary's Girlhood" does not represent itself as an interpretation of the original picture, but as the picture's verbal equivalent: *ut pictura poiesis,* a making like a picture. It strives to eliminate the gap that the symbolic imagination had opened between the *figura* and its interpretation.

Rossetti's purpose emerges with unmistakable clarity in his second (untitled) sonnet on his picture *Mary's Girlhood.* This sonnet devotes itself entirely to an exegesis of the painting's symbolical *figurae:*

> These are the symbols. On that cloth of red
>   I' the centre is the Tripoint: perfect each,
>   Except the second of its points, to teach
> That Christ is not yet born. The books—whose head
> Is golden Charity, as Paul hath said—
>   Those virtues are wherein the soul is rich:
>   Therefore on them the lily standeth, which
> Is Innocence, being interpreted.

Here symbolism is being naively recovered at the level of pure perception. Meaning thus rises up before us as a set of apparitional details, as it does in Rossetti's sonnet "For an Allegorical Dance of Women by Andrea Mantegna." In the latter, however, Rossetti explicitly comments on the kind of art he is trying to imagine, the kind of meaning he is trying to expose, when he concludes his sonnet in this way:

>   It is bitter glad
> Even unto tears. Its meaning filleth it,
> A secret of the wells of Life: to wit:—
> The heart's each pulse shall keep the sense it had
> With all, though the mind's labour run to nought.

The "secret" meaning of this art is its perduring sensoriness, which does not have to be sought beneath the appearances of things, through the abstracted "labour" of the mind.

Essential to the force of the passage is the "wit" playing about Rossetti's line "A secret of the wells of Life." The phrase recalls the symbolistic commonplace, that truth is only found at the bottom of a well. Rossetti's text, however, teases from the word "wells" an unexpected metonymic significance; for the text has exposed another possible meaning of the word, a meaning more connected to the words "tears" and "filleth," which immediately precede the phrase. The great "secret of the wells of Life" may not lie concealed at the bottom, it may rather "well" at the top, like a brimming cup, or like eyes filled with tears. One recalls Blake's proverb of Hell—"The cistern contains, the fountain overflows"—because Rossetti, like the Blake from whom he learned so much, wanted to recover an art of ornamental profusion, an art whose meaning is no more (and no less) than the actual and determinate play of the energetic mind.

This is exactly the inheritance received and passed on by Ezra Pound, and by every modernist who followed a similar constructivist approach toward the making of poetry.

NOTES

1. There is a problem with respect to these cantos because the decorated editions display two distinct sequences (1–16, 17–27). The unit 1–30 does not come into existence until later, in 1930; and when it does, the initial distinction is removed. A critical edition of the *Cantos* will have to make some difficult decisions about how to present these texts.

2. For a clear presentation of the lines of disagreement see Bowers's presidential address to the STS, "Unfinished Business," in *Text* 4, ed. D. C. Greetham and W. Speed Hill (New York: AMS Press, 1988), 1–11, esp. 8; and my paper "The Textual Condition," ibid., 29–37.

3. In his famous "The Application of Thought to Textual Criticism," *Proceedings of the Classical Association* 28 (1921): 67–84.

4. Lawrence Rainey has pointed out (*a*) that the use of roman numerals was a common fascist practice, and (*b*) that the dust jacket of the 1933 edition displays the Xs as the leather thongs binding a fasces.

5. This tendency toward productive comprehensiveness may be seen, in one respect, as a feature of the authoritarianism of the modernist approach. However, to the extent that Pound, like Yeats, drew upon the work of William Morris and the legacy of the Kelmscott Press for his interest in the physical presentation of texts, Pound's work here can be connected to Victorian socialist ideals of medieval-artisanal cooperative production. See my essays "Thing to Mind: The Materialist Aesthetic of William Morris," *The Pre-Raphaelites in Context* (Huntington Library and Art Gallery: San Marino, 1992): 55–74; and "The Socialization of Texts," *Bulletin of the Association of Documentary Editing* 12 (September 1990): 13–37.

6. I refer to the series of articles Pound published in *The New Age* between 7 December 1911 and 15 February 1912 under the general heading "I Gather the Limbs of Osiris"; this eleven-part sequence is reprinted as part 1 of Pound's *Selected Prose, 1909–1965*, ed. William Cookson (Faber and Faber: London, 1973): 19–44.

7. For a good discussion of Pound's vorticism that has a bearing on my argument in this paper, see Hugh Kenner, *The Pound Era* (Berkeley and Los Angeles: University of California Press, 1971), 238.

8. For an excellent discussion of Morris and his projects in decorative printing see Norman Kelvin, "Patterns in Time: The Decorative and the Narrative in the Work of William Morris," in *Nineteenth-Century Lives: Essays Presented to Jerome Hamilton Buckley,* ed. Lawrence S. Lockridge, John Maynard, and Donald D. Stone (Cambridge: University of Cambridge Press, 1989), 140–68. See also Henry Halliday Sparling's classic *The Kelmscott Press and William Morris, Master-Craftsman* (London: Macmillan, 1924).

9. See Joan Friedman's *Color Printing in England, 1486–1870* (New Haven: Yale Center for British Art, 1978); Ruari McLean, *Victorian Book Design and Color Printing* (London: Faber and Faber, 1963).

10. See William E. Fredeman, "Emily Faithfull and the Victoria Press: An Experiment in Sociological Bibliography," *Library,* 5th series, 29, no. 2 (June 1974): 139–64.

11. After Morris's Kelmscott Press, the Yeatses' venture with the Cuala Press was the most notable outlet for finely printed work by contemporary writers.

12. For Morris's bibliographical vision and program see *The Ideal Book: Essays and Lectures on the Arts of the Book by William Morris* (Berkeley and Los Angeles: University of California Press, 1982).

13. The one distinctive feature of the Kelmscott Press format that Pound's early decorative books did *not* follow was Morris's tight arrangement of words and lines. Kelmscott Press texts are hard to read (see discussion below). The style of modernist decorative books, like Pound's, tended to lead out the lines and, in general, to deliver the text on a page that provided generous spacing throughout.

14. But see the article by Steve Ellis, "The Punctuation of 'In a Station of the Metro,'" *Paideuma* 17 (1988): 201–7.

15. See *Poetry* 2 (April 1913): 12. All subsequent printings give the poem in its received (and conventional) typographical form.

16. Pound's directions to the printer show the clear influence of William Morris's ideas about page design, especially on the matter of the margins; see Morris's two papers "Printing" and "The Ideal Book," reprinted in *The Ideal Book,* esp. 64–65, 70–71.

17. Once again the influence of Morris appears, this time in Pound's phrase "the old printers" (see ibid.).

18. See Vincent De Luca, "A Wall of Words: The Sublime as Text," in *Unnam'd Forms,* ed. Nelson Hilton and Thomas A. Vogler (Berkeley and Los Angeles: University of California Press, 1986), 218–41.

19. Douglas C. McMurtrie, *The Book: The Story of Printing and Bookmaking,* 3d ed. (Oxford: Oxford University Press, 1943), 460.

20. For an interesting discussion of the promotional and economic factors that contributed to the "anti-Kelmscott" approach to text layout in fine-book production in the 1890s and afterward, see R. D. Brown, "The Bodley Head Press: Some Bibliographical Extrapolations," *Papers of the Bibliographical Society of America* 61 (1967): 39–50.

21. In his visual treatment of the page Pound is in certain respects closer to Blake than he is to Morris. Both Blake and Pound treat the page as an integral unit, whereas for Morris the visual bibliographical unit was not the page but the "opening" (i.e., the two pages that appear together when a book is opened to view). See *The Ideal Book*, 64–65, 70–71.

22. Cantos 72–73 were first issued not through a commercial printing institution, but through an ideological one, an organ of fascist propaganda; see below for discussion.

23. I am grateful to Paul Wellen for helping me to understand Pound's appropriation of these Western conventions for representing the acoustic dimension of Chinese characters.

24. In the finished typescripts of this canto the word appears at the bottom on the second typed page.

25. My Rossetti texts are all taken from *The Works of Dante Gabriel Rossetti*, ed. William Michael Rossetti (London: Ellis, 1911).

4

"All I Want You to Do Is to Follow the Orders": History, Faith, and Fascism in the Early Cantos

Lawrence S. Rainey

The Cantos is a notoriously erudite book. It bristles with difficulty, teems with obscure quotations, and overflows with names, facts, and dates, rarely dispensing the simpler pleasures of plot or suspense. Yet the closing passage of Canto 10 comes perhaps as close as any to doing so. It depicts a battle, in this case an engagement that took place in 1461, focusing on the scene just as the protagonist Sigismondo Malatesta is about to address his troops. (10.47, 11.48). The narrator, evidently an old soldier who has fought alongside Sigismondo, seems to be reliving the sense of impending conflict, and his tone is taut with anticipation. Sigismondo's forces are badly outnumbered: thirteen hundred cavalry and five hundred infantry arrayed against the enemy's four thousand cavalry and one thousand infantry. The battle has already begun, the enemy is approaching:

> And they came at us with their ecclesiastical legates
> Until the eagle lit on his tent pole.
> And he said: The Romans would have called that an augury
> *E gradment li antichi cavaler romanj*
> > *davano fed a quisti annutii,*
> All I want you to do is to follow the orders,
> They've got a bigger army,
> > but there are more men in this camp.

Sigismondo delivers a brief speech designed to rouse his troops. The language has a soldierly simplicity ("All I want you to do is to follow the orders"), and it makes a direct appeal to manly pride and camaraderie ("but there are more men in this camp"). Its opening gambit, however, is more complex: Sigismondo observes an eagle that has just landed on the top of his tent, and, seizing the occasion, he interprets it as a presage of victory, a sign that his troops will win: "The Romans would have called that an augury," he says, then adding, "And the ancient Romans placed great faith in such annunciations." To the reader outside the text, Sigismondo's invocation of antiquity signals his familiarity with the culture of early Renaissance humanism, with its appeal to ancient practice as a guide to present conduct, while to the common soldier who is the immediate audience within the text, it remains simple enough to convey its general force. Quite abruptly, at this point, the canto breaks off, ending like a serial film on a note of suspense. Will the speech succeed? Will Sigismondo prevail or go down in defeat? To learn the answer, we must turn the page . . .

Canto 11 begins with a flashback to the action of the previous episode. Once more we hear the same phrase, "And the ancient Romans placed great faith in such annunciations," followed by fifteen lines that further delay the conclusion and build up suspense: we receive a lengthy list of Sigismondo's commanders (a miniature variant of the epic catalog), we are told about the size of the respective armies, and then we learn the battle's outcome:

> And we beat the papishes and fought
> them back through the tents
> And he came up to the dyke again
> And fought through the dyke-gate
> And it went on from dawn to sunset
> And we broke them and took their baggage.

Sigismondo has won, at least for the moment; and from the outcome we can infer that his speech proved effective. Yet however much the device of narrative suspense has been highlighted, more than the outcome of a single battle is at stake in this passage. For here theatrical trappings of war serve as the staging ground of a very different drama, a drama of interpretation. Sigismondo achieves his victory by virtue of his capacity to interpret an event as an augury, a sign. He himself becomes an augur, a diviner whose task is to determine whether the gods approve a proposed action, or in the more extensive sense, to foretell the future. He takes on the functions of the poet, the artist, and he becomes "the antenna of the race." His actions, in effect, epitomize some of the deepest structures governing the relations among text, reading, and history within *The Cantos* itself. Confronted with an unexpected event in an environment that threatens his destruction, Sigismondo reads it through the prism of history, interprets its significance for the present, and transforms it into a guide for conduct in the future, doing so in a way that lends interpretation a performative dimension within the "present" of the text, turns it into an exhortation to resolute action in the face of an overwhelmingly hostile reality. Sigismondo, in other words, does more than offer just a reading of a single event, for his actions constitute a reading of reading. They recapitulate the interpretive processes that are also being enacted within the text by the author, processes that are then to be assimilated by the reader who is outside the text. Within the text, that is to say, the reader of *The Cantos* is likewise confronted with apparently random events that occur in an environment implacably hostile to everyday reading, inimical to conventions of narrative and sequence, and is likewise invited to assess them in the light of history, whether furnished by the text itself or secured in a shared background of knowledge, beliefs, and cultural practices. While in the world outside the text, the reader is also solicited to transform that interpretive knowledge into action, be it the action of interpretation itself or the action of living differently in the light of new imaginative experience. At the heart of this paradigm is a reference to interpretive practices from the past, the auguries of ancient Rome, protocols in which the governing term is *faith*, for it is faith that the Romans once gave to such annunciations, and faith that Sigismondo now demands of his men. Faith becomes the term that mediates a transition from an apparently historical discourse that rests on everyday notions of referentiality and representation to another discourse that invokes a notion of experience and that brings that notion to bear on the future. But faith in what?

We might call this the "Sigismondo paradigm" of interpretation, an ideal configuration of event and text, of reading and history, which constitutes one of the principal protocols offered by *The Cantos,* a paradigm of its own interpretive activity and a model of how that activity should be assimilated, reinterpreted by readers. And yet, as readers will have already noticed, our initial summary of this passage has glossed over several cruxes entailed in its interpretation, local difficulties that bear upon similar questions of event and reading, history and understanding. The presence of these questions at both micro and macro levels is not surprising. The question of how one was to interpret history, both past and contemporary, was one that was acquiring a special urgency in the wake of the Great War that had utterly transformed the political surface of European culture. The monarchies that had ruled Germany, Austria, and Russia for centuries had vanished, replaced by new democracies or an extreme and intransigent form of socialism. Still, these were all political orders that had been in existence long before World War I. What made the question of history so pressing in late 1922 and early 1923, when Pound was working on the Malatesta Cantos, was the interpretive challenge posed by the brusque arrival of fascism at the center stage of Europe with Mussolini's accession to power. In turn, that immediate question intersected with issues of history, faith, and modernity that were much discussed throughout the period from roughly 1900 to 1925. At stake, in Sigismondo's brief remarks to his troops, then, is a set of issues that have recently been at the center of debate about modernism, the avant-garde, and fascism. But to address them we must survey briefly Sigismondo's career and its aftermath, then examine the compositional history of this specific passage, and finally return to our primary questions.

Sigismondo Malatesta (1417–68) is known to posterity for a single act that he pursued over the course of more than a decade, his sponsoring the reconstruction of the church of San Francesco (or Saint Francis), often called the Tempio Malatestiano, located in the town of Rimini.[1] The building figures in every introductory work of Western architectural history because it was the first ecclesiastical edifice to incorporate the Roman triumphal arch into its structural vocabulary.[2] The massive central doorway, flanked by two blind arches, plainly owes much to the nearby Arch of Augustus, the oldest triumphal arch in Italy, which is also located in Rimini. The interior, too, is striking: it teems with an elaborate series of sculptures and bas-reliefs by Agostino di Duccio, while the sacristy for the Chapel of San Sigismondo houses a fine fresco by Piero della Francesca. The church's reconstruction, initially undertaken as the refurbishing of a single chapel within an already extant church that dated from the thirteenth century, assumed new dimensions in 1449–50, when Sigismondo entrusted the project to Leon Battista Alberti, one of his earliest and most important commissions. It was Alberti who redesigned the building's entire facade, added the central doorway, and adorned the sides with a series of seven deep arches divided by massive piers. Alberti also planned to add a transept and to crown the intersection of nave and transept with a soaring dome; but a precipitous decline in Sigismondo's political fortunes left him unable to bear the costs of construction. By 1460 work on the project had stopped, and the church was left incomplete.

Sigismondo's political career was shaped by the shifting balance of power that prevailed in the Italian peninsula. Essentially there were five major states: Venice and Milan in the north; Florence in central Italy; and Rome (or the papacy) and Naples in the south. In the course of his lifetime Sigismondo served each of them as a condottiere, though by the later 1450s the major states increasingly regarded him with suspicion, either because his conduct of various campaigns had lacked sufficient vigor or because he was reported to have engaged in duplicitous dealings with his opponents.[3] In 1459 he joined another condottiere, Giacomo Piccinino, in an imprudent attempt to unseat the Aragonese dynasty that ruled Naples and replace it with the Angevin dynasty of southern France. For Milan the scheme raised the specter of invasion from France, and Francesco Sforza, ruler of the Milanese duchy, reacted sharply. So did papal Rome, partly because it too wished to prevent the establishment of a French presence in the peninsula, partly because Sigismondo's actions offered a pretext for the church to reassert its claims over territories long lost to its control. The territories were those of Sigismondo. By law the Malatesta were not the legal rulers of Rimini and the surrounding countryside, but vicars of the church who, in return for an annual fee, were granted absolute control over all taxation and legal matters. After the collapse of the conciliar movement in the 1440s, however, the papacy was increasingly assuming the institutional traits of the Italian *casato*, or extended family enterprise, acquiring its elastic corporate and dynastic structure as well as its ambitious expansionism.[4] The resurgent papacy, in seeking to regain control over territories it had lost in the past, was taking the first step toward the formation of the modern papal state that would rule over central Italy until 1860. Sigismondo's was among the first of the many minor states that would disappear during the next half century. That, of course, was no consolation for him. In 1461 he managed to survive a ferocious campaign that was launched against him, defeating a superior ecclesiastical army at the battle of Nidastore on 2 July of that year, the battle that is the subject of the lines quoted above. The next season his luck ran out. On 12 August 1462 his troops were routed at the battle of Senigallia, and less than a week later those of his ally, Giacomo Piccinino, were annihilated at the battle of Troia. When peace terms were drafted, Sigismondo had lost everything except the city of Rimini and a few nearby towns.

Already during Sigismondo's lifetime the church of San Francesco aroused discussion, and in the centuries that followed it elicited a growing body of scholarly and antiquarian commentary.[5] But it was in the later eighteenth century that a series of new and related arguments about the church's significance began to make their appearance. It was urged, for example, that the church was not a church at all, at least not in the ordinary sense; nor was it just a monument to the Malatesta dynasty or Sigismondo's exemplary status as its preeminent representative. Instead, the building had been designed to commemorate Sigismondo's love for Isotta degli Atti, his mistress and later (after 1456) his third wife. The crucial evidence adduced in support of this view was the entwined cipher, made up of the letters *S* and *I,* that is sculpted everywhere among the church's internal and external decorations. The sign, in the new view, referred to the first letters in the names of Sigismondo and Isotta. This interpretation was first broached in 1718, then debated in 1756, when one scholar accepted it and another rejected it; in 1789 it came up again, and this time it was embraced without argument.[6] From then on it was unquestioned. until early in the twentieth century.

The figure most responsible for diffusing a new understanding of Sigismondo and his career outside of Italy was the great historian Jakob Burckhardt. His *The Civilization of the Renaissance,* first published in 1860, largely created the modern notion of the Renaissance as a distinct historical period that signals the emergence of modern individualism. Burckhardt assigned Sigismondo an exemplary status, presenting him as the crowning figure among "The Furtherers of Humanism." His court had epitomized "the highest spiritual things" and been a stage "where life and manners . . . must have been a singular spectacle." His greatest achievement had been the reconstruction of the church of San Francesco, a project inspired by "his *amour* with the fair Isotta, in whose honour and as whose monument the famous rebuilding of S. Francesco at Rimini took place."[7] Burckhardt turned Sigismondo into the epitome of "the whole man," a new human "type" who represented a form of historical existence crucial for the course of civilization, the type that had ushered in the age of modernity, a figure equally capable in war and art, in contemplation and action, one whose unfettered individuality united ruthless realism with lofty ideals: "Unscrupulousness, impiety, military skill, and high culture have been seldom so combined in one individual as in Sigismondo Malatesta.[8] The "whole man" embodied in Sigismondo became the repository of an immense paradox: he was both the figure who had given birth to modernity and a symbol of all that modernity had later lost and betrayed, a rebuke to modernity itself. Translated into French (1876), Italian (1877), and English (1886), Burckhardt's work placed Sigismondo at the center of European intellectual debates about the nature of modernity—its origins, meaning, and prospects—and so about the very meaning of civilization.

Burckhardt's vision was recapitulated and transformed in myriad ways. Writing in 1874, John Addington Symonds, a popular yet respected English historian, viewed the church of San Francesco as "a monument of . . . the revived Paganism of the fifteenth century," and "one of the earliest buildings in which the Neopaganism of the Renaissance showed itself in full force" (103). Though ostensibly a church, it had "no room left for God."[9] Symonds lingered over the many outrages allegedly committed by Sigismondo (the murder of several wives, etc.),[10] but he tempered their opprobriousness by integrating them within a liberal view of history, one that saw the violence of early individualism as a transient stage within the otherwise benign formation of modernity. Much bolder was a French journalist and art historian named Charles Yriarte, whose lengthy biography of Sigismondo was published in 1882. Yriarte claimed to have discovered a love poem "written by Sigismondo in honor of Isotta."[11] Calling it "the most characteristic of Sigismondo's works" (139), he argued that its many zodiacal references provided "the key to the enigma" of the elaborate bas-reliefs found inside the church of San Francesco (218). "It is not God who is worshiped here; instead it is for her that the incense and the myrrh are burned" (198). His study secured the foundations for a consensus that was uncontested for decades, dominating the period that ran from its publication in 1882 to roughly 1920. Encyclopedias, travel guides, novels, plays, and scholarly monographs repeated his claims again and again. From 1886 to 1929, every edition of the *Encyclopaedia Britannica* reported that the church of San Francesco was built "to celebrate the tyrant's love for Isotta," was "dedicated . . . to the glorification of an unhallowed attachment," and was filled with sculptural decorations "derived . . . from a poem in which Sigismondo had invoked the gods and the signs of the zodiac to soften Isotta's heart."[12] Baedeker travel guides repeated the same claims,[13] while popular novelists such as the British author Edward Hutton, whose *Sigismondo Pandolfo Malatesta* was published in 1906, termed the church "a monument to Sigismondo and Isotta" and lavished pages on "those sculptures so wonderfully setting forth the verses of Sigismondo."[14]

The consensus forged by Yriarte began to come under attack around 1910, in the work of two scholars in Rimini who collaborated in a program of research that entailed reexamining the many original and as yet unpublished documents housed in the city's archives and library. In 1909 one of them, Giovanni Soranzo (1881–1963), published an essay, "The Cipher *SI* of Sigismondo Pandolfo Malatesta," which reconsidered the meaning of the much-discussed sign.[15] There was not a single contemporary document suggesting that the sign referred to both Sigismondo and Isotta. Indeed, the only document to discuss the sign, a chronicle by one of Sigismondo's closest collaborators within the court, specifically stated that it referred to Sigismondo alone. It was a common practice, moreover, among the courts of northern Italy to use the first two letters of someone's name as an abbreviation: Niccolò d'Este was frequently cited as *NI*, while Sigismondo's son, Roberto, was commemorated on numerous ceramics and other artifacts by the cipher *RO*. Worse yet, the most common spelling of Isotta's name during her lifetime was *Ysotta* or *Yxotta*, spellings that appeared in nearly all the contemporary legal documents concerning her. One year after the publication of Soranzo's researches, Aldo Francesco Massèra issued a detailed examination of all the poems and poets allegedly connected with Isotta.[16] The notorious poem that Yriarte had claimed to discover, the work that he had termed "the key to the enigma" of the church's sculptural decorations, had been written not by Sigismondo, but by Simone Serdini, a poet from Siena who had communicated with the court of Rimini during the decade after 1410. Serdini had died in 1419 or 1420, some twelve years before Isotta was born. It was impossible that his poem referred to her or her relations with Sigismondo, which began in 1446.

Yet the work of Soranzo and Massèra scarcely affected the legend of Sigismondo and the church of San Francesco. Soranzo's essay was published in a journal of provincial history devoted to Romagna, of which Rimini is a part, while Massèra's appeared in a journal for professors of Italian literature. But the more important reason was a form of ideological resistance. Burckhardt had placed Sigismondo and the romantic reading of the church of San Francesco at the center of a much wider debate about the culture of modernity, debate only partially responsive to issues of evidence and historical documentation. Some writers chose to ignore the researches of Soranzo and Massèra, such as Edward Hutton, whose 1913 guidebook to the province of Romagna simply repeated the claims of his earlier novel.[17] Others transformed the historical claims into symbolic

ones, such as Luigi Orsini, whose 1915 guidebook to Romagna reformu-
lated Yriarte's argument about the poems as a metaphor: the church of San
Francesco was "a poem of indestructible beauty, uniting all the tenderest
harmonies of art and feeling."[18] But the most important attempt to
address the arguments advanced by Soranzo did not appear until 1924,
when Corrado Ricci (1858–1934), a gifted art historian, published his
monumental study of the church of San Francesco.[19] While it was true, as
Soranzo had shown, that every known document indicated that the sign *SI*
had been understood during Sigismondo's lifetime to refer solely to Sigis-
mondo himself, this had been only the sign's "official meaning." Behind it
had stood an "equivocal meaning" known only to Sigismondo, Isotta, and
perhaps a few of their intimates. Sigismondo himself, in fact, had designed
the sign precisely in order to create this kind of ambiguity.[20] Ricci offered
no evidence for this claim; his argument was a transparent evasion, untyp-
ical and unworthy of a scholar otherwise noted for historical rigor and crit-
ical insight. Yet Ricci himself may not have understood why it so mattered
to him to argue for the validity of the sign's romantic interpretation, an
understanding that merely epitomized the basic structure underlying the
Romantic interpretation of the church itself: in each case the genuine
meaning, the hidden yet true meaning, is one that is not in conformity
with culturally (and therefore historically) given values, but that is
achieved only by the shedding of historical attributes (habits, conventions)
and meanings of the cultural system, a laying bare of something other—a
hidden meaning that stands apart from everyday language and institu-
tional discourse, a privileged site in which the sign and the church express
sheer authenticity, their grounding in pure selfhood. Here, in other
words, is semiosis that has been disembedded from local and temporal
contexts of interaction and restructured in a conceptual time-space that is
more indefinite, autonomous, and universal. Sigismondo acts in confor-
mity not with historically determinate conventions of religious piety or
dynastic self-aggrandizement, but with an experiential impulse deemed
universal, just as the meaning of the sign *SI* is no longer located in the geo-
graphically determinate practices of northern Italy or the temporal context
of the midquattrocento, but in an impulse that is largely disembedded of
time and space. It is a process that recapitulates, in other words, the so-
called disembedding mechanisms that some sociologists have considered
one of the fundamental features of modernity.[21] And Sigismondo was
nothing, in the Burckhardtian understanding, if not the epitome of
modernity itself.

While liberal historiography sought to account for Sigismondo by sit-uating him within a progressive account of modernity, others emphasized the more rebellious implications lodged within the Burckhardtian inter-pretation. Friedrich Nietzsche accentuated them to the point of turning the entire Renaissance into the promise of a modernity that had been sub-sequently thwarted, a modernity not yet realized:

> The Italian Renaissance contained within it all the positive forces to which we owe modern civilization: liberation of thought, disrespect for authorities, victory of culture over the darkness of ancestry, enthu-siasm for knowledge and the knowable past of man, unfettering of the individual. . . . indeed, the Renaissance possessed positive forces which have up to now, *in our contemporary modern civilization,* never been so powerful again. . . . it was the golden age of this millennium.[22]

The implications of this were hardly lost on Antonio Beltramelli, a restless Italian journalist from Romagna whose admiration for Nietzsche is already evinced throughout his 1908 volume, *The Chants of Faunus* (*I canti di Fauno*).[23] Two years later, in 1910, Beltramelli published *A Temple of Love* (*Un tempio d'amore*), a brief narration of Sigismondo's life and his reconstruction of the church of San Francesco in Isotta's honor.[24] His account differed from his predecessors' chiefly in its tone, a note of violent lyricism celebrating the concepts of struggle and will: "the mere presence of Sigismondo was enough to impose subjection, and in this lay the secret of his fascination over the masses" (40). Or again: "if Sigismondo failed in his effort to kill Pope Paul II, it was hardly for lack of will" (43–44). In his hands the salient characteristic of Sigismondo became a ruthless, in-domitable will that also signaled the arrival of a new ethical and cultural order, turning him into an exemplary figure for the imagining of a new man who would address the pervasive sense of crisis that marked the early twentieth century and modernity itself.

Thirteen years later, in 1923, the same year that saw the first publica-tion of the Malatesta Cantos, Beltramelli published another book, called *The New Man* (*L'uomo nuovo*).[25] It was the first biography of Mussolini to be published after his arrival in power in late October 1922. Beltramelli had always been a regionalist with ties to his native province of Romagna, where Mussolini had also been born and begun his meteoric rise through the ranks of the Socialist Party. *The New Man* portrayed him as a son of his native soil, as harsh and violent as the landscape that had nurtured him.

Seeking to furnish Mussolini with a cultural genealogy, Beltramelli located his forerunners in the house of Malatesta, also from Romagna. There was the founder of the dynasty, Malatesta da Verucchio: "He knows what he wants, and he places his life as a pledge for his will" (55). And the culmination was Sigismondo Malatesta, the "warrior" who had "the heart of a poet," a figure whose "desperate energy" and "passionateness" (56–57) impressed itself in his every deed. Mussolini was pleased, and wrote Beltramelli a congratulatory letter reproduced in facsimile at the end of the volume. It was an appropriate gesture. Beltramelli had been a member of the Fascist Party since its inception in 1919, and in the years after 1923 his role as a party militant would expand: serving as a principal speaker at the Convention of Fascist Culture (1925), the keystone in the regime's efforts to organize the nation's intellectual life, and a signatory of its chief document, *Manifesto of Fascist Intellectuals;* then as editor of newspapers for the University Youth movement and the "syndicate" of Fascist writers. He died in 1930, and in 1937 the anniversary of his death was commemorated with an article that reprinted all the marginalia that a young socialist named Mussolini had left in his copy of *The Chants of Faunus.*[26]

Beltramelli's portrait of Sigismondo was not, however, the antithesis of the one given by the more refined and scholarly Ricci, but its complement. Beltramelli's book on Sigismondo, in fact, had originated in a lecture on the church of San Francesco that he had given some years earlier, in 1907, a lecture he had written after consulting the text of an earlier lecture on the same subject by Corrado Ricci.[27] Ricci, it is true, had kept his distance from the National Fascist Party and its activities during the period 1919 to 1922, and in 1923 his distinguished career, marked by his steady ascent through the ranks of the cultural bureaucracy—director of the Brera in Milan (1899–1903), of the Royal Galleries of Florence (1903–6), and of antiquities and fine arts for all of Italy (1906–19)—was culminating in a shower of honors. Now, however, they were being dispensed by the new regime as part of its effort to woo the qualified personnel necessary to run a modern bureaucracy, personnel not to be found among the ill-educated and violent leaders of the squads who had brought the party to power. On 1 March 1923 Ricci was named a senator of the kingdom (*senatore del regno*); on 11 April he was appointed president of the Central Commission for Antiquities and Fine Arts; and on 6 May he was named president of the Casa di Dante, one of the nation's most prestigious cultural institutions. In March 1925 he would participate alongside Beltramelli at the Convention of Fascist Culture held in Bologna, and his role in the cultural politics of the regime would continue to expand, reaching its apogee at the inaugural lecture he gave in 1933 for the series of annual courses offered by the Fascist National Institute of Culture. When he died in 1934, it was reported that Mussolini "knew him intimately and appreciated his deep learning and indomitable energy."[28]

Pound, at one point or another, examined all the works that have been mentioned so far, and when possible he sought to meet their authors. In mid-May 1922, he saw the church of San Francesco for the first time during holiday travels with his wife Dorothy; before leaving he had taken notes from Symonds and purchased a Baedeker guidebook.[29] While in Rimini he purchased a copy of Antonio Beltramelli's book, making detailed use of it a month later when he wrote his earliest drafts for the Malatesta Cantos.[30] When he returned to Paris, he purchased a copy of Charles Yriarte's book, eventually entering 150 marginalia and markings to register his interest in its detailed interpretations.[31] He also purchased Edward Hutton's novel and Giovanni Soranzo's book *Pius II and Italian Politics in the Struggle against the Malatesta, 1457–1463*. In the Bibliothèque Nationale of Paris he consulted still other volumes too rare to be easily purchased.[32] After five months' intense work, he left Paris in January 1923, and, after a brief vacation, he began an extensive tour of historical archives and libraries holding books and primary documents connected with Sigismondo. His travels lasted nine weeks, from 11 February to 14 April, and covered Rome, Florence, Bologna, Modena, Cesena, Rimini, the Republic of San Marine, Pennabilli, Fano, Pesaro, Urbino, again Rimini, Ravenna, Venice, and Milan. While in Rome he met with Corrado Ricci, who furnished him with information about archival sources and a previously unknown inscription hidden beneath a plaque on the tomb of Isotta, as well defending his interpretation of the cipher made up of the letters *SI*.[33] While in Rimini he encountered Aldo Francesca Massèra, though it was a meeting that seems to have been rather less cordial, as we shall see. While in Ravenna he sought out Santi Muratori, a colleague of Ricci who had executed earlier renovations to the church. And while in Milan he attempted to contact Giovanni Soranzo, whose book on Sigismondo and essay on the cipher *SI* he had read in Paris.[34] Ultimately Pound accumulated more than seven hundred pages of notes and over sixty-five drafts and draft fragments. Pound was not just interested in the Tempio Malatestiano; he was possessed by it.

For Pound the Tempio became a resonant symbol that encompassed a broad range of his experiences and aspirations, both literary and extraliterary. Sigismondo, after all, had been a poet, and Yriarte's attribution of the poem by Serdini to him had only given further impetus to a conception of the church as a poem in stone, a lyrical work that expressed a realm of selfhood and desire free from, and in opposition to, the everyday world of socially given meaning. The building's melange of styles, from the severe exterior by Alberti to the luxurious sculptural decorations by Agostino di Duccio, epitomized a polyphonic ecclecticism already typical of *The Cantos*. Alberti's adaptation of motifs from antiquity coincided with Pound's recurrent interest in the renewal of classical tradition. Sigismondo had written in lyrical genres especially linked to the moment when Provençal poetry had influenced Italian, suggesting that he had harbored a genuine sympathy for the culture of Provence, not unlike Pound's own. And a more romantic reading of his biography might suggest that his devotion to Isotta was a continuation of practices sanctioned in the Provençal culture of courtly love; moreover, his fatal political mistake had been to lend his support to the house of Anjou from southern France, the land of Provence; and perhaps the ecclesiastical campaign against him was not simply the outcome of mundane political considerations, but an attempt to suppress a heretical and neopaganizing ethos of the same sort that had been stifled before in Provence.[35] Further, throughout 1922 and 1923 Pound was preoccupied with efforts to garner patronage in support of T. S. Eliot, an episode that formed only part of a persistent pattern throughout Pound's career, from the patronage that he himself had received from Margaret Cravens (1910–12) and John Quinn (1915–23) to his efforts to secure patronage for Joyce, Eliot, and Lewis. Late-nineteenth- and early-twentieth-century historians had long portrayed the Renaissance as an age unrivaled in its patrons, neglecting the link between political power and cultural display that fostered the practice of the Renaissance courts and instead assimilating their activity to post-Kantian ideals of aesthetic disinterestedness. Yet granted the assumptions of this historiographical tradition, Sigismondo could be viewed as one of the greatest of the smaller courtly patrons, one who had commissioned works from Alberti, Agostino di Duccio, Piero della Francesca, Pisanello, the poet Basinio da Parma, and many others. Finally, authors as diverse as Burckhardt and Beltramelli had made Sigismondo into an exemplary figure whose restless individuality and unbridled will had marked a crucial moment in Western cultural history, constituting a resource for the imagining of a new man who would address the endemic crisis that was gripping liberal bourgeois culture. Sigismondo, as constructed in a complex ensemble of works and cultural practices, had become a riveting image: the source of one of the highest cultural achievements in the West and a locus for nagging questions about the cost, meaning, and purpose of that ideal moment, a figure who simultaneously heralded modernity's arrival and rebuked its failure to realize its emancipatory promise. Here were lodged all the contradictions of art and modernity, imagination and power.

Having surveyed the cultural genealogies that led to the invention of "Sigismondo" and the reception of this tradition by Pound, we must reconsider the two lines that Sigismundo speaks at the end of Canto 10 and the beginning of Canto 11. To begin, we can use a word-for-word translation into English, though the result will have a slightly antique word order.

> *E gradment li antichi cavaler romanj*
> And greatly the ancient knights Roman [i.e., ancient Roman knights]
>> *davano fed a quisti annutii*
>> gave faith to these annunciations.

The interlinear translation provides enough information so that, by triangulating cognate terms from English or French or Spanish, even a reader unfamiliar with Italian can extrapolate the passage's basic meaning. Nevertheless, it also obscures several difficulties inherent in the original, some apparently due to discrepancies between contemporary Italian and earlier Italian. The definite article "li," for example, is an older form that has disappeared and is now written only as *gli;* but as the older form occurs frequently in Dante, it is scarcely a difficulty. Similarly, the word "quisti" is evidently a cognate of the word *questi* (*these*). It is not, however, immediately recognizable as either an older form or a dialect variant. Equally puzzling is the word "cavaler"; while it is plainly a cognate of the modern *cavaliere* (plural *cavalieri*), a reader will at least pause and be distracted by the peculiar form in which it appears here. Is it an older form that has vanished, or simply a mistake? And if a mistake, whose is it?

More troubling are three other words: "fed," "gradment," and "annutii." The first one, *fed,* seems to be a variant of the Italian word *fede* (faith), which derives from the Latin *fides,* a root also discernible in English words such as fidelity and fiduciary. But why is the final letter *e* miss-

ing? Is it an older or a dialect form that has since disappeared? More per-
plexing is the case of *gradment,* a word that is not even recognizably Ital-
ian. One might guess that it comes from Provençal, or Catalan, or some
other poorly known Romance language; but then what is it doing here? Of
course no word in itself radically alters the entire passage; yet to find five
words out of eleven written in a manner discrepant with practice both
older and modern, and to be obliged to pause and puzzle over the possi-
ble motives and motivations of each, is plainly to encounter an obstacle to
ready understanding.

We might approach these puzzles by considering the genetics of these
lines. Their source is a fifteenth-century chronicle written by Gaspare
Broglio Tartaglia da Lavello (1407–93), a soldier of fortune and counselor
who served at the court of Rimini from 1443 until Sigismondo's death in
1468, when he withdrew from active political life and resumed the com-
position of his memoirs, a task he had already begun much earlier.[36]
Though the memoirs began with a universal history of the world from its
inception to his own times, they mostly concerned his own age, especially
events he had witnessed or participated in, so becoming an important
source for the life and times of Sigismondo. Giovanni Soranzo, in fact,
devoted several pages in the introduction to his book to praising Broglio's
account: Broglio had consistently been "au courant about the diplomatic
affairs, undertakings, and economic and political conditions of his mas-
ter," and his chronicle was "extremely important, because often it treats
events that he claims to have witnessed himself and that are not reported
in other chronicles or archival sources.[37]

One such event was the battle at Nidastore of 1461, when Sigis-
mondo led his troops to victory over superior ecclesiastical forces.[38]
Broglio vividly recounts how Sigismondo addressed his troops just before
battle at dawn, exhorting them to obey orders and assuring them of vic-
tory; for the evening before he had witnessed an omen—an eagle that had
landed on his tent. Here is the passage, with the lineation following that
of Broglio's manuscript:

> Or considerate se lla victoria è nostra—
> che ieri sera un'aquila gientile se posò sulla cima del nostro padiglione;
> grandemente li antichi e valenti romani davano grandissima fede a
> questi annuntii chiamati agurii; per la quale parte ne pigliamo gran
> conforto perchè essendo noi discessi della progienia e sanguinità dello
> illustrissimo Publio Scipione Affricano, nobile romano.[39]

We can translate this, again adhering to the lineation of the manuscript, as follows:

> Now consider whether the victory is ours—for yesterday evening a noble eagle landed on the top of our tent. Greatly the ancient and valiant Romans placed great faith in these annunciations, called auguries; therefore we take solace from this event, as our house descends from the progeny and blood-line of the famous Roman nobleman, Publius Scipio Africanus.

Broglio's account was still unpublished in 1923, nor had this passage ever been quoted or transcribed in any secondary source prior to that date. Instead, as is clear from a variety of evidence, Pound examined the only extant copy of the work, the original manuscript in Rimini, which he consulted between 21 and 27 March 1923 when he stopped there in the course of his research tour of Italian libraries and archives.[40] Yet what Pound actually saw was something different from the edited and orderly passage above. Instead he saw something that, to most people, appears a tangle of curious letters and cryptic marks. In its own time, of course, the "tangle" was part of a systematic set of graphic signs that could be readily deciphered by competent readers. For it was an example of a script, a standardized system of the same sort we use today when we write notes and letters by hand: a script is the system that lets each of us distinguish and read countless hands, or particular versions of a script. Unlike today, however, fifteenth-century Italy had not just an infinite variety of hands, but also many scripts, each associated with particular social classes and graphic functions. One script, for example, was called merchant's script (*mercantesca*) and was used for the conduct of business by shopkeepers, traders, bankers, and others engaged in commerce. Another script has come to be called humanistic script; not surprisingly, it was used by humanists, or teachers of the disciplines that evolved into the modern humanities, and by secretaries and other members of the bureaucratic elite who served the wealthiest courts and the chanceries of well-to-do republics, such as Florence. Yet another script was called chancery script (*cancelleresca*): it was used by the chanceries of states that were smaller and generally more conservative in their cultural outlook. In the course of the period from roughly 1450 to 1525, chancery script gradually receded before the cultural pressures of the humanists and their script. But as Broglio was from an older generation and had been educated in the provincial hinterlands of the Republic of Siena, he still used a chancery script that, in the course of time, had been somewhat simplified under the influence of the humanistic scripts that he had observed in his long years as courtier, ambassador, and counselor.

For our purposes only one point need be made about chancery script. Though it contained a number of ornamental flourishes (usually at the top of ascenders), it was a script that had evolved largely in response to the shortage and costliness of paper, a development that resulted in its having two important features. One was the use of a fairly extensive set of abbreviations designed, essentially, to save space. Instead of writing out the word *per,* for example, a scribe would typically write only the letter *p* with a short bar across the descender, or bottom part of the letter: *p.* Similarly, a scribe would write only *pte* for the word *parte,* meaning "part." Likewise, a scribe could place a horizontal stroke above a letter in order to indicate an abbreviation of the letters *m* or *n,* and thus one might write *dā,* instead of *dam,* or even *damn.* The other feature was a device known as fusion, which enabled a writer to fuse or meld together the strokes from adjacent letters with commensurate shapes, again saving space and time. Thus a writer could bleed together the finishing stroke on the letter *d* with the *e* to produce something that we can crudely represent as *de,* as in *fede,* or he might meld together the letters *t* and *e.*

These remarks make clear why Broglio's manuscript, when Pound first saw it, probably seemed a tangle of cryptic marks. Figure 1 is a photograph of the passage by Broglio in the original manuscript in his own hand. It gives a fair sense of what Pound himself saw, though of course it fails to register textures that the naked eye can perceive and has been reduced in size in order to fit the smaller dimensions of this book. It was while observing these lines that Pound attempted to transcribe them (Box 63a, Folder 2432). A photograph of his transcription (fig. 2) is given opposite Broglio's manuscript, so that the reader can easily compare them.

To be sure, Pound's hand can also seem daunting to readers not accustomed to it, and therefore we also need a transcription of Pound's transcription from Broglio, which follows below. Our transcription follows the lineation given by Pound, except that we shall move his interlinear and marginal corrections directly into the text and place them in angled brackets; all square brackets are Pound's:

or confidrate sella vittoria
e mā cħ frey stra un a

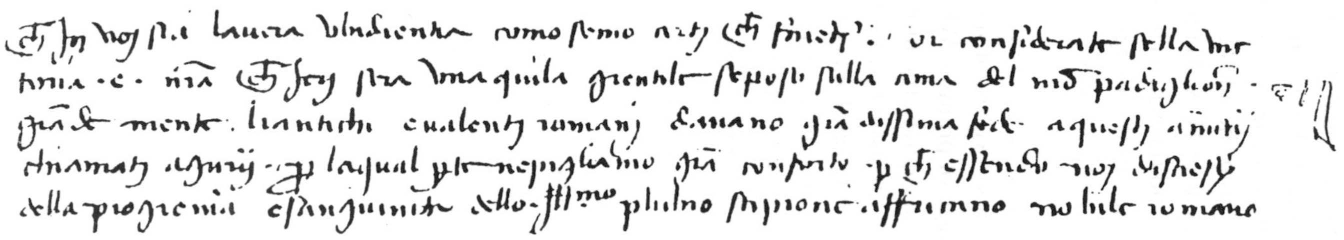

Fig. 1. Gaspare Broglio, *Cronaca universale*, Rimini, Biblioteca Civica Gambalunga, MS SC-MS 1161 (formerly D.III.48), fol. 2465, enlarged by 10 percent.

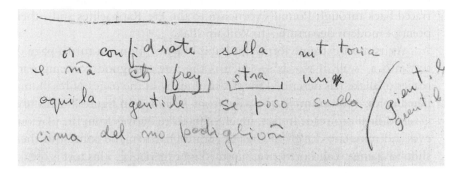

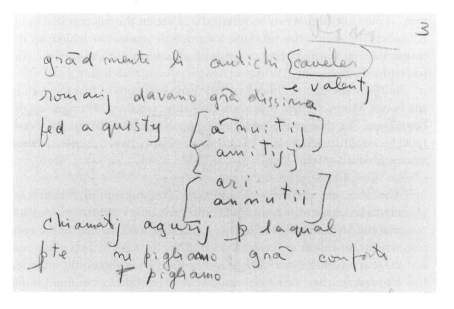

Fig. 2. Ezra Pound, transcription from the *Cronaca universale* of Gaspare Broglio, Beinecke, Box 63, Folder 2432. (For this illustration, parts of leaves 2 and 3 are mounted together.) The Yale Collection of American Literature, Beinecke Rare Book and Manuscript Library, Yale University.

aquila gentile <gientae grentile> se pose sulla.
cima del mo padiglioñ
grādment li antichi [caveler] <e valentj>
romanj davano grādissima
fed a quisty [a⁻nuitij] [amitij] [$^{ari}_{annutii}$]
chiamati agurij p̱ la qual
p̱te ne pigliano <pigliamo> grā conforto.

Pound's transcription recorded his first and only transaction with the original document, and when he was back in Paris and forced to rely on these notes for accurate information about the manuscript, he would face serious difficulties. Quite plainly, his transcription contained many mistakes that fall into several types. Pound has little sense of the conventional abbreviations derived from the tradition of Latin writing and therefore cannot resolve words such as *per* and *parte*. He is also uncertain about the horizontal line above a letter that represents a missing *m* or *n*. He is unfamiliar with fusion and cannot detect its presence in words that make use of it, chief among them *grandemente* (where fusion occurs between *d* and *e* and between *t* and *e*) and *fede* (again between *d* and *e*). He is also uncertain about the value of the letter *j* and has difficulty distinguishing graphemes for the letters *e, c, r, i, t,* and *n*. Finally, he has difficulty distinguishing some versions of the letters *s, f,* and capital *I* (whence his reading of "frey stra" for *ieri sera*).

It is difficult, however, to specify a standard by which to assess Pound's transcription. A typical professor of American literature, at present, will seldom read or speak a foreign language with ease, let alone decipher a written version of it such as Broglio's. Even professors of English literature who have specialized in the Renaissance can seldom read the so-called secretary script used by Shakespeare. Moreover, to compare Pound with modern specialists who have been trained in paleography is not to acknowledge that he occupied a position outside the university, and that his learning, notwithstanding his M.A. in Romance Philology, more closely approximated that of elite bourgeois readers than that of highly trained experts. Yet it is in part because Pound himself highlights his acquaintance with primary documents, because he himself seems to insinuate a deeper and more extensive engagement with archival materials, that some readers may choose to assess his transcription harshly.

Pound did not consult his transcription again until six weeks later in early May 1923, when he referred to it in preparing a typescript preliminary to a final copy of the poem (Box 64, Folder 2452), writing himself a reminder to consult it when readying the final version. The result appeared in his final draft, the typescript that served as setting copy for the first printing of the Malatesta Cantos (autograph corrections are in angled brackets):[41]

> And they c<a>me at us with their ecclesiastical legates.
> Until the eagle lit on his tent pole.
> And he said <: ">The Romans would have called that an augury
>   augury
> E grādment li antichi cavaler romanj
> davano fed a quisti annutii.

A collation shows that Pound has altered his earlier transcription at four points:

1. He adds the word *e* (or *and*) to the beginning of Broglio's text, a device to lend some continuity to his own text.
2. Pound changes final *y* to *i* in the word that Broglio had written as "questi," and that he had mistakenly transcribed as "quisty"; it now becomes "quisti."[42]
3. Pound is apparently uncertain about the two readings his transcription gives for Broglio's *e valenti:* one is the erroneous "cavaler," another the more correct "e valentj." As his notes do not distinguish between secure and uncertain readings, he mistakenly selects his initial reading (*caveler*) and then decides to normalize or "correct" it from *caveler* to *cavaler.*[43]
4. Pound omits the word *grandissima*, even though he had transcribed it diplomatically as *grādissima*. Most likely this was an error of carelessness.

The new rendering also retains three errors from his earlier transcription: *grandemente* still lacks the first and third *e*, while *fede* lacks the final *e*, and *annuntii* the third *n*.

Pound faced special difficulties with the abbreviation sign over the letter *a* in *grandemente*, and for an obvious reason: the typewriter keyboard was not designed to reproduce quattrocento abbreviations. To address this Pound adopted a different solution in each instance where the term occurred, once in Canto 10 (originally XI), and once in Canto 11 (originally XII). In Canto 10 he apparently used the underscore character; he turned the platen by hand until he could strike the key and make it come out above the letter *a,* producing *ā.* But in Canto 11 he used the umlaut character, a much simpler procedure on his European-style typewriter. As neither solution seemed quite satisfactory, he also added instructions in the left margin opposite each instance of *grandemente,* appending an autograph letter *a* surmounted by a mark resembling a tilde (*ã*) in order to instruct the printer that the horizontal line above the *a* should be slightly curved so as to imitate the analogous mark in Broglio's hand. The result was confusing: now there were three different signs that might be placed above the *a* of *grandemente.*

From Pound's typescript derive three printings, each of which introduced another alteration in the text or in font size and style. These appeared in 1923, 1925, and 1930. The earliest was the first publication of the Malatesta Cantos in the *Criterion,* edited by T. S. Eliot. The typesetting was troubled and hasty, and we do not know on what authority the lines in question suffered two changes.[44] First, they were printed in italics, apparently to give them the same treatment accorded elsewhere, though inconsistently to quotations in a foreign language. Second, the crucial *a* in *grandemente* (or "gradment," as it had now become) was rendered with an umlaut above it both in Canto 10 (originally XI) and in Canto 11 (originally XII).

In early 1925 the Malatesta Cantos were published a second time as part of the deluxe and limited edition that first issued the Cantos in volume form. A collation shows that this portion of the new edition was typeset from the 1923 *Criterion* printing. Correspondence indicates that more care was taken with proofreading and that Pound was pleased with the edition as a whole when he received final proofs on 25 January 1925.[45] Presumably he approved the single alteration in the lines quoted from Gaspare Broglio. This time the sign above the *a* in *grandemente* (or "gradmente," as it appeared here) was changed from an umlaut to a straight, horizontal line—*a.* Otherwise the text was unaltered.[46]

The third printing occurred in 1930, again as part of an edition comprising all the Cantos written so far. Initially undertaken by Nancy Cunard and her Hours Press, it soon required technical capacities far beyond those of her artisanal operation, forcing her to entrust the typesetting to François Bernouard, a printer noted for his innovations in French typography and design. Although Bernouard set copy from the 1925 edition, his efforts resulted in two further variants in the passage. One was a question of format: in accordance with his stylistic conventions, Bernouard set the first two words of Canto 11 in full capitals. The other was textual: he omitted the mark above the letter *a* in *grādment* (or *grandemente*), in both instances of its occurrence.

> *E GRADMENT li antichi cavaler romanj*
> *davano fed a quisti annutii*

Bernouard had finally fixed the form in which Broglio's passage would be transmitted.[47]

The textual history of the two lines from Broglio in Cantos 10 and 11 is distinguished chiefly by Pound's solicitude to represent the abbreviation sign above the letter *a* in *grandemente* (as umlaut, horizontal line, or curved mark)—precisely the feature omitted from all versions of the text after 1930. Indeed, the only edition of *The Cantos* that has accurately reflected his intentions is *A Draft of XVI. Cantos* from 1925. Yet why did this minutia matter?

Pound was concerned to represent the abbreviation sign over the letter *a* for several reasons. One was that it attested to the veracity, the historical accuracy, of his portrait of Sigismondo. Some two weeks after he had returned from Italy in April 1923, when asked to describe his recent work during an interview published in the *New York Herald*—the interview has not been previously mentioned in studies of Pound—he stressed the significance of its historical dimension: "I want my work . . . to withstand all historical criticism."[48] "Historical criticism," in this context, implied a kind of captious scrutiny of details that, if they were found to be inaccurate, threatened to undermine the broader vision of cultural life embodied in his depiction of Sigismondo Malatesta and the courtly culture of Rimini. The desire that his work be able "to withstand" such examination presupposes a common knowledge of protocols and procedures, a shared sense of canons of evidence and the treatment of historical sources— agreement that may, on Pound's part, be given only grudgingly or provisionally, but that nevertheless means, at least for the moment, agreement to play the game by "their" rules. The abbreviation sign over the letter *a*, like the footnotes directly incorporated into the text of the poem, like the minute corrections administered to historians who had inaccurately quoted some source or other, like the careful directions to the printer concerning how to simulate the various abbreviations representing quattrocento forms of address, all presuppose an assent, however provisional, to premises and procedures grounded in Enlightenment rationalism and the practices of advanced historiography as they had evolved up to Pound's time.[49]

Paradoxically, however, the abbreviation sign over the letter *a* also epitomized the degree to which Pound's assent to these protocols was provisory, the extent to which it was a tactical maneuver, not genuine assent. For the same sign could suggest a very different set of rules by which the game might be played. Viewed in another light, the meticulous rendering of the documentary grapheme registers the aura of the original document, records the authenticity of Pound's direct encounter with an unpublished source, testifies to the experiential reality at the foundation of Pound's evaluation of Sigismondo and the cultural achievements associated with him. For it is here, in Pound's immediate and lived engagement with such resistant materials, that his perception of Sigismondo finds its genuine sanction, not in the arid protocols of rationalist historiography. The poetic counterpart to the sign, seen in this light, is located not in the punctilious mimesis of scholarly footnotes, but in the almost brutal succession of raw documents, of coarse and contradictory reports that succeed one another seemingly without logic or principle, each bristling with cryptic names and dates. It is from experience and not ideology, life and not theory, that the author has wrested his insight into the nature of Sigismondo's significance, and it is this realm of lived experience that is presented as a substantive reality posed outside and against the merely procedural, merely formal canons of reason.

So deep, so total is Pound's conviction of truth as experience that it is precisely this, the experience in which his vision of Sigismondo has taken shape and from which it derives its authority, that he seeks to represent in his poem. His goal is not to offer "a historical portrait" of Sigismondo, however useful that term may be as a conventional shorthand to characterize the Malatesta Cantos, for that would imply adherence to the ethos of detachment and distance, the conventions and protocols of rationalist historiography. Instead he seeks to recreate, as fully as possible, the experiential immediacy in which his own understanding of Sigismondo's career has crystallized, that dark voyage amid the murmurs of a forgotten history in which, by force of will, he has glimpsed a thread of gold amid the gloom.

The result is that the Malatesta sequence is a test of extraordinary difficulty, one that presupposes and solicits a quasi-heroic reader, one whose labors and intuitions must be responsive to the author's own. No one has described as well as Donald Davie the resistant density, the impediment to reading posed by such a text:

> Indeed, "reading " is an unsatisfactory word for what the eye does as it resentfully labors over and among these blocks of dusty historical debris. We get lost in ever murkier chaos, an ever more tangled web of alliances, counteralliances, betrayals, changing of sides, sieges and the raising of sieges, marches and countermarches; it is impossible to remember whose side Malatesta is on any time or why.

Davie's key verbs are telling: "the eye . . . labors," and "we get lost," and "it is impossible to remember." They record a progressive clotting that turns into absolute blockage. The text becomes an overwhelmingly hostile reality, an assault upon consciousness that confronts the reader with a world as confusing and chaotic as the one that was faced by the readers' predecessor, the poet, which in turn is like that which faced his predecessor, Sigismondo. Each is threatened with being engulfed by irresistible darkness, lost "in ever murkier chaos, an ever more tangled web" that is the expression of a profoundly pessimistic view of human destiny and the basic setting from which an evanescent victory, a momentary order, is wrested in an act of will that is simultaneously an act of memory and vatication:

> *E gradment li antichi counter romanj*
> *davano fed a quisti annutii.*
> [And greatly the ancient Roman knights
> gave faith to such annunciations.]

It is here, in this paradigmatic moment, that the hero realizes his own identity, largely by invoking and assimilating that of a predecessor: just as the ancient Romans are assimilated by Sigismondo, so he is assimilated by the speaker of *The Cantos*, while all these in turn are to be assimilated by the reader.

What is recovered at such moments is difficult to define: an experiential essence, a glimpse of pure being as it stands stripped of historical and social accretions, a laying bare of fundamental identity. Yet it is important that the object of understanding not be defined more precisely, for to do so would subject it to the rationalizing discourse to which it stands inalterably opposed. Precisely, however, because such understanding is posed outside of and against that discourse, the question of verification assumes such prominence, becomes so vexed and problematic: for this form of understanding defies the rationalist criteria of evidence and proof, of logic and argument, and instead can appeal only to a hermeneutics of experience, appeal to what must be only felt and not analyzed, shown and not clarified. Which is why, on the one hand, *The Cantos* as a whole seems to offer a repetitive sequence of models and exempla that are endlessly adduced for the reader's edification, even while it is equally true that the very concept of a model, that is, some definable pattern with normative claims upon the reader's attention, is rejected in favor of presenting the experiential world from which a perception of them has been wrested. The result is to put enormous pressure on the connection between sign and referent, on the linkage between the private experience that the sign encapsulates and the public status to which the exemplary figure is assigned. Indeed, nothing can really forge the linkage between private experience and public exemplum except faith: it becomes the circuit that mediates the transition from (using Pierce's terms) an iconic function (historical portrait) to an indexical function (an index of experience) to a performative function. And that is the importance of Sigismondo's invocation of the ancient Romans. It is faith without substance, faith that need not define its contents: faith that finds its validity not in its congruity with an anterior or prior referent, but in action that is located in the future. It is tested, if we may use that verb, not against a historical notion of veracity, but against the idea of efficacy, which is to say that its validity has been relocated in the realm of experience—in this case the experience of the auditor/reader who is spurred to action.

This complex of hermeneutical motifs—experience, faith, action—was fundamental to Pound's understanding of literature and its social functions, and it furnished the framework in which he assimilated his emerging interest in fascism and Mussolini during the period 1925–35. Writing several notes that were to serve him for the composition of Cantos 31–33 in 1930, Pound assigned himself the task of defining the "biolog[ical] function of lit[erature]." In response he produced a list with five potential answers:

nutrition of impulse
relieve mind of strain

give feeling of being alive
set 'em off = mobilize
energy—start dynamo

Setting aside the second item in Pound's list ("relieve mind of strain"), we see that his answers are of two basic sorts. One function of literature is to nurture the realm of experience: "nutrition of impulse," and "give feeling of being alive." The other is to be a spur to action: "set 'em off = mobilize," and "energy—start dynamo." The two, moreover, are not wholly separate, but overlap: for if one function of literature is the "nutrition of impulse," a form of augmenting experience, it is also the case that impulse is typically a spur to action. Pound, in other words, assumes a continuum between experience and action, even if the action is only that of changing one's beliefs, altering one's understanding. "The aim," writes Pound in another set of notes concerning *The Cantos*, is "to create states of mind in which certain things are comprehensible" (Box 65, Folder 2538).

All these notions recur in an important and unpublished essay that bears the title "Fascism or the Direction of the Will," written by Pound in April of 1933.[50] Intended to clarify Pound's views on Mussolini and Italian fascism, it repeatedly attacks the notion of clarification itself, dismissing rational and coherent accounts as "dogma" and "theory." As he forthrightly states, "I strongly disbelieve in any general definition." In the same vein, he castigates people who "are so full of principle that they won't ride in a train." Indeed, Italy's problem before the advent of fascism was that it had been led by "scoundrels" who were willing to "wreck Italy for the profit or for the satisfaction of dogmas." Fascism, in Pound's view, is precisely the opposite: "Fascism by its founder's own definition is NOT a body of abstract dogma." Or again: "But then fascism hasn't any theories. It has methods." Or as he would put it in a subsequent revision of the essay: "the real point of fascism being that it simply is NOT abstract." Pound, it is true, was doing little more than parroting the self-understanding of the regime. As Giovanni Gentile, the philosopher who took upon himself the task of articulating "The Philosophic Basis of Fascism," had expressed it: "Fascism prefers not to waste time constructing abstract theories about itself."[51]

Instead, Pound's belief in the virtues of fascism is asserted on the grounds of concrete experience. Observations slowly accumulated over time are one form of this:

I have seen Italy off and on since 1898. I have seen Italy for several months a year since 1920. I have lived here for the last eight years. I have seen not one town but a hundred. (*FDW,* 1)

Here the repetitive assertion, "I have seen . . . I have seen . . ."—it is almost a cameo of the structure of *The Cantos*—asserts the primary and constitutive nature of experience itself. But inadvertently it also suggests a merely quantitative distinction between less experience and more, leading to a largely mathematical, hence mechanical and empty, concept of experience. The real test for experience, therefore, is located not in the past, but in the future, in a criterion of efficacy: "FASCISM has meant throughout all this fifteen years that the main and necessary idea should be presented to the Italian people in such a form *that they should take action.* That is the bones and marrow of it" (*FDW,* 4; italics added). Or again: "Fascism . . . continues to be a constructive force, *directed at results* of most possible concreteness" (*FDW,* 1; italics added). Fascism, in short, can be assessed partly through observation and experience accumulated in Italy (history); but it is best understood when one perceives the outcome, the action, to which it leads (the future). Between these two terms, and yet inseparable from them, lies that mysterious terrain that resists definition, that can be understood only in faith: "I can declare faith in Mussolini's instinct," Pound concludes (*FDW,* 1). It is a puzzling comment, after all: we are asked to judge Mussolini not by his words, not by his policies, not even by his actions. but by something as remote and inaccessible as his "instinct," something to which we have access by "faith." And yet this is plainly part of a coherent set of cultural motifs. As the contemporary historian Emilio Gentile (no relation to the philosopher Giovanni Gentile) observes, fascism's appeal to faith was indistinguishable from its cultivation of activism, activism that in turn "was inseparable from fascism's irrationalist conception of politics, which affirmed the priority of lived experience over ideology and *faith* over theory in the formation of a political culture."[52] His assessment is amply confirmed by the writings of fascist theorists. Assaying the distinctive feature that the syndicalist philosopher Georges Sorel had contributed to "The Philosophic Basis of Fascism," the philosopher Giovanni Gentile singled out "faith in a moral and ideal reality for which it was the individual's duty to sacrifice himself, and to defend which, even violence was justified."[53] Or as Mussolini would explain, only six days before the March on Rome in October 1922:

> We have created our own myth. Myth is a faith, a passion. It is not
> necessary that it be a reality. It is a reality in the fact that it is a spur, a
> hope, a faith, a form of courage.[54]

Mussolini, here, equates myth in the sense defined by Sorel with faith, and,
just as it will function later in Pound's writing, so here faith becomes the
term that mediates the transition from a discarded referentialism ("It is not
necessary that it be a reality") to validity testing by performative criteria
("a spur" to action).

Five months after Mussolini had spoken these words, Ezra Pound found
himself in Rimini, on 20 March 1923. It was his third visit to the city. The
first, in May 1922, had yielded his first view of the church of San
Francesco. The second, however, had taken place only a week earlier, on
12 March 1923, when Pound had come to the city to examine documents
held in the municipal library, the Biblioteca Gambalunga. He had been
disappointed, as he explained to his wife Dorothy the next morning in a
previously unpublished letter written at the "Palace Hotel, Rimini":[55]

> Blood And Thunder.
> Library here closed *at least* until the 20th as the damn *custode* [cus-
> todian] has flu, and the boss is too lazy—or has to teach physics else-
> where.
> Am going to San Marino by the *trenino* [little train] in a few min-
> utes and shall try to fill in time in Pesaro, Fano, etc. till the bloody *cus-
> tode* recovers. IF he recovers.

Plainly annoyed with the city librarian ("the boss"), Pound spent the next
week traveling to San Marino (13–14 March), Pennabilli (15 March),
Fano (16–17 March), Pesaro (18–19 March), and Urbino (19–20
March). He returned to Rimini in the late afternoon of 20 March, once
more staying at the Palace Hotel, from where he wrote another letter to
Dorothy the next morning.[56] His trip had been "laborious," he admitted,
and he was glad to be "back here in comfort." Already he had acquired an
ally in his efforts to resolve the question of the library's closure: "I go to
library here at 10:00 o'clock this a.m. Hotel-keeper ready to sack the place
and have up the mayor if it isn't open; he is a noble fascist." Ending his let-
ter as he headed out the door, he concluded: "Will now try the library."

Whether Pound found it open is unclear. In any event, its resources were soon at his disposition, and he spent the next week examining documents related to Sigismondo Malatesta—among them, the manuscript of Gaspare Broglio.

Pound's "hotel-keeper" was named Averardo Marchetti (1890–1942).[57] The son of Ferdinando and Rosa Rambelli Marchetti, he had served in the armed forces from 1915 to 1918, the entire time of Italy's participation in the war. Wounded once and repeatedly decorated, he achieved the rank of lieutenant and then captain. In early 1918 he married Antonia Vittoria Podrecca (1890–1969), with whom he eventually had two sons, Ferdinando in 1921 and Federico in 1926. By 1921 he was listed in municipal records as a hotel-keeper (*albergatore*), and by 1923, when Pound came to Rimini, he was managing the Palace Hotel, located near the railway station and yet close to the Tempio and the center of town. Little is known about the evolution of Marchetti's political views, but his course of development suggests a familiar pattern. During World War I many soldiers, especially officers from the lower ranks, felt a profound sense of camaraderie that suggested the possibility of a "new" Italy, a potential betrayed by corrupt politicians of the old order at the war's end. Their numbers were to swell the ranks of emergent fascism. On 24 May 1921 Marchetti, together with seven other men, founded the *Fascio riminese,* or the the Fascio of Combatants of Rimini, the local chapter of the Fascist Party that had been created two years earlier in Milan.

The fascio was soon actively participating in the so-called *squadrismo,* the harassment and beating of opponents. In September 1921 the Riminese fascio joined a march on Ravenna by three thousand fascists under Leandro Aprinati. "Everyone had to remove his hat when the Fascist emblems and banners went by, and some priests who did not react quickly enough were beaten until they bled."[58] In the summer of 1922 Arpinati organized and coordinated a systematic offensive of squads from Bologna and Ferrara against the Socialist administrations of Romagna, including the one that had governed Rimini since the elections of October 1920.[59] Their victory was swift. On 6 July 1922 the Socialist administration resigned, citing partly the failure of local banks to extend credit, chiefly "the violence committed today against the persons of the administration." Six days later the city was formally consigned to Dr. Arcangelo Leggieri, who, with the title of royal commissary (*reggio commissario*), was to manage its affairs under an "extraordinary administration."[60] In early February 1923 he was was succeeded by Dr. Luigi Marcialis, a former subprefect of the city who liked to vaunt his title of *Gran Cordone Mauriziano* (or member of the Order of the Knights of Saint Maurice and Saint Lazzarus). Marcialis served from February to November 1923, doing little to conceal his sympathies: when he reported to the Fascist administration that followed, he praised "the living flame of faith and duty which has burned in your hearts, whether on the fields of battle or in the recent deeds of sacred civil resistance," and he looked forward to "the rebirth of our Italy under the guide of our supreme Duce and artificer, Benito Mussolini."[61] There must have been many occasions when he collaborated with Marchetti, a founder of the local fascio and one of its chief leaders. When Mussolini organized the Volunteer Militia for National Security (MVSN) in December 1922, Marchetti had been named *commandante della piazza,* charged with maintaining law and order in the city.

It was at this conjuncture of events that Pound stayed in Rimini from 21 March to 27 March. He left the city early the morning of 28 March, and soon after his arrival in Ravenna that evening he wrote to Dorothy to report on his recent activities.[62] He began with his typical salutation to her: taking on the voice of a cat:

> M a O ! !:
> Triumphal exit from Rimini.
> *Reggio Commissario* descended on the librarian (who may die of the shock). *Very* sympatique the *Gran Cordone.*

Pound's report makes it difficult to specify exactly what occurred, but its basic import is plain enough. Alerted by Marchetti to the presence of a foreign poet and scholar in town, the royal commissary Marcialis had publicly paid his respects to Pound and reproved the library's director, Aldo Francesco Massèra, for not having shown more solicitude in meeting his needs. Here, for Pound, was swift action replacing bureaucratic delay. He would never forget it.

The same evening that he wrote to Dorothy, he also sent a postcard to Nancy Cox-McCormack (1885–1967), an American sculptor whom he had met in Paris in July 1921.[63] In subsequent months the two had become friends, and in December 1921 Cox-McCormack cast a life mask and also modeled a portrait bust of the poet.[64] Though she soon left Paris for Rome, where she would reside the next eighteen months, the Pounds continued to keep in touch with her. When Pound and his wife went to Italy in the spring of 1922, Cox-McCormack hastened to Siena to visit them for a week; when they came to Rome in early 1923 (from 16 February to 1 March), their housing was arranged for them by Cox-McCormack, whose company they frequented throughout their stay.[65] She had observed the March on Rome at first hand. She later recalled the "armored wagons . . . rushing with soldiers to all critical points," and on the day after Mussolini had assumed power she stood "under a threatening sky" and "watched the Duce, Balbo and others heading this blackshirted procession" from the Piazza del Popolo to the Altar of the Nation. Much later in 1939, in her unpublished memoirs, she remembered: "The creative impetus back of it all swept most of my Italian friends into a world of bright expectations. Their eyes blazed with the blinding light of Fascist 'glory.'"[66] In reality she was describing not her friends, but herself.

A gregarious and gracious Southerner, Cox-McCormack had rapidly developed two circles of acquaintances in Rome. The first centered around the figure of Lilliana de Bosis, whom she met in the summer of 1922; she was the wife of Adolfo de Bosis, a poet formerly associated with D'Annunzio and now a frequent guest of the royal family. When Mussolini came to power, Adolfo defined him as "the King's expedient for avoiding worse conditions." Similarly, she recalled, "Every artist I knew . . . was enthusiastic about the 'stellone' (great star) who had appeared in the sky 'to save Italy from utter ruin.'"[67] The de Bosis family soon introduced her to Giacomo Boni, a famous archaeologist who would be appointed a senator by Mussolini in March 1923 and cast the decisive vote against the first motion of no confidence presented a month later; Boni would go on to design the official insignia of the party, an archaeological reconstruction of the fasces that had been carried by the magistrates of ancient Rome.[68] The de Bosis family also introduced her to Ansel Edgar Mowrer, a correspondent for the *Chicago Daily News,* who in turn introduced her to Vittorio de Santa, a journalist working for the *Chicago Tribune.*[69] On 3 January 1923, de Santa wrote a letter to Mussolini urging him to accept Cox-McCormack's proposal that she undertake to sculpt his portrait.[70] Yet it was more than just chance that led Cox-McCormack to Mussolini, for her second circle of acquaintances pointed in the same direction. In the autumn of 1932 she met Thomas Judson, an American expatriate who had come to Rome in 1914 to study archaeology and had remained as a consultant to dealers in arts and antiquities. Judson, in turn, had introduced her to Lidia Rismondo, a young and attractive demimondaine who had cultivated contacts with the fringes of the Fascist leadership in Milan and now was hosting a political salon conveniently located near

Mussolini's residence. In an apartment "crowded with treasures" she entertained "groups of officers and their wives," for whom she would "sing a few arias" while "accompanying herself on the piano." On 18 March 1923 she took Cox-McCormack to watch Mussolini open the meeting of the International Chamber of Commerce. Some five weeks later she introduced Nancy to Mussolini himself. In early May, at a second meeting in Mussolini's apartment in Palazzo Trittoni, he agreed to let her sculpt his portrait. It was the first bust to be made of the new leader. By the end of their ten sittings in May and June, Nancy was captivated.[71] In October 1923 she published an essay that praised him for being "wholly concerned with welding Italy into a prosperous and happy entity." He was "a creative force evolving and directing the beginnings of a renaissance." He was "much an artist," and his eyes, "the kindliest I have ever looked into," revealed "a man guided by tremendous and admirable qualities of heart."[72] Two years later, in her preface to the English translation of Mussolini's *My Diary*, she hailed him as "the inspiration of the new epoch in Europe."[73] (She lost faith in the regime in the early 1930s, after a member of the de Bosis family incurred the government's wrath by dropping antifascist leaflets from an airplane over Rome, leading to a programmatic harassment of the entire family that finally disillusioned her.)

When Pound had visited Cox-McCormack in Rome in February 1923, she had introduced him to Giacomo Boni, who, in turn, had introduced him to Corrado Ricci, the art historian and cultural administrator who was completing his monumental study of the Tempio Malatestiano.[74] And no doubt Pound had also learned of her contacts with Lidia Rismondo, her efforts to secure Mussolini's approval of a portrait, and her favorable view of the new regime. Certainly he was aware that she was moving among influential circles close to the government, which explains the force of his unpublished postcard to her, dated 28 March 1923:[75]

Dear Nancy—

If you have *any real political power*, please see that the Gran Cordone Mauriziano Dr. Luigi *Marcialis, Reggio Commissario pel Comune di Rimini* [royal commissary for the City of Rimini] and also Signor *Marchetti*, Direttore del Fascio [of] Rimini, both receive *all* possible honors and advancements. They deserve well of Italia.

Yrs,

Ezra

In late March Cox-McCormack was scarcely able to secure rewards for either Marchetti or Marcialis, and Pound had to make do with a more spiritual token of esteem. When he returned to Paris he sent Marchetti a copy of the Knopf edition of *Lustra* with an inscription reading: "*Al amico Marchetti, done del autore suo amico. Ezra Pound 1923.*"[76] (The mistakes in *al* and *del* will be noted by some observers.) That, however, was only the beginning.

Pound's postcard was more than just a hasty gesture. His experience in writing the Malatesta Cantos was important to him, as scholars have long known. After completing the four Malatestas in April and May 1923, Pound suddenly understood the shape that he had been seeking for his long poem; he swiftly revised all the previous cantos, added five more, and completed the first sixteen cantos in their modern form, leading to the publication of *A Draft of XVI. Cantos* in January 1925.[77] Pound himself understood the significance of Marchetti's aid for his work. In June 1925, he returned to Rimini for a fourth visit, this time to commemorate Marchetti's actions by presenting him with a proof copy of *A Draft of XVI. Cantos,* an event that was duly recorded in the newspaper of the local fascio, *The Bridgehead* (*La Testa di Ponte*) in its issue of 6 June 1925. (See the appendix for the text of the article.) As Pound described it weeks later, a copy of *The Cantos* "was carried through the village, not on a triumphal ox-cart draped with scarlet, but at any rate with due order by il Commandante. . . . Marchetti stated that he had shown my poem 'anche a Domini Deo.' " Pound even asked his publisher for a special set of page proofs containing only the Malatesta Cantos, as he would be "sending them to il Commandante" in Rimini.[78]

Nor was this the last time that he commemorated Marchetti. Eight years later he recalled him again in *Jefferson and/or Mussolini:*

"NOI CI FACCIAMO SCANNAR PER MUSSOLINI" [We're willing to cut our throats for Mussolini], said my hotel-keeper in Rimini years ago, thinking I knew nothing about the revolution and wanting to get it in my head. Nothing happens without efficient cause. My hotel-keeper was also Comandante della Piazza, we had got better acquainted by reason of his sense of responsibility, or his interest in what I was doing. The local librarian had shut up the library, and the Comandante della Piazza had damn well decided that if I had taken the trouble to come to Romagna to look at a manuscript, the library would cut the red tape.

"Scannar" is a very colloquial word meaning to get scragged. It has none of the oratorical quality of "we will die for," but that's what it means. And my friend M. was expressing a simple fact.

This kind of devotion does not come from merely starting a boy-scout movement.[79]

Pound's recollection of "my friend Marchetti" is cited as a landmark in his understanding of fascism, and Marchetti's willingness to "cut his throat" as an index of fascism's virtue: what can inspire "this kind of devotion" must have something to it, Pound reasons. Again the critical notion is faith, and again it is inseparable from action, Marchetti's resolve that "the library . . . cut the red tape." Taken together, Pound commemorated his encounter with Marchetti at least six times between 1923 and 1933: in letters to his wife and Nancy Cox-McCormack, in the dedication copy of *Lustra* that he gave to him, in his visit to Rimini to present *il Commandante* with *A Draft of XVI. Cantos,* in a later gift of page proofs for the Malatesta Cantos, and in published recollections in *Jefferson and/or Mussolini.* For him their encounter marked a turning point: only thus had Pound been able to secure access to that world of experience epitomized by the abbreviation sign over the letter *a* in Broglio's manuscript.

Pound's experiences with Cox-McCormack and Marchetti in February and March of 1923 were not his earliest encounters with fascism in the years 1922–23. His first had already taken place in Paris during the latter half of 1922. In August, when his wife Dorothy was away in London, he wrote her that he had recently dined on several occasions with the Marchesa Luisa Casati, a former mistress of D'Annunzio who frequented the Paris salon of Natalie Barney and Romain Brooks, the latter having once painted her portrait. A few days later Pound noted that the marchesa had finally left Paris, together with her "squad of fascisti"—it is his first use of this term in all his correspondence. When Dorothy replied with a salacious anecdote about the marchesa and the portraitist Augustus John, Pound was nonplussed: she was "exactly the type," he replied. "She has all the carefree qualities of the sculptures in Rimini."[80]

A month later, in September, Pound was introduced to the famous American journalist Lincoln Steffens. In late October he went to hear Steffens lecture on the Russian Revolution and his firsthand impressions of Lenin. When Steffens came back to Paris a month later, returning from the Lausanne Peace Conference at which Mussolini had made his debut before the international press, he gave another lecture on revolutions, synthesizing his earlier experiences in Mexico and Russia with his recent observations of Mussolini. Steffens had found Mussolini as impressive as Lenin, and he especially admired his disdain for parliamentarian politics: "He despises the old game of politics and diplomacy, democracy as we pretend it is. . . . He has risen into an empty throne by dint of his contempt for the present type of government." Mussolini, as he put it in his contemporary *Autobiography,* was "as bold as Einstein." He and Lenin alone were the contemporaries who knew how to "read history, and not as scholars do, for love of a growing body of knowledge, not even as scientists seeking the laws that govern events, but as men of action, reading a record of human experimentation to find out what can be done and how." By the end of his first interview with Mussolini, Steffens had "come out of it sure that here was a man and that that man knew something and meant something and had the will to and the way to do something. I would go and live in Italy," he recalled, "to see . . . this dictator work."[81] Pound attended, having "dragged" along the Irish critic Mary Colum. To her the lecture offered only "appalling dreariness," but Pound listened with "rapt attention, his eyes glued to the speaker's face, the very type of a young man in search of an ideology, except that he was not so young."[82] What Steffens had done was to sketch an answer to the question of history that had acquired such urgency in the aftermath of World War I. He might almost have been outlining the project of *The Cantos.*

If Pound's experiences with Marchetti had been anticipated by preliminary encounters with fascism in Paris, they were also followed by others that took place when he returned there. Once more it was Cox-McCormack who provided the occasion. After completing her portrait of Mussolini on 1 July 1923, she returned to Paris for a period of several months. To Pound she avidly recounted her experiences with Mussolini, her impressions of his abilities, and her belief in the sincerity of his interest in the arts. After one such conversation, Pound wrote her at length on 15 August (a month after publication of the Malatesta Cantos); the letter has not been previously published.

> To clear up what I said the other day, it would be quite easy to make Italy the intellectual centre of Europe; and that by gathering ten or fifteen of the best writers and artists. . . .
>
> The experiment would not be expensive: the whole thing depends on the selection, and on the manner of the invitation. I shouldn't

trust any one's selection save my own. There is no use going into details until one knows if there is or could be any serious interest in the idea; that is to say, if the dictator *wants* a *corte letteraria;* if he is interested in the procedure of Sigismundo Malatesta in getting the best artists of his time into Rimini, a small city with no great resources. I know, in a general way, the fascio includes literature and the arts in its programme; that is very different from being ready to take specific action.

You have to avoid official personages, the deadwood of academies, purely pedagogical figures. The life of the arts is always concentrated in a very few individuals; they invent, and the rest follow, or adapt, or exploit.

Italy has an opportunity *now,* an opportunity she would not have had thirty years ago, or even ten years ago. Germany is busted, England is too stupid, France is too tired to offer serious opposition; America is too far from civilization and won't for a hundred years distinguish between the first rate and the second rate; she will always stay content with copies.[83]

The terms of Pound's proposal are remarkably revealing. When he defines a "serious interest in the idea" as desire to have "a *corte letteraria,*" he is quoting from the title of a study that had surveyed the humanists who worked at the court of Sigismondo,[84] a parallel that is reinforced when he urges that Mussolini follow "the procedure of Sigismundo Malatesta in getting the best artists."

Cox-McCormack evidently decided not to act on Pound's proposal until she was back in Italy and could make use of her personal contact with Lidia Rismondo. But her return had the unintended effect of multiplying Pound's requests for contact with Mussolini. In early January 1924 he wrote her anew, this time asking her to use her influence with Mussolini to secure an essay by him for the *Transatlantic Review,* Ford Madox Ford's new literary journal:

Dear Nancy:

CAN you get a few choice words from Muss. exclusively for the Transatlantic, one or two pages, or as much more as he likes on his scheme for restoration of ROME; tell Judson that the Trans. is THE intellectual organ. (Jud. can have a try writing for it himself re Etruscan research.)

Get Muss. to write a line on new building in Rome, new paving, etc. (possibly as link in revival of Italian intellectual life—that leads on to our other affair).

Ford wants this message at once; i.e., as soon as possible. ANY how in time for second number.

The Transatlantic is a free international avenue of communication. Muss. wd. reach the PENSEURS partout; and they "make the opinion of next week."

yrs.

E.P.[85]

Cox-McCormack evidently declined this request, but it was hardly long before Pound returned to "our other affair," his proposal for Mussolini to pursue a program of cultural patronage that would turn Italy into an international cultural center. On 13 January 1924 Pound wrote, "I would come [to Rome] if the moment were opportune," to discuss his earlier proposal for cultural patronage.[86] On 28 January he raised the subject again, this time at length. He dismissed as "slither and blah" the notion that his proposals be forwarded to Mussolini in a letter; he wanted something quite different:

> The matter will be settled man to man between M[ussolini]. and me, or else it will be merely bitched, botched, and bungled, bureaucratized, bastardized, bootied, boggled, and altogether *zum wasser.*

As if momentarily acknowledging the difficulties posed by his truculent demand to meet a head of state, he also proposed another scheme:

> It [the topic] can be *opened* by *your* asking M. one simple question— or even getting R[ismondo]. to ask it—so long as you get a direct definitive answer. And the question is . . . Does he want Italy to be *veramente IL centro, non UN centro, della vita europea (centro dell'intelletto e della coltura della Europa).*
>
> *COME ERA nel quattrocento e nel cinquecento.*
>
> *If so* he can have *il mio sostegno* and I will come to discuss or tabulate *QUALCHE MISURA SEMPLICE che si può prendere con piccolissimo spese e ANCHE SENZA SPESE ALCUNO.*
>
> That is about as briefly as I can put it.[87]

What became of these discussions is not clear. Most likely Mussolini's confidantes informed Cox-McCormack that he had no time for such matters with the approaching elections, and shortly afterward Cox-McCormack left Rome for good, ending the opportunity. To be sure, the affair is not without touches of the comic, as when Pound offers "my support" to Mussolini on the egocentric assumption that it might really matter to him to have it; or even the absurd, as we are left to contemplate an issue of the *Transatlantic Review* that might have contained the first sections of what became *Finnegans Wake* alongside writings by Pound, Hemingway, Gertrude Stein, and Benito Mussolini! Yet beyond that, there is also a thread of connection that winds its way among all these events: from Pound's admiration for the Marchesa Casati with "all the carefree qualities of the sculptures in Rimini" (August 1922); to his encounters with Boni and Ricci in Rome (February 1923) or with Marchetti in Rimini (in March 1923); to his proposal that Mussolini adopt "the procedure of Sigismundo Malatesta in getting the best artists" (August 1923); even to his hope that Mussolini will want to make Italy "as it was in the quattrocento" (January 1924). That thread is the intricate complex of motifs, both ideological and practical, that were invested in the cultural invention of Sigismondo, a complex by which Pound is able to address and assimilate the emerging culture of fascism.

Critics have often explained Pound's turn to fascism as a response to the global economic crisis that followed the Great Crash of 1929. His interest in Mussolini is the result of good will marred by naïveté, a noble urge to better the world that is diverted into mistaken hero worship. More recently this argument has been reproposed, with modifications, by scholars who urge that Pound's "conversion to fascism," be dated to 1931— it was in 1931 that Pound began dating most of his letters by the fascist calendar—and who argue that Pound's "growing sympathy for Italian fascism was always based in part upon Mussolini's socialist roots; . . . Pound's was a left-wing fascism."[88] His "version of Italian fascism," in short, "emphasized its socialist roots." His earliest reference to the "left wing of the fascist party," which appears in a letter of early April 1934, "is an accurate reflection . . . of the roots of many of [fascism's] programs in Mussolini's early advocacy of Syndicalism and Socialism." Evidence to support this view is found in a letter from Pound to Oswald Mosley in July 1934 advising him that "The only fascism that CAN work in Engl' or France or America is fascismo di sinistra [left-wing fascism]."[89]

Several points in this view are dubious. I doubt whether "many of [fascism's] programs" really had "roots . . . in Mussolini's early advocacy of Syndicalism and Socialism." None is cited, most likely because there is none to cited. What Mussolini knew of syndicalism was Georges Sorel's *Reflections on Violence* with its theory of myth, the notion that the revolution would come into being only if workers believed in a myth, a transfixing image of cataclysmic change and social transformation that would seize the imagination, not appeal to reason or logic. Mussolini reviewed the book at some length in 1909, and from it he learned much about a politics of the imagination and myth that he would use both as radical socialist and as early fascist.[90] But that is a far cry from the kind of governmental legislative initiative usually encompassed by the term *program*. Indeed, syndicalism had no program to offer. It urged violent revolution, not programs.

It is still less tenable to urge that Pound's interest in fascism stemmed from a systematic comparison of the guild syndicalism that had appeared in the *New Age* with the economic policies of the regime. Such arguments confuse rationalizations with reasons. Pound, in his letter of April 1934, was not indicating that his "sympathy for Italian fascism was always based in part on Mussolini's socialist roots." He was parroting a commonplace of fascist propaganda, which consistently called attention to Mussolini's earlier socialism in order to imply that he would bear in mind the interests of workers. Likewise, in his letter to Mosley, he was dispensing advice about tactics for success in England, not affirming principles that had guided his intellectual development. To be sure, Pound did come to believe that Mussolini would eventually adopt economic policies of the sort that Pound espoused in the years after 1935. But these were much later developments: they were elaborate self-deceptions with which he rationalized his ongoing support of a regime whose brutality and moral bankruptcy were, by that time, clear to most observers. They were never the reasons that had sparked and sustained his initial interest. Those more genuine reasons were already fully formed by late 1923 and early 1924, as Pound himself acknowledged. As he put it in early 1933, all but echoing Lincoln Steffens's view: "I bet on Italian fascism years ago and came here to live in the middle of it."[91] Pound, we recall, had left Paris for Italy in late 1924.

When drafting his original notes for Canto 41, which offers its famous portrait of Mussolini, Pound included a sketch of Mussolini's military service in World War I that says much about the origins of his attraction to Mussolini.

"would have called that a portent"
saw then the white thorn hedges, albassina,
stiff silvered [w]ith frost, by San Casciano
twenty metres between their trenches.
"identified as the hospital where Mussolini . . . ["]
from cliché in the Corriere and therefore bombed
by the austrians, that was his worst day in the war.

                                        (Box 66, Folder 2548)

Pound's sketch follows a commonplace of fascist propaganda, which
urged that the Austrians had bombed the hospital that housed Mussolini
in order to kill him. More important, however, is the opening line, "would
have called that a portent," for it is Pound's recollection of Sigismondo's
speech to his troops at the end of Canto 10: "And he said: The Romans
would have called that an augury." Pound's evocation of the earlier pas-
sage suggests how fully his understanding of Mussolini was shaped in, and
by, the experience of writing the Malatesta Cantos in 1922 and 1923. The
echo becomes a cipher in which the mystery of the protagonist's identity
is finally resolved: he is a reincarnation of Sigismondo Malatesta, and it is
faith, rooted in experience, that will enable us to perceive his identity amid
the apparent confusion of contemporary history.

The question of identity, after all, is one of the major motifs of *The
Cantos*, one already thematized in the work's opening lines:

And then went down to the ship,
Set keel to breakers, forth on the godly sea!

Who performs these actions? The subject is conspicuously absent, and it is
not until the next line that the reader learns: "We set up mast and sail on
that swart ship." But in that momentary yet crucial gap in the poem's first
two lines, in that suspended space where actions occur without a subject
to perform them, the text lays out its great theme of a subject internally
split and dispersed through time, defining its heroic task as the reconstitu-
tion of that lost identity, an effort that will consist in closing the gap
between narrator and hero, author and reader—so forming "we." That is
also what is at stake in the closing lines of Canto 10, when Sigismondo
assumes the vatic function of the augur who interprets the eagle's landing
on his tent. For a moment the figure of Sigismondo becomes blurred, his
identity attenuated amid the multiple embedding of quotations: the

speaker of the poem quotes Gaspare Broglio, who quotes Sigismondo (cited only by the pronoun "he"), who in turn quotes the ancient Romans, who in turn . . . : "And he said: The Romans would have called . . ." Identity is fragmented and dispersed, then reconstituted in an experience that demands faith. Which leads to action: "All I want you to do is to follow the orders." Heroic individualism, the discursive sweep of this passage tells us, is the other side of corporate conformity, and the question of the subject is resolved in the affirmation of subjection. The identity of the speaker is reestablished in the restoration of clear distinctions between "I" and "you," between the subject and the object, between active volition ("I want") and passive obedience ("follow the orders"). That is also the distinction that was at stake in the strained relations between Pound ("I want") and the librarian of Rimini ("follow orders"), Aldo Francesca Massèra, the sedate scholar who was so underpaid that to make ends meet he had to teach physics at a local naval academy and who felt reluctant to assume as well the functions of a custodian for an American tourist, living in Paris, who vaunted his erudition about a historical subject that Massèra, in many ways, understood in greater depth. But Massèra also knew what a visit from Marchetti could mean: the report of those priests who had been bloodied in nearby Ravenna, the sight of the city officials of Rimini (his employers!) being beaten seven months before—they were not matters to be weighed lightly. He too had experienced what "this kind of devotion" on the part of Marchetti could portend, though his assessment of its merits probably differed somewhat from Pound's. Thus, during Pound's last day in Rimini, when Massèra saw Pound and Marchetti huddled together with Marcialis, who now wielded absolute and unbridled power over the city government, he may well have feared the loss of his job. Swallowing his pride, he accepted the public rebuke of Marcialis, a humiliating experience: no wonder, as Pound put it, he seemed ready to "die of the shock."

And yet to use Pound's words, it was Massèra's public humiliation that defined his "triumphal exit from Rimini," just as that triumphal exit signaled the beginning of his inexorable entry into the ranks of militant fascism. We err, I think, in urging that that adherence had its basis in a reasoned examination of competing economic theories or a sustained comparison of Mussolini's programs with those of guild socialism or revolutionary syndicalism. No one, that day in Rimini, is reported to have mentioned those subjects to Aldo Francesca Massèra. Yet I suspect that he understood only too well the genuine basis of fascism: the solemn language of "faith" and "action" scarcely concealed the taut fist of terror and unbridled power.

APPENDIX

The following article appeared in *Testa di Ponte* (Rimini, Italy), 6 June 1925, page 1. The original Italian version follows the English translation.

ENGLISH POET SINGS DEEDS AND HISTORY OF THE MALATESTA

Ezra Pound is an English poet who, while visiting Italy, or more precisely Rimini, exactly two years ago, became so deeply taken with the charm of our monuments, those mortal traces of an immortal history, that he found himself enwrapped in the mantle of inspiration.

Thus, after returning to his homeland, Pound set about the task of finding a form to express, in a superb book, everything that was churning about in his poetic mind.

And he has written an artistic masterpiece that is titled *Cantos* and that will be published by *Tkree* [*sic*] *Mountains Press Paris.*

Yesterday we saw the printer's proofs of this poem written in English, proofs shown to us by Captain Marchetti, to whom the poet has given a copy as a token of his esteem during his recent return to Italy, and we were quite amazed at the work's elaborate typographical ornamentation.

We thank Ezra Pound and congratulate him, too. We also offer him our best wishes for the task that lies ahead, given that the complete work will consist of a hundred cantos, while the first volume contains only sixteen.

UN POETA INGLESE | CANTA LE GESTA E LA | STORIA DEI |
MALATESTA

Ezra Pound è un Poeta Inglese il quale venendo in Italia, e precisamente in Rimini due anni or sono si è sentito tanto tenacemente conquistato dal fascino dei nostri monumenti, segni mortali di una storia immortale, da trovarsi avvolto nel manto dell'ispirazione.

Così, Ezra Pound ritornando in patria s'è accinto a fissare sulle pagine di un superbo libro, tuttociò che turbinava nella sua mente di Poeta.

Ed à scritto un capolavoro d'arte che s'intitola "Cantos" e che sarà edito da *Tkree* [*sic*] *Mountains Press Paris.*

Abbiamo visto ieri ia bozza tipografica di questo poem scritto in inglese, bozza mostrataci dal Cap. Marchetti al quale il poeta oggi ritornando in Italia à voluto farne omaggio, e siamo rimasti sbaorditi dalla veste tipgrafica dell'opera.

Ringraziamo e ci congratuliamo col Ezra Pound al quale facciamo anche vivi auguri per ciò che deve ancora compiere, giacchè l'opera complete consterà di cento canti ed il primo volume non ne contiene che sedici.

NOTES

I am grateful to Michael Keller for comments on an early draft of this essay. Readers should note that the first section of this essay offers a synthetic account of matters that I have treated more amply in *Ezra Pound and the Monument of Culture: Text, History, and the Malatesta Cantos* (Chicago: University of Chicago Press, 1991). I've assumed that most readers will not be familiar with that work and have repeated several points here.

1. On Sigismondo Malatesta, the best treatment in English is that of Philip J. Jones, *The Malatesta of Rimini and the Papal State: A Political History* (Cambridge: Cambridge University Press, 1974), chap. 7. Also important is a collection of essays by Philip J. Jones et al., *Studi malatestiani* (Rome: Istituto Storico Italiano per il Medio Evo, 1978), which includes an essay by Jones, "Le signorie di Sigismondo Malatesta," 5–20. The most coherent treatment of Sigismondo's life is still that of Francesco Gaetano Battaglini, "Della vita e de'fatti di Sigismondo Pandolfo Malatesta Signor di Rimino, commentario," in his *Bassinii Parmensis poetae, opera praestantiora nunc primum edita et opportunis commentariis illustrata* (Rimini: ex typographia Albertiniana, 1794), 2: 257–699.

2. For a representative discussion of the building see Nikolaus Pevsner, *Outline of European Architecture,* 7th ed. (Harmondsworth: Penguin, 1963), 189–90. The most complete account of the church's construction is furnished by Corrado Ricci, *Il Tempio Malatestiano* (Rome: Bestetti and Tumminelli, [1924]; reprint, Rimini: Bruno Ghigi Editore, 1974). See also Rudolf Wittkower, *Architectural Principles in the Age of Humanism* (1949; reprint, New York: W. W. Norton, 1971), 1–41. On the iconography of the sculptural decorations see Charles Mitchell, "Il Tempio Malatestiano," in Jones et al., *Studi malatestiani,* 71–104. And for the viewpoint of more recent architectural history see France Borsi, *Leon Battista Alberti: L'opera completa* (Milan: Electa Editrice, 1980).

3. On this later stage in his career see Giovanni Soranzo, *Pio II e la politica italiana nella lotta contro i Malatesti, 1457–1463* (Padua: Fratelli Drucker, 1911).

4. See Gioacchino Paparelli, *Enea Silvio Piccolomini: L'umanesimo sul soglio di Pietro,* 2d ed. (Ravenna: Longo Editore, 1978), 175.

5. See, for example, Giorgio Vasari, *Le vite de' più eccellenti pittori, scultori e architettori* (1550; Novara: Istituto De Agostini, 1967; 2:138, 358–59, 414.

6. For the first mention of this notion in 1718 see Giuseppe Garuffi, "Letter apologetica, scritta all'Illustrissimo Signor Carlo-Francesco Marcheselli, Nobile Riminese, dal Signor Arciprete D. Giuseppe Malatesta Garuffi, in difesa del Tempio famosissimo di san Francesco, eretto in Rimini da Sigismondo-Pandolfo Malatesta in tempo, che teneva il dominio di detta città," in *Giornale de' Letterati d'Italia* 30 (1718): 181. For the discussion in 1756 see Gianmaria Mazzuchelli, *Notizie intorno ad Isotta da Rimino*, 2d ed. (Brescia: Dalle Stampe di Giambattista Bossini, 1759), 32, 38–39; as well as Giovanbattista Costa, "Il Tempio di S. Francesco di Rimino, o sia descrizione delle cose più notabili in esso contenute," in *Miscellanei di varia lettura*, ed. Giuseppe Rocchi (Lucca, 1765), 5:88. For the discussion in 1789 see Francesco Gaetano Battaglini, *Memorie istoriche di Rimino e de' suoi signori artatamente scritte ad illustrare la zecca e la moneta riminese*, ed. Guid'Antonio Zanetti (Bologna: Nella Stamperia di Lelio dalla Volpe, 1789; reprint, Rimini: Bruno Ghighi, 1976), 38–39 n. 60. For a more detailed and extensive discussion of this debate and its effects on Pound see Rainey, *Monument of Culture*, 186–209.

7. Jacob Burckhardt, *The Civilization of the Renaissance in Italy*, trans. S. G. C. Middlemore (New York: Harper and Row, 1958), 235 for all quotations to this point.

8. Burckhardt, *Civilization of the Renaissance*, 50.

9. John Addington Symonds, *Sketches and Studies in Italy and Greece*, 2d series (London: Smith, Elder, 1898), 103, 20.

10. John Addington Symonds, *The Renaissance in Italy*, vol. 1, *The Age of the Despots* (New York: Henry Holt, 1888), 428 n. 1. For the history of these charges see Rainey, *Monument of Culture*, 77–154, 257 n. 38.

11. Charles Yriarte, *Un condottiere au XVᵉ siècle. Rimini: Études sur les lettres et les arts á la cour des Malatesta* (Paris: Jules Rothschild, 1882), 218–19.

12. Pasquale Villari, "Rimini," in *Encyclopaedia Britannica* (Edinburgh: A. and C. Black, 1886), 20:558; and *Encyclopaedia Britannica* (Cambridge: Cambridge University Press, 1911), 23:346.

13. Karl Baedeker, *Italy: Handbook for Travelers*, 13th ed., vol. 2, *Central Italy and Rome* (Leipzig: Baedeker, 1900), 104. See also the same author and title, 1908 edition, 98. See also André Maurel, *Les petites villes d'Italie*, 2d series *Émilie-Marches-Ombrie*, 10th ed. (Paris: Librarie Hachette, 1920), 137–56, esp. 152–53.

14. Edward Hutton, *Sigismondo Pandolfo Malatesta—Lord of Rimini: A Study of a Fifteenth-Century Despot* (London: J. M. Dent, 1906), 295–96, 207–15.

15. Giovanni Soranzo, "La sigla SI di Sigismondo Pandolfo Malatesta," *La Romagna* 6 (1909): 306–24.

16. Aldo Francesco Massèra, "I poeti isottei," *Giornale Storico della Letteratura Italiana* 57 (1911): 1–32.

17. Edward Hutton, *The Cities of Romagna and the Marches* (London: Methuen, 1913), 105–11.

18. Luigi Orsini, *Il Tempio Malatestiano* (1915; reprint, Florence: Fratelli Alinari, 1927), v, vi.

19. See Ricci, *Il Tempio Malatestiano.*

20. See Ricci, *Il Tempio Malatestiano*, 315–19.

21. See Anthony Giddens, *The Consequences of Modernity* (Stanford: Stanford University Press, 1990), 21–27.

22. Friedrich Nietzsche, *Menschliches, Allzumenschliches I*, no. 237, in *Sämtliche Werke: Kritische Studienausgabe*, ed. Giorgio Colli and Mazzini Montinari (Munich: DTV and de Gruyter, 1980), 2:199. For the English edition contemporary with Pound see Friedrich Nietzsche, *Complete Works*, ed. Oskar Ludwig Levy (1909–11; reprint, New York: Russell and Russell, 1965), 6:220–21.

23. *I canti di Fauno* (Naples: Editore Francesco Perrella, 1908).

24. Antonio Beltramelli, *Un tempio d'amore* (Palermo: Remo Sandron, [1912]).

25. Antonio Beltramelli, *L'uomo nuovo* (Rome: Mondadori, 1923).

26. On Beltramelli's career see R. Bertacchini, "Beltramelli, Antonio," in *Dizionario biografico degli italiani* (Rome: Istituto della Enciclopedia Italiana, 1966), 8:56–60. On his participation at the congress see Emilio R. Papa, *Fascismo e cultura* (Venice: Marsilio, 1974), pp. 161–62 for signers of the program and p. 165 for the program itself. For the regime's tributes to Beltramelli upon his death, see *Il Popolo d'Italia*, 16 March 1930, 3; the newspaper was founded by Mussolini and edited by his brother Arnoldo after 1922; Arnoldo's obituary notice for Beltramelli appears on the same page.

27. For Beltramelli's unpublished letters to Ricci documenting their collaboration in 1907 see Rainey, *Monument of Culture*, 324 n. 114.

28. For Ricci's life see Rainey, *Monument of Culture*, 193–94 and the relevant notes indicating sources.

29. On his notes from Symonds see Rainey, *Monument of Culture*, 117–18; on his purchase of the Baedeker, 290 n. 105.

30. For Pound's reading of Beltramelli while writing his earliest drafts in June 1922 see Rainey, *Monument of Culture*, pp. 29–31; for Beltramelli's influence on a later draft in October 1922, pp. 172–73.

31. Pound's copy of Yriarte is held at Yale University, the Beinecke Rare Book and Manuscript Library, call number ZA P865 +Zv 882y; the various notes, calling cards, and newspaper clippings that he kept inside the volume currently have the call number Uncat. Za file 204. Quotations and discussions of his marginalia and marginal markings appear in Rainey, *Monument of Culture*, 30, 41–42, 121–22, 154, 163–64, 176, 182, 189–90, 316 n. 87, 319 n. 106; with reproductions on 164, 175, and 319 n. 106. The marginalia are also discussed by Daniel Bornstein, "The Poet as Historian: Researching the Malatesta Cantos," *Paideuma* 10 (1981): 283–91.

32. Soranzo, *Pio II*. For his purchase of Soranzo's book on 21 July 1922 see Rainey, *Monument of Culture*, p. 123, and for its immediate influence on his drafts, pp. 123–26; for his work in the Bibliothèque Nationale, pp. 103–4.

33. On his meeting with Ricci see Rainey, *Monument of Culture*, 191–97.

34. For his efforts to contact Santi Muratori see Ezra Pound to Dorothy Shake-spear Pound, 28 March 1923, Lilly Library, Pound MSS 2, 1923; for his inter-est in contacting Soranzo see Ezra Pound to Isabel Pound, 24 February 1923, Box 52, Folder 1968.

35. For drafts connecting Maltestan Rimini with the culture of Provence see Rainey, *Monument of Culture*, 37–42.

36. On his life see A. S. Strnad, "Broglio, Gaspare," in *Dizionario biografico degli italiani* (Rome: Istituto della Enciclopeida Italiana, 1972), 14:437–39.

37. Soranzo, *Pio II*, 11: he argues that Broglio was "al corrente delle pratiche diplomatiche, delle imprese, delle condizioni politiche ed economiche del suo signore," and he terms the chronicle "importantissima, perchè spesso verte intorno a fatti, dei quali egli si dice testimone oculare e che invano si recercano nelle altre cronache o nelle carte degli archivi."

38. On the background of the battle and the many sources describing it see Jones, *Malatesta of Rimini*, 230 and 230 n. 2. A fuller account of the battle is given by Soranzo, *Pio II*, 247–50.

39. Gaspare Broglio, *Cronaca universale*, Rimini, Biblioteca Civica Gambalunga, MS SC-MS 1161 (formerly D.III.48), fol. 246^r according to the modern enu-meration, fol. 273^r according to the older one. The work has been partially published as Gaspare Broglio Tartaglia, *Cronaca malatestiana del secolo XV (dalla cronaca universale)*, ed. Antonio G. Luciani (Rimini: Bruno Ghigi Edi-tore, 1982), but this edition contains only excerpts and does not include the passage in question. All transcriptions from the manuscript and all translations from it are my own.

40. For Pound's visit to Rimini on these days see Ezra Pound to Dorothy Pound, 21 March 1923, Lilly Library, Indiana University, Bloomington, Pound MSS 3; Ezra Pound to Agnes Bedford, 25 March 1923, Lilly Library, Pound MSS 2, Bedford 1923. See Ezra Pound to Ernest Hemingway, 26 March 1923, Boston, Kennedy Library, Hemingway Collection, E. Pound. See Ezra Pound to James Sibley Watson Jr., 26 March 1923, New York Public Library, Berg Collection; Ezra Pound to Dorothy Pound, 28 March 1923, Lilly Library, Pound MSS 3.

41. Beinecke, William Bird Papers, series II, item no. 37.

42. In effect this accords with conventional transcription practice, which normally resolves a final *j* as *i;* however, Pound does this by virtue of an accident, rather than deliberate choice.

43. The reason for this change is not clear. Pound may have thought that his tran-scription was mistaken; or he may have thought that Broglio had made an orthographical error; or he may have altered the letter through simple care-lessness.

44. Eliot accepted the new group of cantos of 14 May 1922, apparently without having seen them (see T. S. Eliot to Ezra Pound, 14 May 1923, Lilly Library, Pound MSS 2, T. S. Eliot). On 18 May Pound sent him the manuscript, and on 20 May Eliot replied that he wanted to print them in the next issue, sched-uled for July—if he could find the space. (See Ezra Pound to T. S. Eliot, 18

May 1923, private collection, Mrs. Valerie Eliot. See also T. S. Eliot to Ezra Pound, 20 May 1923, Lilly Library, Pound MSS 2, T. S. Eliot.) On 22 May an arrangement was found that would create some new space, and the decision to print was made firmer. Transmitting the manuscript to the printer and typesetting took roughly three weeks: sometime between 13 and 17 June Pound received proofs and corrected them (see Ezra Pound to T. S. Eliot, 12 June 1923, private collection, Mrs. Valerie Eliot), and by 18 June they were already back in the office of the *Criterion*—clearly a very short time (see Richard Aldington to Ezra Pound, 18 June 1923, Lilly Library, Pound MSS 2, 1923). The proofs for the Malatesta Cantos are probably conserved in the archives of the *Criterion,* which are held by Faber and Faber and Mrs. Valerie Eliot, but as they are not accessible to scholars, we cannot be certain which changes were approved by Pound; Eliot himself commented in late July of 1923 that the new cantos were "not perfect in typography, owing to the muddle in which this no. was produced" (T. S. Eliot to Ezra Pound, 23 July 1923, Lilly Library, Pound MSS 2, T. S. Eliot).

45. Ezra Pound to William Bird, 25 January 1925: "Vurry noble work, and to date *no* misprint of any importance," Lilly Library, William Bird MSS, 1925.

46. Except for one change: in the Canto 11 occurrence of the Broglio passage, the 1923 *Criterion* printing had contained a period at the end of the second line. It was eliminated from the 1925 edition and from all subsequent ones.

47. Upon its fourth appearance in the 1933 edition by Farrar and Rinehart it underwent a last, minor change in typographical format, but one that did not affect the text, which has remained unaltered until the present—unusual in comparison with most of *The Cantos.* Farrar and Rinehart altered the majuscules that had been introduced by Bernouard, changing them to small capitals and altering the font of the opening words from italic to roman in the version that appeared at the beginning of Canto 11. They made no changes to the quotation as it appears in Canto 10.

48. "Medieval History Condensed in Verse: Ezra Pound Writing Results of Research in Italy," *New York Herald,* 29 April 1923, sec. 2, p. 3, col. 6.

49. Pound gives a footnote citing Yriarte, *Un condottiere,* in Canto 10, page 44; he also corrects Yriarte's transcription of a document in Italian, altering Yriarte's *gettata via* to *buttato via* to make it accord with the original letter housed in Florence; for his motives in doing so see Rainey, *Monument of Culture,* 71. For his instructions to the printer telling him how best to simulate the quattrocento abbreviations, see below.

50. Ezra Pound, "Fascism or the Direction of the Will," Box 89, Folder 3359 for the earlier version (hereafter *FDW*) and Folder 3360 for the revised version. The essay's date is inferred from Pound's references to having written *Jefferson and/or Mussolini* two months earlier, in February 1933. The title's allusion to Dante's letter to Can Grande is obvious and need hardly be mentioned. Pound, of course, also used the phrase to define his aims in *The Cantos,* implicitly urging a common program shared by his poem and fascism.

51. Giovanni Gentile, "The Philosophic Basis of Fascism," *Foreign Affairs* 6 (1927–28): 290–304.

52. Emilio Gentile, "The Conquest of Modernity: From Modernist Nationalism to Fascism," *Modernism/Modernity* 1, no. 3 (September 1994): 73.

53. Gentile, "Philosophic Basis of Fascism," 296.

54. Benito Mussolini, "Discorso a Napoli," 24 October 1922, quoted in Gentile, "The Conquest of Modernity," 73.

55. Lilly Library, Pound MSS 3, 1923, Ezra Pound to Dorothy Shakespear Pound, [13 March 1923].

56. Lilly Library, Pound MSS 3, 1923, Ezra Pound to Dorothy Pound, "Wednesday" [21 March 1923].

57. My account of the life of Averardo Marchetti is based on photocopies of his birth, marriage, and death certificates, as well as the birth certificate of his first son and the death certificate of his wife, all from the Anagrafe of Forlì. These materials were kindly furnished to me by Dr. Paola Delbianco of the Biblioteca Civica Gambalunga, together with her letter of 26 October 1988, which also contains her own two-page typescript entitled "Averardo Marchetti," including information from her interview with Averardo's son, Federico Marchetti; a clipping from *L'Opinione* (Philadelphia), 8 December 1917; and a photocopy of *La Testa di Ponte* (Rimini) II.21 (6 June 1925), p. 1; and a photocopy of the title page from the copy of *Lustra* that Ezra Pound gave to Averardo Marchetti in 1923, now in the possession of his son Averardo. Some of these materials are discussed at more length below. I am deeply grateful to Dr. Delbianco and the library's director, Dr. Piero Meldini, for their generous assistance in locating and forwarding these materials.

58. Max Gallo, *Mussolini's Italy,* trans. Charles Lam Markmann (New York: Macmillan Publishing, 1973), 127.

59. On Arpinati's campaign see Liliano Faezna, "Prima passi del fascio riminese," *Storie e Storia* 2 (October 1979): 45–61, esp. 53–54.

60. Niccolò Matteini, *Rimini negli ultimi due secoli* (Santarcangelo di Romagna: Maggioli, 1977), 380 and 382. Matteini cites a manifesto published by the administration upon its resignation: "La lunga aspra lotta sostenuta per circa 20 mesi contro ogni sorta di difficoltà, di contrasti, diffidenze—dall'eredità finanziaria disastrosa all'assenteismo degli Istituti di Credito locale, alla resistenza dei contribuenti, alle more degli uffici e dei poteri di stato—è culminata oggi nella violenza contro le persone degli amministratori." From Matteini, too, comes the information regarding the appointment of Dr. Marcialis, which follows immediately below. His calling card, evidently given to Pound when they met one another in 1923, is preserved among the papers that Pound kept in his copy of Yriarte, *Un condottiere,* now in the Beinecke Library (see note 31).

61. Dottor Luigi Marcialis, *Relazione in merito alla gestione straordinaria, 6 febbraio–9 novembre 1923* (Rimini: Comune di Rimini, but printed in Santarcangelo di Romagna, Tipografia Fratelli Giorgetti, 1923), [5].

62. Lilly Library, Pound MSS 3, 1923, Ezra Pound to Dorothy Pound, "Ravenna, Wednesday night" [28 March 1923].

63. On Nancy Cox-McCormack the only published study is Lawrence Rainey's introduction to Nancy Cox-McCormack, "Ezra Pound in the Paris Years,"

Sewanee Review 102 (1994): 93–95. In the account below I also draw on her unpublished papers and memoirs at Smith College, the Sophia Smith Collection, Nancy Cox-McCormack Papers; hereafter this is abbreviated C-M P, followed by the box and folder numbers.

64. The life mask is conserved at the Beinecke Rare Book and Manuscript Library of Yale University, call number 1980 152, while the portrait bust is held at the State University of New York at Buffalo, Poetry and Rare Books Collection, without call number.

65. See Ezra Pound to Nancy Cox-McCormack [circa 30 January 1923], in which Pound enquires about the price of a room at Nancy's *pensione;* Buffalo, State University of New York at Buffalo, the Poetry/Rare Books Collection, Nancy Cox-McCormack Papers, call number B745, Folder 13. See also Ezra Pound to Nancy Cox-McCormack, 3 February [1923], B745, Folder 10, in which he specifies the room that he wants.

66. All quotations are from Nancy Cox-McCormack, "Mussolini," an unpublished typescript containing her memoirs and conserved in C-M P, Box 7, Folder 2. The typescript is signed by Cox-McCormack and dated "1939." It was evidently intended to form part of a larger project, her autobiography, and a canceled heading on the first page of the manuscript reads: "PART TWO | Chapters 7–18." As it stands now, the typescript consists of two blocks of material. The first is given the title in typescript, "Fascist Thunder," with an additional title added by hand, "Mussolini, 1922 fall." The pages of this section are numbered 141–56. The second is given the title in typescript, "Man from Romagna," also with an additional title by hand, "Mussolini, early 1923," and the pages of this section are numbered 239–83. The three quotations given here are from typescript pages numbered 152–53, 152, and 155.

67. All quotations are from Nancy Cox-McCormack, "An Italian Memoir, Incorporating the Story of Lauro de Bosis," an unpublished typescript recounting her experiences with the de Bosis family, conserved in C-M P, Box 8, Folder 1, p. 19. The memoir was apparently written between 1954 and 1960.

68. On Boni see P. Romanelli, "Boni, Giacomo," in the *Dizionario biografico degli italiani* (Rome: Istituto della Enciclopedia Italiana, 1870), 12:75–77. For Cox-McCormack's introduction to him see her unpublished reminiscences, "An Italian Memoir," 24–25. See also her published essay, "Giacomo Boni: Humanist—Archaeologist of the Roman Forum and the Palatine," *Art and Archaeology* 28, nos. 1–2 (July–August 1929): 35–44.

69. Cox-McCormack, "An Italian Memoir," 20.

70. Carbon of letter from Vittorio de Santa to Benito Mussolini, dated 3 January 1923, C-M P, Box 7, Folder 2.

71. "Mussolini," pp. 247–50 for her remarks on Judson Lida Rismondo; p. 255 for her attendance at the International Chamber of Commerce; pp. 251–53 for her first meeting with Mussolini in late April; and pp. 257–58 for her second meeting with him in early May 1923. Her bust of Mussolini is conserved at the Herbert F. Johnson Museum of Art, Cornell University, Ithaca, New York. Another copy of the bust, formally held in the Philadelphia Museum of Art, was "deaccessioned" some time in the past. The bust is dated 1 July

1923. Cox-McCormack reports that her second and crucial interview with Mussolini took place in early May, in "Mussolini," p. 257, and that she began the first of ten sittings with him "the next day," p. 258.

72. Nancy McCormack, "Gifted Sculptor Gives Vivid Pen Picture of Mussolini," newspaper clipping from unidentified source, dated "Oct. 1923," in C-M P, Box 1, Folder 10.

73. Nancy Cox-McCormack, preface to Benito Mussolini, *My Diary* (Boston: Small Maynard Co., 1925), ix. An echo of her view that Mussolini was "much an artist" can be heard in Pound's assessment of him: "take him as anything but an artist and you will get muddled with contradictions"; Ezra Pound, *Jefferson and/or Mussolini* (1935; reprint, New York: Liveright, 1970), 34.

74. Rainey, *Monument to Culture*, 191–93.

75. Ezra Pound to Nancy Cox-McCormack, 28 March 1923, Buffalo, State University of New York at Buffalo, the Poetry and Rare Books Collection, Nancy Cox-McCormack Papers, call number B745, Folder 5.

76. The copy is still in the possession of Federico Marchetti in Rimini. I am grateful to Dr. Paola Delbianco for obtaining a photocopy of the volume for me.

77. See Myles Slatin, "A History of Pound's *Cantos* I–XVI, 1915–1925," *American Literature* 35 (1963): 183–95.

78. Ezra Pound to William Bird, 24 August [1925], Lilly Library, William Bird Papers.

79. Pound, *Jefferson and/or Mussolini*, 26–27.

80. Letters from Ezra Pound to Dorothy Pound, Lilly Library, PM2.

81. On Pound's attending the lecture of 29 October 1922 by Steffens, see letter from Ezra Pound to Homer Pound, 30 October 1922, Beinecke, Box 52, Folder 1967. For Steffens's views of the Lausanne, see his letters of 25 and 30 November 1922, in Lincoln Steffens, *Letters*. Steffens's views on Mussolini, which were published in the *Los Angeles Times*, 23 December 1922, are quoted from Justin Kaplan, *Lincoln Steffens: A Biography* (New York: Simon and Schuster, 1974), 259. Quotations from *The Autobiography of Lincoln Steffens* (New York: Harcourt Brace, [1931]), 816, 817, 819.

82. Mary Colum, *Life and the Dream* (Garden City, N.Y.: Doubleday and Company, 1947), 307–8.

83. Letter from Ezra Pound to Nancy Cox-McCormack, 15 August 1923, State University of New York at Buffalo, Poetry Collection, Box 745, Folder 16.

84. See Angelo Battaglini, "Della corte letteraria di Sigismondo Pandolfo Malatesta signor di Rimini commentario," in F. G. Battaglini, *Basinii Parmensis poetae*, 2:1–257.

85. Letter from Ezra Pound to Nancy Cox-McCormack, [circa 5 January 1924]; Tennessee State Library and Archives, Manuscript Section, Nancy Cox-McCormack Papers, Accession no. 413. I have capitalized the word "Rome" in the second paragraph. A portion of this letter was previously published in my introduction to Cox-McCormack's memoirs of Pound, "Ezra Pound."

86. Letter from Ezra Pound to Nancy Cox-McCormack, 13 January [1924], State University of New York at Buffalo, Poetry Collection, Box 745, Folder 15.

87. Letter from Ezra Pound to Nancy Cox-McCormack, 28 January 1924, State University of New York at Buffalo, Poetry Collection, Box 745, Folder 17.

88. See Timothy Redman's essay in this volume.

89. Timothy Redman, *Ezra Pound and Italian Fascism* (Cambridge: Cambridge University Press, 1990), 156–57.

90. Benito Mussolini, "The General Strike and Violence" (Lo sciopero generale e la violenza), a review of Georges Sorel, *Considerazioni sulla violenza* (Bari: Laterza, 1908, or as it is known in English, *Reflections on Violence,* first published in *Il Popolo* no. 2736, 25 June 1909, 10; reprinted in Enzo Santarelli, *Scritti politici di Benito Mussolini* (Milan: Giangiacomo Feltrinelli Editore, 1979), 115–20. See also his "Syndicalist Theory" (La teoria sindicalista), a review of Giuseppe Prezzonlini, *La teoria sindicalista* (Naples: Editore Francesco Perrella, 1909), first published in *Il Popolo* no. 2713, 27 May 1909, 10, and reprinted in the same edition by Santarelli, 109–14.

91. "Fascism or the Direction of the Will," revised version, 2.

The Middle Years

5

An Epic Is a Hypertext Containing Poetry: *Eleven New Cantos* (31–41) by Ezra Pound

Tim Redman

Ezra Pound's *Eleven New Cantos* were published as a group in 1934. Including cantos appearing in various publications from 1931 to 1934, *Eleven New Cantos* inscribes an arc stretching from Jefferson to Mussolini; it offers witness to Pound's momentous conversion from Social Credit to fascism, a conversion that would powerfully affect the second half of the poet's adult life. In this essay I propose first to present a brief overview of *Eleven New Cantos,* examining aspects of those cantos that provide some understanding of Pound's conversion; second, to take an extensive look at passages in Canto 33; and third, to consider how several new software tools grouped variously under the rubrics hypertext, hypermedia, and multimedia provide us with the first adequate metaphor for understanding the structure of *The Cantos.* I will argue that in several important ways *The Cantos* may be considered a protohypertext, a new poetic form intuited by its author, and that there may be a new kind of poetics, a poetics of hypertext, that offers a valuable way of approach to Pound's difficult epic.

To understand Pound's voyage in *Eleven New Cantos* from a dead president-philosophe to a live tyrant, we should look briefly at their progression. That Pound understood or planned this group as a sequence can be seen from his notes for *The Cantos* now at the Beinecke Library at Yale. On two different pages he jotted the following (I present one version in the left column, the other in the right):

XXXI	TJ	
II		TJ JA
III	JA	
IV	JQA	JQA
V	Mittle europe	Mittel Europa
VI	DMP	GC
VII	Van B.	Van B.
XXXVIII	Contemporary	contemp - ness.
	Blogget. Krupp	
IX	Κίρκη	Κίρκη
	Kantago Morgan	
XL =	Hanno	material order
XLI	Dux	moral order ethics[1]

Such a schematic for the group helps us see its unity: it has a beginning, a still center in Cavalcanti's canzone "Donna mi prega," and a conclusion. Despite this overall cohesion, Pound's brevity and precision of reference pull both indifferent and curious readers away from the text, the former to set it aside, the latter to search for sources.

Eleven New Cantos initiates a new phase in Pound's epic, the beginning of what have been termed the "Middle Cantos," those cantos (31–71) published in the tumultuous decade of the 1930s. The first three cantos of the middle group (31–33) are drawn largely from Pound's copy of *The Writings of Thomas Jefferson* (Washington, D.C.: Thomas Jefferson Memorial Association, 1905) published in twenty volumes. These volumes, a gift from T. S. Eliot, were heavily marked and annotated by Pound, who drew from them in order to pay homage to the great American president as well as to reflect obliquely upon events of his own time. No finished portrait of Jefferson can be seen in these cantos, which were published as a group in *Pagany,* but Pound does present us with a Jefferson who is *polumetis,* of many devices, showing his range of interests, observations, and accomplishments. Pound's turn to the works of the American founders in the Middle Cantos demonstrates both a growing interest in political matters and an attempt to articulate his own American identity after so many years of expatriation.

Of course, Pound's choices of passages to excerpt reveal his state of mind. As later with John Adams in Cantos 62–71, he presents a life of Jefferson with occasional elements drawn from the life of Pound. This can be seen most clearly in one typescript note for these cantos:

Item: to my good and affectionate servant Bunwell, his freedom and
the sum of three hundred dollars / necessities to his trade of glazier;
to good servants Hemings and Fosset, their freedom at the end of
one year and to each all tools of their callings n [*sic*] a log house to be
built for each. T. J. XVII 470.
Item: to the late Thos. Hardy, my thanks for instruction.
Item: to the late Robert Bridges, ditto for a caution 'gainst homo-
phones. (Box 66, Folder 2548)

Jefferson's last will and testament recall to Pound his own obligations,
though with an interesting reversal: instead of Jefferson who will in death
pay his debts to the living, Pound acknowledges his indebtedness to the
dead. In addition to serving as reticent autobiography, Pound's frequent
use in *The Cantos* of quotations, citations, and allusions shows his epic's
great indebtedness to its many sources. A hypertext or hypermedia envi-
ronment would best actualize all the various contexts of the poem and
their relations to each other.

Another mixture of the presidential and the Poundian comes within
these cantos. In Canto 31, President Jefferson is quoted: "'English papers
. . . their lies . . .'" The remark about English newspapers, found in vol-
ume 6, page 207 of the Jefferson, reflects Pound's own disenchantment
with the English press, born of his experience of its role in World War I
and his work for A. R. Orage's journal the *New Age*. To find such a view
in Jefferson provided Pound with further confirmation of his own belief.
To some extent this pattern will become typical of Pound during the
period. He will arrive at some conclusion about public affairs and then find
what he takes to be confirmation of his views in his historical readings.
Such a method of examining history is both richly suggestive and seriously
misleading at the same time; it will be used by Pound to construct his par-
ticular view of history that becomes a constant subject of his poetry and
prose until the end of World War II.

Pound's turn to the political continues in Cantos 32 and 33, both of
which begin with John Adams, who will occupy his own decade of cantos
(62–71) that close the middle group. Canto 33 finds Adams writing to Jef-
ferson on 28 June 1812 "Litterae nihil sanantes" [Literature curing noth-
ing], echoing yet concealing Pound's own ongoing crisis: whether in
response to the world turmoil of the Great Depression his poetry was not
merely frivolous. Pound's typescript notes to these cantos reveal that he
was questioning his own role as a writer:

```
Func. of Lit in Stato.      = propaganda?? = keep clean the
tools.                        d'accordo - laws
                              muddle - command . . . .
Propaganda - to teach       specific =
russia              Mus              tessera
to keep clean the tools    = clarity & vigour of any & every
thought
```
_____

```
Biolog. function of lit.   nutrition of impulse
relieve mind of strain
give feeling of being alive
set 'em off = mobilize
energy - start dynamo (Box 65, Folder 2537)
```

His need to justify his own activity is apparent here, as his new concern with literature's propagandistic value emerges. Another note reveals his discontent:

> For a thinking man not a scientist there are two sane courses worth attention. Art which is search for an absolute statement, just as absolute as the solution of a geometrical problem; and to which the answer shd. not only be true but stay true as a conclusion of Euclid/
>   and there is, secondly, action, say political or economic action, in which a given limited field is dealt with in a particular time, the goodness or badness lying in proportion to what is possible in particular given conditions. The two categories for Albertus Magnus wd. have been [as] different as the noun and the verb (Box 65, Folder 2537).

Pound felt the need to become more engaged with political and social problems throughout the years of the 1930s and World War II. His own notes for these cantos are overwhelmingly concerned with the history of economics.

Canto 34 is devoted to the life of John Quincy Adams, as taken from his diary. Pound attempts to give the reader some sense of the diverse activities of the sixth American president (1825–29), who had been secretary of state from 1817 to 1825, but attempting to condense a diary into a single canto results in excessive fragmentation, for most readers. Such fragmentation is increasingly a feature of these middle cantos, but it is a problem that could be remedied in a hypertext environment. Pound's notes to this canto provide us with insight into his thinking:

J.Q.A. Diary/ merely notice June 10/ 1819 general denunciation of Banks/ impertinent and prostrating every principle of polit. econ. no sign that he understood or greatly thought//

mental habit strong/ we just slide over. however/ J.Q. seems to differentiate between debtors and BANK DEBTORS, which latter are so powerful as to controll the press. . . .

Both J/A & T/J J.Q/A and Van B. vs/ bank power. unanimity in all the honest presidents of that time

vs./ Hamilton/ Webster

definitely corrupt. Ham granted honest. but royalist. (Box 65, Folder 2537)

Canto 35 purports to be a portrait of Central Europe, one whose accuracy is questioned by Pound at the very outset of the canto: "So this is (may we take it) Mitteleuropa." Little in it is flattering. It was written after Pound's extensive visit to Vienna (28 April–15 June 1928), and it was meant to show a society in decline. Canto 36 is another attempt by Pound to translate Guido Cavalcanti's canzone "Donna mi prega" which is a close examination of the nature and effects of love and virtually incomprehensible without extensive annotation. Pound does not provide annotation, but it could be provided either in a footnote to a new edition of *The Cantos* or in a hypertext version of the poem. The latter would offer the reader an opportunity to explore themes and phrases (such as "Dove sta memoria") from Cavalcanti that occur elsewhere in *The Cantos*. Canto 37 is an account drawn from the life of Martin Van Buren, the eighth president of the United States (1837–41) who supported Andrew Jackson in his war against the Bank of the United States. The bank, under the direction of its president Nicholas Biddle, engineered a nationwide panic to try to force the renewal of its charter. Pound's notes reveal his growing understanding of the relevance of these old battles to his own time:

National Currency belongs to the nation; there is no reason why the nation shd. pay rent for this currency to any group of persons, however clever a camouflage may be constructed to cover such payments.

The available currency must equal the available goods, or must come so near it as to leave only such fraction of goods undistributed as will serve as reserve in case of emergency.

Here Jackson dictum applies, (Pockets of the people as good a
place for to keep that reserved as anywhere else.) (Box 65, Folder
2537)

Pound's evolving understanding of the economic crisis of Van Buren's
time was conditioned by the contemporary situation in the United States,
Italy, England, and France; it was also informed by his reading of history,
Social Credit, Karl Marx, and soon Silvio Gesell.

Pound's frustration and anger at public corruption would grow as he
read about the same problems recurring again and again throughout his-
tory. Canto 38 reflects these concerns, discussing how the international
arms trade was leading inevitably to further war. A few bright spots occur:
a mention of the public works of Mussolini, the successes of Leo Frobe-
nius, and an extended discussion of Major C. H. Douglas's A + B theo-
rem, the foundation of Social Credit, and, Pound thought, a way out of
the crisis of the Great Depression. In Canto 39, Pound returns to his time-
less world of Homer and the gods that offers refuge from oppressive con-
temporary problems. He never lost sight of the goal that he articulated in
the notes to these cantos: "The aim is to bring back the gods, that is to say,
the aim is to create states of mind in which certain things are comprehen-
sible" (Box 65, Folder 2538).

In Canto 40 Pound is reimmersed in the corrupt world of banking, in
particular in the various schemes and manipulations of the powerful
House of Morgan. The canto undergoes an abrupt transition at midpoint
as Pound seemingly throws up his hands in despair and changes course:
"Out of which things seeking an exit / PLEASING TO CARTHEGEN-
IANS: HANNO." The second half of the canto is devoted to the story of
the Carthaginian navigator and king Hanno, whose adventure is re-
counted by Pound as an exemplary tale of a bold man who acted for the
public good.

This story provides Pound with a perfect transition to Canto 41,
whose principal figure, Mussolini, is meant by Pound to demonstrate a
way out of the various problems and corruptions that he had been cata-
loging in nine of the previous ten cantos. Although most contemporary
readers will react differently to Pound's account of Mussolini, there is lit-
tle doubt that Pound intended to highlight Mussolini's ability to cut
swiftly through corruption, his public-works projects, and his immediate
intuition of the point of Pound's *Cantos*.

The canto was written after Pound had met Mussolini on 30 January

1933. The *Duce* was an immensely charismatic individual, and Pound succumbed to a kind of hero worship. "The Boss"'s remark on Pound's use of foreign accents in *The Cantos,* that it is "amusing," is sanctioned by the poet as the correct response, demonstrating for Pound Mussolini's quick perception rather than what it undoubtedly was: a polite, offhand remark made to yet another visitor during a busy day. The *Duce*'s public-works projects, a genuine achievement, are then mentioned before Pound recounts the anecdote that seems to be the principal point of the canto and the culmination of *Eleven New Cantos.* The story is told to Pound by "the mezzo-yit," a derogatory term of Pound's invention made up of the Italian word for half and an English slang word for a Jew. The "mezzo-yit," however, is a friend or acquaintance of Pound and clearly one who shares Pound's high regard for Mussolini. The story of businessmen forming a consortium to profit privately at public expense contains a degree of sadism in Mussolini's toying with the men before announcing that they would all be sentenced to internal exile. Its lesson is clear: Mussolini is an individual of quick perception and impeccable virtue who keeps an eye on the public good and punishes those who attempt to profit privately at public expense. The niceties of a trial or even of legal or civil rights are summarily dispensed with as Mussolini metes out swift justice.

Pound's notes to this canto enlarge somewhat our understanding of his intent. One note is not entirely clear: "story told by the mezzo=yit / (shall we say X Buh [?] of Tobias)" (Box 66, Folder 2572), where the second line was not used in the canto. The original notes for the story of Mussolini's service in World War I do add to our understanding of the canto:

> "would have called that a portent"
> saw then the witch [?] thorn hedges, albasiina,
> stiff silvered [w]ith frost, by San Casciano
> twenty metres between their trenches.
> "identified as the hospital where Mussolini . . .
> from cliché in the Corriere["] and therefore bombed
> by the austrians, that was his worst day in the war.
> after he had been in the o;t;c; for six days
> Mr. Giolitti or some other thoughtful shitsack
> ordered that he be sent back to the fighting. . .
> which also be call'd a portent, and to show
> how much genius was valued but shitsack who governed in
> them days; (Box 66, Folder 2548)

This note reveals to what a great extent Pound accepted fascist hagiography: that after Mussolini was wounded, the war began to go badly for Italy; that the Austrians, learning where he was hospitalized, shelled the hospital in order to kill him; and that the prime minister himself ordered him back to the front. All of this is a great deal of attention to be paid a corporal; Pound's use of it, even in his notes, shows to what extent he had abandoned his judgment in favor of his need to believe.

One final note confirms this:

```
                      1° atto
1918----------------------------------------------1920
                      2° atto
1920---------------------------------------------<1922>
                      3 atto
1922----------------------------------------------1932
```

This division for Pound of history into three acts—the first act the postwar crisis that formed the climate for the onset of fascism, the second act Mussolini's road to power culminating in the March on Rome, and the third act the first ten years of Mussolini's rule, the *decennio* of fascism whose celebration in 1932 so impressed Pound—show how captivated Pound was by the Italian dictator. Pound's *Eleven New Cantos,* therefore, conducts us on a journey from Jefferson to Mussolini, who, in turn, will presumably lead Italy to the condition of an Earthly Paradise. The illumination provided by even the brief notes I have added to this summary show to what degree our appreciation of those cantos would be enhanced by the rapid three-dimensional text processing of a hypertext environment.

Although it is difficult to pinpoint a precise moment of Pound's conversion to fascism, I do believe that Canto 33 provides evidence of a decisive change of sympathy and focus in his thought. Two passages in particular, one occasioned by his reading of Marx and the other by a speech by Senator Smith Brookhart, show Pound's turn to the political, to his obsession with social issues during the 1930s as opposed to his narrowly focused concern during the 1920s on only selected public issues affecting artists. Since these passages will also illustrate the need for a poetics of hypertext for an understanding of Pound's project, I will examine them closely.

Pound's reading during this time was becoming largely political, economic, and historical in subject matter. Following his generally eclectic bent, he was reading extensively in Karl Marx's Das Kapital, issued in an Italian edition (*Il Capitale* [Torino: Unione Tipografico–Editrice Torinese, 1924]) that is among the most heavily marked and annotated volumes in his personal library. Pound was clearly horrified by the accounts of the exploitation of labor given by Marx in volume 1, parts 3 ("The Production of Absolute Surplus-Value") and 4 ("Production of Relative Surplus-Value"). Although Pound, through the works of Silvio Gesell, would soon become a disciple of Proudhon, he never abandoned his conviction that Marx had exposed fundamental evils in British capitalism of the mid-nineteenth century. Pound's growing sympathy for Italian fascism was always based in part upon Mussolini's socialist roots; as I have argued elsewhere, Pound's was a left-wing fascism.[2]

Canto 33 contains extensive quotations from *Das Kapital*. Since Pound was attracted to the socialist element in Italian fascism, these quotations merit careful consideration. What is clear from these examples is that Pound's *Cantos* are radically intertextual in nature, and that they undermine notions of textual autonomy that have been a staple of most poetic and aesthetic theory and practice for centuries. We shall return to this question in the third section of this essay.

Take the first quotation, "limits of his individuality (cancels) and develops his power as a specie." This sentence is drawn from volume 1, "The Process of Capitalist Production," part 4, "Production of Relative Surplus-Value," chapter 13, "Co-Operation," of *Capital*. In the Moore-Aveling translation the section from which the sentence is drawn reads:

> the special productive power of the combined working-day is, under all circumstances, the social productive power of labour, or the productive power of social labour. This power is due to co-operation itself. When the labourer co-operates systematically with others, he strips off **the fetters of his individuality and develops the capabilities of his species.**[3] [I have added boldface throughout the quoted passages to highlight Pound's use of his sources.]

The chapter is devoted to exploring the synergistic effects of a number of individuals working cooperatively rather than singly on a project; under many circumstances, combined labor produces a greater amount of use value than would the same number of individuals working alone. Although this passage does not fit into Pound's usual interest in Marx, it is not difficult to see why he seized upon it. The passage corresponds to the Social Credit idea of the increment of association, a cornerstone of Pound's economic thought. It also suggests the central symbol of Italian fascism, the fasces, a rod made up of a group of bundled sticks whose striking force is greater than an equal number of individual sticks because they are subsumed to a collective purpose. Throughout the '30s and throughout the period of World War II, Pound would attempt a synthesis of the best Marxist, Social Credit, and fascist ideas into a coherent political and economic philosophy.

The following lines from that paragraph in Canto 33 are taken from part 4, chapter 15, "Machinery and Modern Industry," section 9, "The Factory Acts: Sanitary and Educational Clauses of the same. Their General Extension in England":

> (Das Kapital) denounced in 1842 still continue
> (today 1864) report of '42 was merely chucked into the
> archives and remained there while these boys were ruined
> and became fathers of this generation.

The relevant section from Marx is:

> Already in 1840 a Parliamentary Commission of Inquiry on the labour of children had been appointed. Its Report, in 1842, unfolded, in the words of Nassau W. Senior, "the most frightful picture of avarice, selfishness and cruelty on the part of masters and of parents, and of juvenile and infantile misery, degradation and destruction ever presented. . . . It may be supposed that it describes the horrors of a past age. But there is unhappily evidence that those horrors continue as intense as they were. **A pamphlet published by Hardwicke about 2 years ago states that the abuses complained of in 1842, are in full bloom at the present day. It is a strange proof of the general neglect of the morals and health of the children of the working-class, that this report lay unnoticed for 20 years, during which the children 'bred up without the remotest sign of comprehension as to what is meant by the term morals, who had neither knowledge, nor religion, nor natural affection,' were allowed to become the parents of the present generation."** (492–93)

A third passage that appears in Canto 33:

> for workshops
> remained a dead letter down to 1871 when was taken from
> control of municipal . . . and placed in hands of the factory
> inspectors, to whose body they added eight (8) assistants
> to deal with over one hundred thousand workshops and
> over 300 tile yards.

This is condensed from Marx's:

> **The Workshop Regulation Act,** wretched in all its details, **remained
> a dead letter in the hands of the municipal and local authorities
> who were charged with its execution. When, in 1871, Parliament
> withdrew from them this power, in order to confer it on the Fac-
> tory Inspectors, to whose province it thus added** by a single stroke
> **more than one hundred thousand workshops, and three hundred
> brickworks, care was taken at the same time not to add more than
> eight assistants to their already undermanned staff.** (494)

Pound had little respect for Marx as an economist, stating, correctly, that
Marx did not grasp the nature of money. He did admire Marx, however,
for his savage indignation, his passion for justice, and his skill and effec-
tiveness as a social crusader. Pound was undoubtedly drawn to the two
passages cited above because they exposed the extreme abuses of Victorian
capitalism. However, he probably chose to include them because they
illustrate the failure of the British Parliament, either due to lack of will or
to downright corruption, to take any effective action to curb those abuses.
The inability of various democratic and parliamentary governments to
remedy the widespread suffering caused by the Great Depression was
another reason why Pound and others turned to charismatic leaders such
as Mussolini for solutions.

Pound particularly admired part 3, "The Production of Absolute Sur-
plus-Value," chapter 10, "The Working-Day," of Marx's *Capital.* He
commented a few years later:

> The errors of Marxist materialism are much clearer in its results than
> in the pages of Marx where his noble indignation clouds the mind of
> the reader, for example, in Chapter X of *Das Kapital.*[4]

Not surprisingly, all of the remaining quotations from Marx in Canto 33 are drawn from his lengthy chapter 10. Mark's text reads:

> Belgium is the model bourgeois state in regard to the regulation of the working-day. **Lord Howard Walden, English Plenipotentiary at Brussels,** reports to the Foreign Office, May 12th, **1862: "M. Rogier, the minister, informed me that children's labour is limited** neither by a general law nor by any local regulation; that **the Government,** during the last three years, **intended in every session to propose a bill on the subject, but always found an insuperable obstacle in the jealous opposition to any legislation in contradiction with the principle of perfect freedom of labour."** (277)

becomes in Pound's hands this imperfect transcription:

> Rogier (minister) told me that this government (Brussels)
> had been intending to introduce such a law but found itself
> (re/ child labour not limited to 12 hours per day) always
> blocked by the jealous uneasiness that met any law tamp-
> ering with the absolute freedom of labour.
> Lord H. de Walden from Brussels. 1862

Marx's account of how manufacturers, by reducing wages in correspondence with the legal reduction of the working day, caused workers to agitate for repeal of a law meant to protect them reads:

> The new Factory **Act of** June 8th, 1847, enacted that on July 1st, 1847, there should be a preliminary shortening of the working-day for "young persons" (from 13 to 18), and all females to 11 hours, but that on May 1st, **1848,** there should be a definite limitation of the working-day to 10 hours. . . . **the manufacturers . . . denounced the Factory Inspectors as a kind of revolutionary commissioners like those of the French National Convention ruthlessly sacrificing the unhappy factory workers to their humanitarian crotchet.** (283–85)

becomes in Pound's version:

> They (the owners) denounced the inspectors, as a species of
> revolutionary commissar pitilessly sacrificing the unfortu-

nate labourers to their humanitarian fantasies (re/ the law
of 1848).

Pound's change of commissioners to commissar is a nicely ironic touch
that would go unnoticed without this kind of extensive annotation.

Sometimes Pound's use of Marx stays very close to the original text.
Marx writes:

> By I. and II. Will. IV. ch. 24, s. 10, known as Sir **John Hobhouse's
> Factory Act, it was forbidden to any owner of a cotton-spinning
> or weaving mill, or the father, son, or brother of such owner, to
> act as Justice of the Peace in any inquiries that concerned the
> Factory Act.** (289)

Pound condenses: "that no factory-owner shall sit as a magistrate in cases
concern- ing the spinning of cotton . . . (Factory Act of John Hobhouse)
/ nor shall his father, brother, or son." Marx's

> Already, in December, 1848, Leonard Horner had a list of 65 manu-
> facturers and 29 overlookers who unanimously declared that no sys-
> tem of supervision could, under this relay system, prevent enormous
> over-work. **Now the same children and young persons were
> shifted from the spinning-room to the weaving-room,** now, dur-
> ing 15 hours, **from one factory to another. How was it possible to
> control [such] a system [?]** (290)

is condensed by Pound as

> And if the same small boys are merely shifted from the spinning
> room to the weaving room or from one factory to another,
> how can the inspector verify the number of hours they
> are worked? (1849, Leonard Horner).

And finally, Marx's

> Soot is a well-known and very energetic form of carbon, and forms a
> manure that capitalistic chimney-sweeps sell to English farmers. **Now
> in 1862 the British juryman had** in a law-suit **to decide whether
> soot, with which,** unknown to the buyer, **90% of dust and sand are
> mixed, is genuine soot in the commercial sense or adulterated**

soot in the legal sense. The "amis du commerce" decided it to be genuine commercial soot, and non-suited the plaintiff farmer, who had in addition to pay the costs of the suit. (248)

is improved by Pound to the humorous

> Case where the jury ('62) was to decide whether soot adul-
> terated with 90% of dust and sand was "adulterated-in-
> the-legal-sense" soot or in the commercial "real soot." As
> friends of commerce decided (the jury decided) it was
> "real soot" against the plaintiff with costs.

Pound's use of Marx in Canto 33, therefore, ranges from an inadequate or inaccurate summary that merely mystifies the reader, to an exercise of wit that cannot be appreciated without reference to its source, to a condensation that improves the intended humor of the original. A hypertext version would enhance our appreciation of Pound's various intentions and his successes and failures.

Canto 33 thus shows clear evidence of Pound's extensive absorption of Karl Marx; it also shows how rapidly his own thought was evolving during this time. An excellent example of this turn in Pound's thinking closes the canto, and we will also consider it in depth:

> and he even
>
> (to change the subject)
> put into the mouths of the directors of the Federal Reserve
> > banks the words that they should say . . . "You have got more
> > than your share, we want you to reduce, we can not let
> > you have any more."
>
> (Mr. Brookhart)

Such economic subjects will become frequent in Pound's work during this period. What is remarkable and revelatory here is the context from which Pound drew this quotation and how it demonstrates Pound's radical shift of position. By considering the full context in which this remark appeared in the *Congressional Record,* I hope to both illuminate Pound's drastic change of view and provide an illustration of how a hypertext version of *The Cantos* can reveal the unity of Pound's epic.

During the 1920s, Pound had crusaded against "the passport nuisance" and article 211 of the U.S. Penal Code, the antiobscenity statute that, as Pound complained in a letter of 8 November 1930 to Senator

Bronson Cutting of New Mexico, "confuses smutty postcards, condoms, and Catullus." But the crusade closest to his heart was that against the antiquated copyright laws of the United States. Cutting, a newspaper publisher before he became a politician, was a natural ally for Pound in this effort, and they corresponded about it and other matters. Cutting was working to enroll the United States in the international Bern Convention for the protection of literary and artistic works, and he wished to draw his efforts to Pound's attention. Thus he sent Pound the *Congressional Record* that highlighted his activity.[5]

In that *Congressional Record* Pound would have read of a concerted effort on behalf of writers, an effort that he had repeatedly called for during the 1920s. House Resolution 12549, "to amend and consolidate the acts respecting copyright and to permit the United States to enter the Convention of Bern for the Protection of Literary and Artistic works," was debated and amended before passing the House of Representatives. It then went to the Senate, was referred to the Senate Committee on Patents, reported out of committee with amendments, and debated in the Senate. Senator Cutting, a supporter of the bill, took a vigorous role in the debate, a role of which he was evidently proud. The struggle to get the bill passed was directed not so much against concerted opposition as to the pressures of time before the close of the session. The House-Senate conference committee even went so far as to agree in advance to accede to *any* amendments the Senate would make to the bill so as to pass the bill before Congress adjourned. They were not successful, and the United States did not subscribe to the Bern agreement until more than fifty years later.[6] The Seventy-First Congress ended 4 March 1931, without time to finish consideration of the bill, which therefore died in the general flurry of last-minute business.

One would have expected Pound to react violently to the recurrent failure of the United States to protect its artists and writers, his principal social concern of the 1920s. But his letter of acknowledgment indicates a sudden change of direction. Passing over Cutting's activity and indeed the extensive debate on copyright, he focuses instead on a new interest. He wrote to Cutting on 20 March 1931: "Thanks for the Congressional Record of 28 ult. Brookhart's speech against Meyers seems to me very important."

Senator Smith Brookhart's speech was delivered over two days, 24 and 25 February 1931, and takes up approximately twenty double-columned pages in the *Congressional Record*. The speech was occasioned by the nomination of Eugene Meyer for membership on the Federal

Reserve Board. Senator Brookhart's speech is worth a close look, both because it captured Pound's imagination and because it offers such clear evidence of his abrupt change of direction at this time. The senator began by considering Eugene Meyer's previous positions as "a member of the New York Stock Exchange . . . engaged in what I shall call stock gambling" (*Congressional Record—Senate* 1931, 5839) and then as head of the War Finance Corporation, where, "instead of using the fund provided for it to sustain and benefit agriculture, as was contemplated by the law, those funds were used mainly in speculation in Government bonds, and agricultural conditions continued to grow worse" (5840). As the speech develops, this abuse of trust is clearly Brookhart's main theme, a populist theme dear to Pound's heart:

> Mr. Meyer is the worst enemy of the farmers in the United States and, as will be shown before I get through, that means the worst enemy of general prosperity, because agriculture is the foundation and basis of all enduring prosperity. (5840)

Pound's developing beliefs, that the farmer can never go into debt except through financial chicanery and that natural abundance is the only basis of wealth, are echoed here. After discussing Meyer's career at more length, Brookhart continued with an analyis of the general economic situation of the United States.

One of Brookhart's themes in this analysis is that capital is taking a disproportionate share of the national wealth, at the expense of "labor, invention, genius, and management" (5843), and particularly at the expense of agriculture. Banks are especially suspect: "big New York banks earned more in 1930 than they did at any other time, right during the year of the depression" (5843). He summarizes:

> The policy followed in administering the War Finance Corporation which I have described, the policy adopted in administrating the Federal land bank and the intermediate credit bank which I have described, have contributed heavily to destroy the credit of agriculture throughout the United States. (5843)

From this condemnation of banks, Brookhart turns to consider the cause of depressions, drawing on the work of Yale economist Irving Fisher and on the alternating boom-and-bust business cycles of the fifty-year period from 1880 to 1930, a period that witnessed eight major and seven minor depressions. As a general conclusion, after focusing on some federal railroad legislation, Senator Brookhart finds the roots of the problem in laws favoring some groups over others, in lack of regulation of interlocking directorates and insider deals, and in greed. After that he turns to an examination of banking laws, in particular the Federal Reserve Law of 1913.

Smith Brookhart's attack on the banking system fits a typical pattern of populist rhetoric. The villains are "the Wall Street crowd" who send "the protecting tentacles" of a reserve bank "out all over the country" (5847). The ability of the reserve banks to issue reserve notes to circulate as money upon the credit of its assets had been delegated to it by Congress, using its constitutional authority to "coin the money and regulate the value thereof" (5847). The reserve bank expands and contracts the currency according to business demands. Senator Brookhart expressed a key point: "some of us think that the Government itself ought to take care of this elastic money proposition; that it is a governmental function and ought not to be delegated to any bank" (5847). Pound, of course, would agree, and this belief would form the cornerstone of his economic writings and political allegiances during the next three decades.

Senator Brookhart goes on to examine the counterclaims by the supporters of the Federal Reserve System: that it financed the war and that it had the ability to stop panics and runs on banks. He hastily dismisses the first, by saying that the purchase of Liberty Bonds financed the war, and grudgingly admits the second. For Brookhart, however, the primary function of the Federal Reserve banks "is to insure a more efficient use of the credit supply of the country and thereby, under the law of supply and demand, reduce the interest rate to the people at large" (5848). This desirable result has not transpired; instead, "the law and the manipulation together have reduced it only to gamblers" (5848). Drawing upon the proceedings of the Sixty-third Congress during its debate on the Federal Reserve Law, Brookhart finds that one intent of the law was to prevent collusion between the large banks and stock speculation: "the Federal Reserve Act was enacted to stop the accumulation of this surplus credit in New York for these speculative purposes" (5849). We can see clearly in Senator Brookhart's speech an articulation of some of the American populist principles that were at the base of many of Pound's political beliefs.

On the next day, the senator continues his speech opposing the nomination of Eugene Meyer. At that time he brings up his most damning charge, at least from Pound's perspective and the perspective of anyone sensitive to the economic crisis of the time—the ability and willingness of the Federal Reserve Bank to pursue a deflationary policy. Brookhart examines in some detail the deflation policy of 1920, but there are so many similarities between 1920 and the country's situation in 1931 that his speech raises serious questions of national policy in face of the Great Depression. He states: "I think a reserve bank has no right ever even to consider a general policy of deflation. I think such a policy is always an economic crime. But, notwithstanding that fact, they did consider it in 1920" (5922).[7] Brookhart reminds his colleagues of Federal Reserve policy during the aftermath of World War I. He recounts that early in 1919 the Federal Reserve banks in the Northwest sent letters to member banks encouraging them to make more loans. Relying on these letters, the member banks complied. Rumblings about inflation, he says, began in late 1919, and in response to that the Federal Reserve Board met on 18 May 1920. Here is Brookhart's account of the meeting, with Pound's selection for the canto in boldface:

> The meeting started with a speech by the Governor of the Federal reserve Board, Governor Harding. In that speech he pointed out that the country was inflated; that there were too many Federal reserve loans, and that they must be reduced. Then he even **put into the mouths of the directors of the Federal [R]eserve banks the words they should say** to the member banks in order to bring about deflation. On page 8 of these minutes he says: "Thus the directors of the Federal reserve banks are clearly within their rights when they say to another member bank: 'You have gone far enough; we are familiar with your condition; **['Y]ou have got more than your share, and we want you to reduce[,] we can not let you have any more.'**" (5922)

After discussing the board's recommendations on railroad rates to the Interstate Commerce Commission, Brookhart's speech continues:

> Then, Mr. President, **they adopted another resolution;** they did not stop with this one. On **page 42** is found a resolution in accordance with the terms of which they appointed a **committee** to go to the **Interstate Commerce** Commission to **ask** for an **increase of railroad rates**. . . .
>
> I would have the Senate and the country think for just a moment about that situation. Think of a great board with greater economic

power than any board ever had in the history of the world, greater than the combined economic power of the Kaiser and the Czar in their palmiest days, meeting for the purpose of considering a general deflation of the country, and then at the same time proposing to inflate the railroads of the country by raising their rates! . . . When the meeting came to adjourn, Governor Harding **said to them:**

"**I would suggest, gentlemen,** that **you be careful not to give out anything about any discussion of the discount rates.** This is one thing there ought not to be any previous discussion about, because it **disturbs everybody,** and if people think rates are going to be advanced there will be an **immediate rush** to get into the banks before the rates are put up, and the policy of the Reserve Board is that that is one thing we **never discuss with the newspaper man.**" . . .

Under that injunction of secrecy the meeting adjourned. **I have asked about a million people if they knew about that policy at that time, and no hand has ever yet been raised in assent.** . . .

Mr. President, while the ordinary banker and the ordinary business man knew nothing about this meeting, big business men knew about it. In defense of this action it has been stated to me that the question of discount rates ought always to be kept secret. I would concede that, if it could be kept secret for everybody alike; but, Mr. President, for instance, **Armour & Co.'s banker was in that meeting, and the next day he was out after a loan for $60,000,000** for Armour & Co. for 10 years, thus predicting a 10-year depression that was to follow the action contemplated by this meeting. Eight per cent was offered for that money, **and** Armour & Co. **got it.** . . .

There was no open discussion of this deflation policy until October. Then they came out publicly, and let the whole public know they intended to force a deflation.

Swift & Co. got a loan of $50,000,000 just a little later for the same purpose. The **Sinclair** Oil Co.—and all Senators have heard of that patriotic institution—got a loan for $46,000,000; and they were forehanded; they got their loan a few days before the meeting was even held. I have here the testimony of Mr. Sinclair before the committee presided over by the then senior senator from Wisconsin, Mr. La Follette—the elder La Follette—when he was investigating the oil business. I, myself, asked Mr. Sinclair why he got that loan at that time, and he said, substantially, that he got it to guard against the Federal Reserve Board's deflation policy. At that time they had no policy, so far as was known; they had not even held their meeting at the time to formulate a policy; yet Mr. Sinclair knew what the baby was before it was born. In that way, Mr. President, big business was informed of this policy, and big business went out and protected itself against the depression that would surely follow, by gathering in all the available credit there was in this country.

Yes, Mr. President; even more than that was done. **This meeting decided we were overinflated,** that there were too many Federal reserve loans, and they must be reduced. (5922–23)

This becomes in Canto 33:

> page 34 of the minutes then they adopted another resolution
>   page 42 committee of interstate commerce, ask increase
>   of railroad rates, said to them: wd. suggest, gentlemen,
>   you be careful not to give out anything about any dis-
>   cussion of discount rates disturbs everybody immediate
>   rush never discuss in the newspapers.....
> ...... & Company's banker was in that meeting, and next day
>   he was out after loan of 60 millions, and got it. Swift-
>   amoursinclair but the country at large did not know it.
>   The meeting decided we were over-inflated.

And so the Jefferson group of cantos ends with this tale of government corruption as exposed by an American senator. Carroll Terrell's *Companion* correctly identifies the principle theme of the section, though erring in one detail. He states: "privy to the deliberations of the Federal Reserve Board . . . [they] knew that the depression [of 1921–22] was coming, but nevertheless they could make huge loans because of anticipated deflation of interest rates." In fact the planned deflation would make money scarce and therefore more valuable, thus raising interest rates; these businesses took advantage of their insider knowledge to secure huge (for the time) loans before credit dried up entirely. Terrell makes no mention of Pound's "Swiftamoursinclair," whether it is a typographical or printing error, or an odd bilingual pun substituting the French *amour* for the name of the giant American meatpacker and hinting at sin *clair*—clear sin.[8]

Although it is not easy to discern how the quotation from Senator Brookhart's speech fits into the end of the three cantos (31–33) devoted to Thomas Jefferson, there is a connection for Pound. His letter to Bronson Cutting (cited above) continues:

Have long thought Wilson wrecked the govt. but lacked detailed information. There is no reason the Federal Reserve Board shd. be a private instrument of the executive. . . . That effectively bitches the Jeffersonian system. Destroys balance between execut. judic. and legislature.

Beyond the Jeffersonian connection, though, there is an old story in Smith Brookhart's speech, one that Pound had encountered before from A. R. Orage. The story tells of the way in which the ordinary farmer and laborer are swindled through the fraudulent manipulations of bankers. The senator from Iowa gives a succinct account of what happened when, as a result of the Fed's deflationary policy, demand loans were called in and farmers were forced to sell their Liberty Bonds or crops below their real value in order to avoid ruin:

> They raised the discount rate up to 7 per cent, as planned in that secret meeting; and when the discount rate is 7 per cent, the ordinary interest rate is about 9 per cent—about 2 per cent higher. When New York money will yield 9 per cent, a $4\frac{1}{4}$ per cent bond goes down below par, just as water runs downhill. Then the big men who had gathered in all this credit had money to buy bonds and they bought them at these low figures. After they have bought them in, then they take a look into this high discount-rate proposition again, and they say it is unsound and that it ought to be reduced. Then it is reduced back down to 3, $3\frac{1}{2}$, even down now to 2 per cent. Then the $4\frac{1}{4}$ per cent bonds come back up to par, and even go above par, and two or three billions of speculative profits are taken from the pockets of the common people of the United States. (5924)

The populist strain in Pound's economic and political thought has been remarked upon before. His interest in Brookhart's speech exhibits it and would reinforce it. Increasingly, Pound would be convinced that the financial powers preyed upon the small landholder in a way analogous to the way the capitalist preyed upon the British laborer. The senator from Iowa goes on to make the point that the cause for these acts is not partisan—partisan animosities disappear when more fundamental class interests are at stake and the opportunity for large profits presents itself:

> Therefore if the people of this country want to understand the fundamental causes in this history of speculation and depression, they must

realize that the cause is not partisan; party lines fade away whenever the big crowd comes along with a big proposition of that kind. (5925)

Brookhart suggests a remedy: government operation of the railroads, government ownership of patents (with a fee to the inventor), government purchase of all crops at a fair price (as it had done during World War I under Herbert Hoover's Farm Board), and strict government regulation of the banking and Federal Reserve System to begin with and ultimately a system of cooperative local banking to supplant it (which recalls Proudhon) with a limit to the earnings allowed to capital. Many similar measures had already been taken or would be taken in Mussolini's Italy.

The crux of the matter was summed up by Senator Frazier (North Dakota): "The Federal reserve law turned the credit of the Nation over to the Federal reserve banking system, and gradually the Federal reserve banking system has come under the control of Wall Street banking interests. . . . Much might be said about Mr. Meyer's connection with some of the big financial interests of the Wall Street group. Some of those interests are largely controlled by foreign capital, at least very largely so. Of course as I see it, Mr. Meyer belongs to the so-called international group in New York" (5931).

That these concerns were very much on Pound's mind can be seen in an interview with him published in the *Paris Tribune* of 14 May 1931:

Ezra Pound, American poet and archfoe of hokum, let loose another broadside yesterday in an interview with *The Tribune,* firing verbal grapeshot and canister at the United States Federal Reserve System, American universities, and the methods used by American foundations or endowments to foster learning and the fine arts.

Mr. Pound is stopping at a hotel in the Rue de Gramont before going in a few days to his home at Rapallo, Italy. . . .

"I see someone is taking up the pamphleteering idea. Senator Brookhart is bringing out in pamphlet form his speech on Mr. Eugene Meyer, head of the Federal Reserve Board, which had been carefully concealed in the *Congressional Record.*

"I have no adequate means of verifying Senator Brookhart's statements, but the speech is most interesting and indicates that the Federal Reserve Board should get more attention than it does from the public."

As I have already demonstrated in my book *Ezra Pound and Italian Fascism,* despite their frequently querulous or eccentric formulation, most of Pound's economic ideas were firmly grounded. They also coincided with what some U.S. senators advocated. Thus in response to historical accounts by Marx and accusations of corruption by Brookhart, to Pound living in Italy, Mussolini might seem to offer a way out.

Pound's use of the material from the *Congressional Record* is as revealing for what he did not read as for what he did. He was meant to read and appreciate Senator Cutting's efforts on behalf of the copyright bill, but he passed over these to focus upon the economic debate, as we have seen. He also passed over, also without remark, another section of the *Record* dealing with a denunciation of actions by Italian Fascist officials to manipulate public opinion in the United States. In the *Record* for 27 February 1931, the "Resolution Approving Senator Heflin's Bill," there was a request to Senator William E. Borah, a Pound correspondent and chairman of the Senate Foreign Relations Committee, for his committee to report favorably on the bill introduced by Senator J. Thomas Heflin. Although the Heflin bill could not be reported by the end of the session, discussion surrounding it illuminates the ill favor that Pound's advocacy of Mussolini found in the United States.

In support of his bill, Heflin added a letter to Secretary of State Henry L. Stimson, signed by the national chairman of the "Defenders of the American Constitution," Dr. Charles Fama of New York City, and other Italo-Americans. The letter requested that the Italian ambassador to the United States, Giacomo De Martino, "be declared persona non grata by this government." Among the reasons cited for this action was the accusation that he was conducting himself as the special agent of the Fascist Party of Italy and of its secret police, the OVRA (Volunteer Organization for the Repression of Anti-Fascism; *Organizzazione Volontaria per la Repressione del Antifascismo*) and that he was deceiving American public opinion "with regard to the un-American principles and warlike ambitions of the present Fascist Government of Italy and its outstanding exponent Mussolini." The letter goes on to charge that under the direction of De Martino, the Fascist Party

> has flooded the United States with paid propagandists who before American audiences profane American democratic institutions and achievements and great men like Lincoln by favorably comparing to

them Fascist principles and pretended achievements and men of the type of Mussolini. (6234)

Pound's book of this period, *Jefferson and/or Mussolini,* would thus be seen by some as fitting into a calculated propaganda effort sponsored by the Italian government. Although Pound wrote it on his own initiative, the fact that it was turned down by forty publishers, as he claimed, should not surprise us. And although Mussolini still enjoyed an excellent reputation at this time among most Americans, there was already a determined antifascist effort on the part of many Americans of Italian extraction, who learned firsthand from friends and family back in Italy of the evils of the regime.

> Senator Heflin told Borah that his bill would let the world know by an act of Congress . . . that we do not propose to have a secret and invisible government in the United States conducted by Mussolini, naming his marshalls and his commanders in the United States Italian counts and the like. (6236)

The *Record* shows that Hefflin and many Italo-Americans were disturbed by the Mussolini government's practice of rewarding its supporters in the United States with Italian noble titles. This early indication of American sentiment was ignored by Pound; in fact, his later correspondence with Borah contains elaborate defenses of the Italian Fascist position.

Such a detailed examination of the background to just a few lines of Pound's cantos show the centrifugal pull away from the text that his poetics demand. This pull has been remarked upon before by using computer analogies.[9] What I propose to do in the final section is to explore the ways that hypertext illuminates some of Pound's strategies in *The Cantos* and to what extent there is a poetics of hypertext.

Hypertext (I use the word to also include hypermedia and multimedia) must be thought of both as a software tool useful in recording associative thinking and as a model for understanding complex intertextual relations. I will discuss its instrumentality briefly to orient those who have not yet encountered the software, so as to proceed to the major focus of my discussion, its metaphoricity and the implications it has for literary studies in general and difficult modernist texts such as *The Cantos* in particular.

Hypertext as software tool is best described as a three-dimensional word, sound, and image processor; it records and manipulates texts. In its easiest form, hypertext is merely a handy way to present footnotes or to register intertextual linkages. Click (with cursor and mouse or key) on "Tempus loquendi, Tempus tacendi" at the beginning of Canto 31 and it would simply present us with a translation: "A time to speak, a time to keep silent." Or we could be told that the quotation is a reversal of Ecclesiastes 3:7 in St. Jerome's Latin Vulgate, "Tempus tacendi, et Tempus loquendi." A more complex hypertext might also inform us that it was the motto of Sigismundo Malatesta, who had it inscribed on the tomb of his beloved Isotta degli Atti in Rimini. After we have absorbed this information, clicking another button will take us back to the main text. So far, all we have is an electronic version of a footnote, something that a good edition of *The Cantos* would provide. In fact, I've taken all of this from Carroll Terrell's *A Companion to the Cantos of Ezra Pound*.[10]

With a hypertext version of *The Cantos* we could go much further. In the text of the above notes we could embed other notes, notes for Ecclesiastes, Sigismundo Malatesta, Isotta degli Atti, and Rimini. By clicking on the note for Ecclesiastes we would be taken to a third screen, perhaps to get a more complete version of the biblical text. Each screen "underneath" another screen would have buttons to click to return to the previous screen or to the main text of *The Cantos*. Each screen containing a page of *The Cantos* would have buttons to take us to the prior or subsequent page. So far, not too much new, no real departure from a sequential and traditional text.

The difference would come with the addition of electronic paths that would transport us to other cantos. Notes on Sigismundo and Isotta would lead us to the Malatesta Cantos, to photos and drawings of the Tempio and a discussion of its place in early Renaissance architecture, or to photos of its sculptures and the relation they bore to Hermetic philosophy. A hypertext, then, is an electronic text that allows the reader to traverse it in a number of different ways. It can take two forms, a read-only hyptertext, where readers could discover paths already embedded by the creator of the hypertext, and a read/write hypertext, where readers could add their own links and screens.[11]

Walter Benjamin, in "The Work of Art in the Age of Mechanical Reproduction," stated that "the history of every art form shows critical epochs in which a certain art form aspires to effects which could be fully obtained only with a changed technical standard."[12] As we have glimpsed through our consideration of one canto, large sections of Pound's epic can only be fully appreciated by referring to the material that he drew upon in constructing his poem. A hypertext Canto 33 would link Pound's readings of Marx and his views on the Federal Reserve to the many other pieces of his writing where these subjects reappear. Pound's *Cantos,* then, illustrate Benjamin's observation in that they are a kind of protohypertext, aspiring to effects that were not yet possible. What I would argue, therefore, is that the idea of hypertext provides a metaphor through which Pound's intent in *The Cantos* can be better understood. A working knowledge of hypertext helps us to understand Pound and other experimental modernists.

Critics have been moving toward such an understanding of Pound for a half century. Joseph Frank first articulated a version of it in his influential essay "Spatial Form in Modern Literature" of 1945, though he still believed in the New Critical dogma that "the primary reference of any word-group is to something inside the poem itself."[13] Max Nanny followed Marshall McLuhan into a new reading of Pound: "By advocating highly implicit or inclusive language and literature Pound wanted the old literate habit of racing along uniform lines of print to yield to a depth reading which is not proper to the printed word."[14]

John M. Slatin observed in his "Hypertext and the Teaching of Writing" that

> it was the modernist poets of his century . . . who really began to challenge the strict linearity of print as they re-defined the art of poetry. . . . Pound had devised an aesthetic based on the unexplained (not unmotivated) juxtaposition of discrete images.[15]

Jay David Bolter remarks that writing in hypertext is a "natural extension" of the work of modernists such as Joyce, Woolf, Pound, and Eliot, who were already writing "topographically . . . using the medium of print, which is not well suited to that mode of writing. . . . It is as if these authors had been waiting for the computer to free them from print."[16]

Jerome J. McGann has invented a term, "radial reading," to describe a kind of reading that "regularly transcends its own ocular physical bases." For McGann, such reading can be as simple as looking up a word or a reference or as complicated as pausing to decode the various contexts "that interpenetrate the scripted and physical text."[17] Pound's *Cantos* demand this kind of radial reading, which "assumes that the physical texts of Pound's work are not only linguistic and spatial but multiple and interactive as well" (124), in other words, that they are hypertextual. Such attributes of Pound's epic are not accidental. McGann argues that *The Cantos* is a poem that has "already theoretically imagined a critical edition of itself. . . . with *at least* the equivalent of footnotes, bibliography, and other scholarly paraphernalia" (129; emphasis added). This observation should not surprise us, for Pound's primary model for *The Cantos*, Dante's *Commedia*, in Pound's day came complete with scholarly apparatus. But whereas Dante had an "Aquinas map" to bring his epic to unity, Pound, following Dante and Browning's *Sordello*, had to imagine something closely resembling a hypertext to contain his heteroclite material.

While such a metaphor (or model) may be helpful in understanding Pound's *Cantos*, it also brings with it new problems. For the centrifugal, dispersive force of hypertext calls ancient organic models for a poetic work, with their ideas of unity, wholeness, and closure, into question. Is there, then, a poetics of hypertext? What would such a poetics be like?

To begin, let us examine some features of the poetics of *The Cantos*. One key question for modernist poetics was whether a long poem could be written using imagist techniques. Epic structure (mythopoeia) and imagist concision (phanopoeia, melopoeia, and logopoeia) would seem to pull against each other in a reader's experience of poetry. Either to be swept forward in the story of the conventional epic or absorbed in the local detail and allusion of the modernist poem: that seems the choice that no poet or reader could avoid. Pound's solution was to try for both. What for Dante was the anagogical became for Pound the hypertextual, invoking a more inclusive idea of order that he intermittently apprehended.

Theorists of hypertext have noticed some startling similarities between hypertext and imagism. John M. Slatin observes:

> the image being, as he [Pound, in *Gaudier-Brzeska: A Memoir*] put it in terms strikingly appropriate to the discussion of hypertext, "not an idea" but rather "a radiant *node* or cluster . . . from which and through which, and into which, ideas are constantly rushing.[18]

Landow defines hypertext as "text composed of blocks of text [Roland Barthes's *lexia*] . . . and the electronic links that join them."[19] Pound's *Cantos* are written in such blocks, with associational linkages and recurrences.

Another feature of Pound's poetics, the ideogrammic method, also applies here. Max Nanny observes that this method, "being a mosaic of particulars that has no favoured point of view, lineal connection or sequential order . . . demands an instant, condensed and total experience."[20] Pound's ideograms could be thus seen to anticipate the conjunctions of various lexia experienced in a hypertext environment. Jay David Bolter has even predicted that texts written in a hypertext environment will "favor short, concentrated expression because each unit may be approached from a different perspective with each reading."[21] Although Bolter's prediction was probably influenced by the initial hypercard software bundled with the old Apple computers, where each "card" was limited to the size of the small screen, Pound's *Cantos,* with their imagist background, their ideogrammic method, and their multiple allusiveness, are already constructed to be read in this manner. As David Hughes explains:

> The spatial element of Pound's work . . . and his use of the graphic meant that meaning, both within each page, and across the particular work (*The Cantos*) as a whole, was deferred, couldn't be fixed. A connection set up by the reader between any two clusters might be undone by another connection set up between either of those two clusters and any other.[22]

And if one reader can have this kind of aesthetic experience from a relatively linear reading of *The Cantos* in their present book form, what kind of experience will readers have if the poem is presented in a hypertext? What is the difference between hypertext and, say, an afternoon browsing in the library?

If we are to have a hypertext poetics, it must allow readers freely directed associations, but within a structure. At the end of every path through *The Cantos,* hypertext readers must come back to the text—perhaps or even probably in a different place.[23] If we are to have works, instead of just "an ongoing system of interconnecting documents,"[24] we need boundaries. Indeed, the problem of boundaries can be thought of as the first problem to be solved in any poetics of hypertext.

George P. Landow discusses this problem. Hypertext leads to what he calls "the dispersed text," as individual lexias acquire an autonomy and linkages of their own.[25] Is there then a minimal, discrete poetic unit, a *poeme* equivalent to the morpheme or phoneme of linguistics, that might be some equivalent to the autonomous text of traditional aesthetics?

The question of boundary and magnitude is an ancient one. Aristotle, in the seventh chapter of *Poetics,* states:

Now a whole is that which has beginning, middle, and end. A beginning is that which is not itself necessarily after anything else, and which naturally has something else after it; an end is that which is naturally after something itself either as its necessary or usual consequent, and with nothing else after it; and a middle, that which is by nature after one thing and also has another after it. A well-constructed Plot, therefore, cannot either begin or end at any point one likes. . . . to be beautiful, a living creature, and every whole made up of parts, must not only present a certain order in its arrangement of parts, but also be of a certain definite magnitude. Beauty is a matter of size and order, and therefore impossible . . . in a creature of vast size—one, say, 1,000 miles long—as in that case, instead of the object being seen all at once, the unity and wholeness of it is lost to the beholder. Just in the same way, then, as a beautiful whole made up of parts, or a beautiful living creature, must be of some size, but a size to be taken in by the eye, so a story or Plot must be of some length, but of a length to be taken in by the memory.[26]

This sense of a whole that has been essential to aesthetics for millennia is challenged by the experience of a complex hypertext. A beginning is where you log on, and an end is where you log off.

A sense of author and authority, considerably revised in the last thirty years, is also challenged by a read/write hypertext. Since readers can create their own elements and links, the author and the original developer of the hypertext (if different) fade into the background. What replaces them is a kind of value-added secondary authorship. In a sense, that is what critics and scholars already do, but the field of commentary would be opened up a great deal in an unlocked hypertextual environment, and questions of quality and qualification would become secondary. As Nancy Kaplan has persuasively argued, perhaps unwittingly echoing Pound's "if the garden of literature is to remain a garden, it needs to be weeded," the new possibilities of read/write hypertexts require a vigorous possibility of erasure.

It may be countered that although a passive aesthetic experience needs a shape, a beginning, middle, and end, an active aesthetic experience, where the reader is caught up in the process of forging new linkages, can yield aesthetic pleasure without traditional shape. Fundamental to a sufficiently complex hypertext is the fact that each reader can find a different path through the "same" hypertext. Can we even talk about a poetics or an aesthetics if the odds are millions to one that another reader will traverse the same path?

Hypertext is an environment that is yet to be fully realized. Existing hypertext programs are merely "first approximations" of what is to come.[27] Yet we already know enough about the parameters of the new environment to begin to define a hypertext poetics. As we have seen, fundamental to our current idea of the aesthetic is a sense of ending. The centrifugal pull of hypertext makes the experience of artistic closure impossible. One doesn't end; one just stops. Freed, then, from our traditional poetics, what suggests itself in its place? Discussion by Latin American (and to a lesser extent Iberian and Italian) poets and critics over the last thirty-five years suggests some ways in which this new poetics might proceed.

António Aragao has proposed that "the creative consequence of the man-machine action produces a unique text under the authorship of the two."[28] Without entering into discussion of machine agency, it seems clear that future hypertext poets must become concerned not just with using existing hardware and software, but in actively participating in the development of the new hardware and software in which their poetry will be, virtually speaking, enacted. Just as Pound sixty years ago intuited the new technology that would be necessary to display his poetry, producing a protohypertext in *The Cantos*, so too the new poet-engineer must not just receive the prepackaged and commodified software and hardware from Apple or IBM, but must play an active role in saying what the new technology will be.

As far back as 1960, the Noigandres Group (its name showing the group's Poundian roots) proposed to measure the significant value of literary production "by obtaining the informational temperature of the aesthetic text."[29] Pound's *Cantos* by such a measure are feverish indeed, and such a proposal, that "Beauty is information, information beauty—that is all / Ye know on earth, and all ye need to know," would serve well for a poetics of hypertext, with its easy inclusion of visual and musical, as well as verbal, elements. Moacy Cirne goes on to say that "concrete poetry was in the beginning a generator of elevated informational temperatures, to be regulated by a *richness of structures*."[30] Although the structural metaphor may seem a bit dated and inadequate to conveying fully what happens in a hypertext environment (as, I believe, are all multidimensional metaphors), it does serve to point us toward a new poetics of hypertext.

Thus, provisionally, we can come to three conclusions. First, although works such as *The Cantos* can and have been understood by several generations of readers, hypertext offers a new model by which they may be better appreciated and more fully articulated.[31] Just as a hologram seems to be a flat and fragmented surface before being resolved by a beam of coherent light into a three-dimensional image, so too Pound's *Cantos,* at first glance a shattered traditional text, are resolved in a hypertext environment into a new kind of poetic coherence and complexity of astonishing beauty. Second, some future edition of *The Cantos* should be published in hypertext. And third, the protohypertext of *The Cantos,* developments in poetics since 1960, and the new hypertext environment all suggest the onset of a new kind of poetics, a poetics of hypertext, where beauty lies in richness of information (not data) and where the poet, "the antenna of the race," works to reunite techne and poesis.

NOTES

1. Box 65, Folder 2534, for material in the first column. The material listed in the second column for Cantos 31–39 is from Box 66, Folder 2565, and gives us the possibility of dating its composition, since a note on its verso is dated "Aug. 7 anno X"(1932). The material listed in the second column for Cantos 40–41 is from Box 65, Folder 2536. Pound draws a line linking [XXX]V [(3)5] and XXXVIII [38] in the second schema. Other notes of relevance: "XXXI-III [31–33] > condensare - means of communic - fra intelg. men" (Box 65, Folder 2537); "XXXVIII [38] incapable of general concept" (Box 65, Folder 2539.

2. I have discussed this at length in my book *Ezra Pound and Italian Fascism* (New York: Cambridge University Press, 1991).

3. Karl Marx, *Capital: A Critique of Political Economy,* vol. 1, *The Process of Capitalist Production,* trans. Samuel Moore and Edward Aveling (New York: International Publishers, 1967), 329.

4. Pound, "Toward an Orthological Economy," *Rassegna Monetaria* 9–10 (September–October 1937): 1104. Translated from Italian.

5. "The *Congressional Record* is published in three forms: (1) the daily *Record* which appears on the morning after the day to which it relates, (2) the paperbound bi-weekly *Record* which is simply an assemblage of the daily issues . . . primarily for the use of members of Congress," and (3) the bound and edited final volumes (Laurence Schmeckebier, *Government Publications and Their Uses,* 1936, rev. ed. [Washington, D.C.: Brookings Institution, 1969]). It is highly probable that Cutting sent Pound the biweekly record.

6. The United States' ratification of the Bern Convention was signed by President Ronald Reagan on 31 October 1988.

7. For a contemporary perspective on these questions see William Greider, *Secrets of the Temple: How the Federal Reserve Runs the Country* (New York: Simon and Schuster, 1987). U.S. Representative Henry B. Gonzalez of San Antonio, ex-chair of the House Banking Committee, has also raised similar concerns.

8. Carroll Terrell, *A Companion to the Cantos of Ezra Pound* (Berkeley and Los Angeles: University of California Press, 1980), 1:132. In my *Ezra Pound and Italian Fascism*, 87, I mistakenly interpret this passage as referring to the Federal Reserve Board's similar decision in 1930. Vincent Sherry pointed out the hidden pun on Sinclair.

9. At the Pound Centennial Conference (1985) in Orono, Maine, I compared this aspect of the *Cantos* to a loop in a computer program that pulls the machine out of the main program to perform a calculation before returning with the new information to the principal program. That was before I knew about hypertext (my Maine talk, "Poking around Pound's Library," was published in *Pembroke Magazine* 20 [1988]: 184–87. John M. Slatin in his "Hypertext and the Teaching of Writing" noticed that "hypertext is an essentially literary concept" (113) and that the modernist poets were the first to challenge the linearity of the print medium with poetry that anticipates hypertext (in *Text, ConText, and HyperText: Writing with and for the Computer*, ed. Edward Barrett [Cambridge, Mass.: MIT Press, 1988]).

10. Terrell, *Companion,* vol. 1.

11. I am indebted to discussions with Richie DeRouen, Dene Grigar, Nancy Kaplan, and Stuart Moulthrop on these subjects.

12. Walter Benjamin, *Illuminations,* ed. Hannah Arendt, trans. Harry Zohn (New York: Schocken Books, 1969), 237.

13. Joseph Frank, *The Idea of Spatial Form* (New Brunswick, N.J.: Rutgers University Press, 1991), 15.

14. Max Nanny, *Poetry for the Electronic Age* (Bern, Switzerland: Francke, 1973), 97.

15. Slatin "Hypertext," 114–15.

16. Jay David Bolter, *Writing Space: The Computer, Hypertext, and the History of Writing* (Hillsdale, N.J.: L. Erlbaum Associates, 1991), 132.

17. Jerome J. McGann, *The Textual Condition* (Princeton, N.J.: Princeton University Press, 1991), 116–19.

18. Slatin, "Hypertext," 115.

19. George P. Landow, *Hypertext: The Convergence of Critical Theory and Technology* (Baltimore: Johns Hopkins University Press, 1992), 4. This work is now available in an expanded, hypertext edition.

20. Nanny, *Poetry,* 72.

21. Bolter, *Writing Space,* ix.

22. David Hughes, "Post-Structuralist Dance: Some Notes Towards a Working Definition," *Dance Theatre Journal* 8, no. 2 (summer 1990).

23. When I and Sharon Sloan, a doctoral candidate at the University of Texas at Dallas, constructed a hypertext version of Canto 45 (the "Usura" canto) in the fall of 1990, we did so in such a way that all paths came back into the canto

or led into another canto. It was so easy to accomplish this goal that I began to think of *The Cantos* as a protohypertext.

24. Theodor Nelson, *Literary Machines,* 3d ed. (Swarthmore, Pa.: T. H. Nelson, 1981), 2.
25. Landow, *Hypertext,* 52.
26. Aristotle, *The Basic Works of Aristotle,* ed. Richard McKeon (New York: Random House, 1941), 1462–63.
27. Landow, *Hypertext,* 7.
28. António Aragao, "The Writing of Sight," in *Corrosive Signs: Essays on Experimental Poetry (Visual, Concrete, Alternative),* ed. César Espinosa, trans. Harry Polkinhorn (Washington, D.C.: Maisonneuve Press, 1990), 83.
29. Cited in Moacy Cirne's "From Concrete Poetry to Process-Poem," in *Corrosive Signs,* 66. The phrase first appeared in Haroldo de Campo's article "A temperatura informacional do texto," *Rivista do livro* (Rio de Janeiro) 18 (Junc 1960): 61–70.
30. Cirne, "From Concrete Poetry," 66.
31. George Landow, following J. David Bolter, has also made this observation.

6

Visualizing History: Pound
and the Chinese Cantos

Ira B. Nadel

Cantos 52–61 are the most annotated of any section of the poem. Pound himself provided a summary table of contents, explanatory note, marginal annotations, and guiding ideograms to his complex redaction of Chinese history from the pre-Christian era to the mid–eighteenth century. The Faber edition, fully titled *Cantos LII–LXXI* and published 25 January 1940 (not February as the verso of the title page states), contained an explanatory statement by Pound on the jacket; the first five hundred copies of the New Directions edition, published 17 September 1940, included a sixteen-page pamphlet on the structure and metric of *The Cantos*. No other section of the poem possessed as much apparatus, a sign that Pound recognized Cantos 52–61 as the most difficult he had so far published—largely because of Western unfamiliarity with Chinese history, a point he elaborated in the "Kung" section of *Guide to Kulchur*.[1] However, an unpublished map prepared by Dorothy Pound for use as endpapers in the volume confirms the importance of "visual history" not only for the Chinese Cantos but for the entire poem.

Pound believed *Cantos LII–LXXI* his "best book" up to 1940 and thought that the volume was "easier to understand than the earlier ones. . . . 52/71 ought to establish the fact that I am an AMERICAN writer, not a collector of bric a brac," he concluded in a letter to Lulu Cunningham of Hailey, Idaho.[2] To Agnes Bedford, on 4 April 1939, he explained that the section was "a progruss on the earlier ones/ tenny rate somfink different," while to F. V. Morley, a Faber director, he announced, "you are gettin something NEW in the Cantos; not merely more of the same. Trust at least two advances in mode will be perceptible by you and the PSM [Eliot]."[3] The two advances were the wholesale borrowings from eighteenth century sources like de Mailla's *Histoire generale de la Chine* and the *Works* of John Adams, and the separation of the new sections from the preceding volumes.

By 1937 Pound believed the use of glosses or explanatory notes damaged the integrity of a literary work, which an unpublished essay entitled "Second fytte" confirmed. Commenting on *The Fifth Decad*, published in June 1937, he declared, "I do NOT want it read with a paraphernalia such as J/J seems to think 'Ulysses' ought to have tied to it." "The proper way to read is to run on when anything isn't comprehensible," he adds (Box 77, Folder 2946). To J. L. Brown in April that year he explained that "part of the job is *finally* to get all the necessary notes into the text itself. Not only are LI Cantos a part of the poem, but by labelling most of 'em draft, I retain right to include *necessary* explanations in LII-C or in revision.[4] This last comment explains why Pound included the many annotations to the Chinese Cantos in the form of introductory glosses or marginal notes that a passage from an unpublished essay from his "Collected Prose" project of 1929–30 elaborates: "one of the diseases of contemporary thought (and probably running back 100 years or more) is due to the loss of custom of making commentaries. I mean marginal commentary on important texts" (Box 77, Folder 2945).

The first volume of *The Cantos* published by New Directions, *Cantos LII–LXXI,* posed immediate challenges. When he saw the typescript, James Laughlin suggested to Pound that he provide a preface or guide: "you see the attitude over here is that the CANTOS are incomprehensible," he told Pound, and added that he ought to write a preface "explaining what is what" (5 February 1940, Box 26, Folder 949). Laughlin even offered to visit Pound in Italy to help write the introduction. Pound vigorously objected and responded that same month by explaining that "Cantos [52/71] can not have a preface IN the book. Cover gives ample space for blurb. . . . The new set is not incomprehensible" (Box 26, Folder 949). Pound may have been thinking of the Faber jacket, which on its front flap contained this statement:

> Poetry: the WORKS, action or process. The German 'DICHTEN' meaning to condense. A note in explanation of foreign words, although very few are used in this section of the Cantos. These are almost always underlinings or repetitions, enforcements of something stated in the English text, are used only as sort of sounding board for a note struck.

As for the form of the decad cantos 62/71, if the critic will read through them before stopping to wonder whether he or she is understanding them; I think he or she will find at the end that he or she has.[5]

Nevertheless, in his letter Pound explained to Laughlin that

Nobody can summarize what is already condensed to the absolute limit. The point is that with Cantos 52/71 a NEW thing is.
    Plain narrative with chronological sequence. Read 'em before you go off half-cocked.[6]

In a letter of 29 February 1940 written after he had read the Adams Cantos, Laughlin told Pound he was convinced that an explanation was essential. By 25 April, Laughlin, persisting in his view, suggested a small pamphlet with an essay by himself and one by Delmore Schwartz on metrics. Pound's reply of 24 May 1940 is curt: "Yes/ I like the idea of YOUR doing a pamphlet/ whether you hand it out, or sell it. I dunno az Mr S/ knows any more bout metric than you do" (Box 26, Folder 949). As production proceeded, Pound requested proofs, but Laughlin explained to Pound that it would be difficult to meet the publication schedule if they were to mail them, writing, "we will read careful and make hidentical with Faberzed, unless you happen to think of ennything you want differunt in which case you better hanswer by clip-clop" (9 August 1940, Box 26, Folder 949). Apparently, this was a misunderstanding, because Pound only wanted proofs of the pamphlet:

WHAT about PROOFS of that pamphlet.
        America in that EVEN a John Quinn or an Harriet Monroe
                        Gheez I orter see proofs/
does you no comfort.
            send in duplicate?
                        (2 November 1940, Box 26, Folder 949)

A pasted-in envelope inside the back cover of the first five hundred copies of the New Directions *Cantos LII–LXXI* contained *Notes on Ezra Pound's Cantos: Structure and Metric,* the first and only time a commentary accompanied an actual volume of the poem. It contained two essays, the first "Notes on *The Cantos*" by Laughlin but signed by "H.H.," the second "Notes on the Versification of *The Cantos*" by Delmore Schwartz and signed "S.D." Laughlin's eight-page essay is an effort to overcome resistance to the poem by explaining Pound's use of foreign quotations, narrrative fragments, and such transitional periods of history as fourteenth-century Italy. The influence of Confucius and the importance of the elliptical style precede the now well-known structural analogy of *The Cantos* to the *Divine Comedy* based on "certain of Pound's revelations to his publisher [Laughlin] about the work in progress" (11). The poem, Laughlin suggests, is an "attempt to x-ray the modern mind" through continual cross-referencing. Pound's aim? To paint "in vast detail, the mind-body-soul of Twentieth Century man" (8, 7). The antisocial use of money becomes the great evil Pound confronts, and although he lives in Italy, he is not a "fascist at heart" (9). In the following three-page essay, Delmore Schwartz discusses Pound's deconstruction of Victorian meter and ability to make history and experience poetic. He focuses on Pound's use of the trochee instead of the iamb and reliance on anapestic and spondaic variations. He concludes that *The Cantos* is "nothing less than a revolution in English versification, a new basis for the writing of poetry" (15).

A variety of textual problems, however, quickly surfaced with the publication of the Faber and New Directions texts of 1940: ideograms were irregularly placed, reversed, turned upside down, or dropped; punctuation was inadequate—or added by compositors; Chinese transliterations were erratic; and factual errors were reprinted.[7] Given the difficulties of printing such a work, these mistakes were not surprising. A letter by Pound to A. B. Drew of Faber's production department dated 7 November 1939 begins with "*Canto* appears in heading where it is intended to be read aloud (if one is reading aloud), so please retain it on page 88" and continues with this directive:

> The one thing that is *not* wanted is uniformity in lots of places where a variant is *intended*. This also goes for hyphens in Chinese words. No need to go into all Lin Yutang has been writing on how to help Europeans remember Chinese names. . . .
>
> I put in the page numbers for the Cantos. The contents is grouped under the cantos. Can't very well be sorted out as to pages as the topics are frequently spread or used on various pages.[8]

One sentence in the letter suggests the liberality of Pound' s punctuation and laissez-faire attitude toward text. Referring to page 158 of the Faber edition (Canto 67), he says to Drew, "you can lard in some lines of three or four dots . . . in the Latin if you like. I can't put in a whole page of Cicero's prose at that point. Got to abbreviate" (329).

Textual changes and errors continued with the printing of the first collected and partially reset edition published by Faber in 1950 as *Seventy Cantos* (the 1948 New Directions *Cantos* merely reprinted the letterpress plates of the individual volumes). Using photo-offset, Faber was able to add thematic ideograms to the Chinese Cantos and make some additional authorial changes, but as layout determined the visual form of the poem, discrepancies and contradictions between printings of the Faber and New Directions editions appeared. The use of offset by Faber meant corrections could easily be made by pasting over changes and rephotographing the page; New Directions' letterpress method meant corrections were a costly undertaking, since a new set of plates had to be made for every change, a laborious and expensive proposition. However, the second printing of the 1951 New Directions edition of *The Cantos* corrects a number of errors in the Chinese Cantos, while additions clarified the text; for example, Pound adds an ideogram and its transliteration to Canto 52, although the Faber resetting ended the canto on page 271, leaving no room for the addition of the character; the date Tching Tang opened a copper mine is corrected to 1760 from 1766 in Canto 53; the upside-down ideogram "Kao Yao" in Canto 53, an error Pound noted in the first edition was righted. [9] But some factual errors remained (and continue). Pound has "Souan yen" kill fifteen tigers in 53.262, transposing his source—page 15 in volume 1 of de Mailla—into the number of dead tigers.[10]

Pound also provided additional punctuation for the Chinese Cantos, as well as corrections to, or additions of, transliterations, partly explained by a note written by Laughlin on the flyleaf of the Faber master copy of 1950 used for the 1951 New Directions reprinting, which included nine stop-press corrections in the second printing: "EP did not correct second proofs on Chinese Cantos just before war. Feels some more commas are now needed for clarity."[11] Most changes were never added to the New Directions text of 1951, however, despite the Faber editor's marking several hundred errors in the Chinese Cantos, particularly in Chinese names. In 1964 Eva Hesse took charge of the changes required to regularize the Chinese transliterations in *The Cantos,* adding superscripts to indicate tone numbers and accents to conform with the modified Wade method used by Mathews in his *Chinese-English Dictionary.*[12] Two notes by Laughlin from conversations with Pound explain the presence of these errors and the rationale for maintaining them:

"No unscrabbling of Chinese names, some of which came out of French, some English translations."

E.P.

"I hadn't a Chinese dictionary in Paris when I had the Fenollosa notebooks. Later in U.S.A. I had the dictionary and not the Fenollosa. Place to start from!"

E.P.[13]

Among the striking features of the first edition of *Cantos LII–LXXI* is a set of black bars censoring the text in Canto 52, another first in that no other part issue of the *Cantos* contains such markings. Fearing a libel suit and acting with the consent of the Faber board of directors, T. S. Eliot inserted them, the result of an extended exchange with Pound over anti-Semitism in the poem. Eliot carefully explained his views to Pound on 15 July 1939:

> I don't find anything libellous about Chinese emperors that isn't made safe by lapse of time, similarly about Adams's, but they [the Faber directors] now agree with me that if you remain keen on jew-baiting, that is your affair, but that name of Rothschild should be omitted. Obvious to me from the start, but you can't expect all minds to work as fast as mine. Alternative blank or fancy name, and if you care to have it will present you with Bleistein which is almost of equal value METRICALLY. (Box 13, Folder 513)

Pound objected and suggested Faber use "a line of ten dots. To hell with Bleistein, a mere Baerlein. If you must have it scan, at least conserve a few implications and use the form STINKSCHULD" (18 July 1939, Box 26, Folder 948). On 1 September 1939 Pound again wrote: "I find I must have my 'Stinkschuld' on galley one/ as the dots repeated 3 times have no phonetic body/ just a silence with no coherence to make a body for the verse."[14] Two weeks later Eliot agreed with Pound's objection to the dots but still demanded censoring of the reference to Rothschild. By 21 September 1939, Pound agreed: "I should prefer a blackout by slugs to a line of dots.—but do as you see fit. every word I write is for England[']s good," he sarcastically added.[15]

James Laughlin, who had purchased John Farrar's interest in Pound's American publications, also made it clear that "in regard to *The Cantos* I will not print anything that can be fairly construed as an outright attack on the Jews and I want that in the contract in the libel clause."[16] Pound, however, battled Laughlin, only partly acquiescing on 24 February 1940: "I don't mind affirming in contract, so long as I am not expected to alter text. . . . think LII/71 ought to be got out as soon as they can be got off the press/ I also think the black out on first two pages, shd. be restored to original as I believe in proofs."[17] But by 15 August 1940, Pound reconsidered, as he explained to his wife, Dorothy: "no use holding up Cantos for those lines.—& no use in saying STink etc. in U.S. either Hank or Will Rothschild—anyhow." On 16 August 1940 he added to Dorothy, "I think ref enc. the *fact* of cancellation more interestin' in view of subsequents, than the text."[18]

Although at one point Pound thought Laughlin added the blackouts,[19] Faber published its edition with the bars eight months before New Directions. On 4 August 1940 Laughlin actually asked Pound what was in the canceled sections, suggesting that if he sent the missing text quickly, Laughlin could slip them into the edition. The bars, however, remained, although in 1948, when resetting the text for the first collected *Cantos,* Laughlin again inquired about removing them; Pound wanted them kept. In March 1963, the issue reappeared when Laughlin wrote to Mary de Rachewiltz suggesting that the blackouts be removed and the original text restored, "provided that it does not appear so objectionable as it must have then, and that Mr. Gleason does not consider it dangerous from any legal point of view." "The trouble is," he adds, "that I cant remember what the lines were that we deleted! It is the same way in the London edition, so that is no help."[20] Here, what had been done to a text had been forgotten, confirming a stage in the socialization of a work. In 1984 Laughlin suggested to Mary de Rachewiltz that it was perhaps time to take them out, and the original lines were restored for the tenth printing of the complete text in 1986, having originally appeared in the Faber bound page proof dated 13 October 1939 now at the Beinecke Library.[21]

The offending lines from the opening page of Canto 52, with the excised portions in carets, read:

<Stinkschuld's> sin drawing vengeance, poor yitts paying for
<Stinkschuld>

Galley proofs show, however, that "Stinkschuld's" substituted twice for "Rothschild's." The following six lines were also blacked out, with "Rothschild" crossed out and "Stinkschuld" added on the galleys:

> <specialite of the Stinkschuld
> > bomb-proof under their house in Paris
> where they cd/ store aht voiks
> > fat slug with three body-guards
> soiling our sea front with a pot bellied yacht in
> > > > > the offing.>[22]

The immediate reference is to the Rothschild yacht, which visited the harbor at Rapallo at the time Pound was composing the section.

The obscurity of the history and ignorance of China by Western readers necessitated Pound's detailed table of contents, something he continued for the Adams Cantos. He also identified the source of the final lines in Greek of Canto 71, the last of the Adams Cantos, and expressed his belief that the "foreign words and ideograms both in these two decads and in earlier cantos enforce the text" but seldom add anything "not stated in english, though not always in lines immediately contiguous to these underlinings."[23] He furthermore anticipated the disagreement over his transliteration of Chinese ideograms, citing his use mainly of French forms, most likely those found in J. P. G. Pauthier 's *Confucius et Mencius: Les quartre livres de philosophie morale et politique de la Chine* (Paris, 1852) and possibly Pauthier's *Chine, ou description historique* (Paris, 1837). Further linguistic confusion originated in Pound's reliance on a Latin translation of the Confucian odes, Alexandre Lacharme's *Confucii: Chi-King*, from which he directly borrows material in Canto 53. But despite Pound's general resistance to including a guide to *Cantos LII–LXXI*, in November 1939 he realized that an annotated table of contents, several introductory paragraphs, and marginal dates accompanying the text were not enough.

On 13 November (1939?) the following letter from Rapallo was received at the offices of New Directions:

> MAP to serve as end paper to Cantos   52/71

> It shows the various invasions of China. Aim being to aid the reader through Cantos 52/61/ see also dates in page margin/ AND th[e] table of contents.

got to London too late for Fabers edition.

idea was to do it on yellow paper; both inside front and back cover/ opening to double page. carefully measured to size of Faber pages.[24]

Pound is not quite accurate, since Faber records indicate that the map did arrive in time, but, because of wartime austerity and restrictions on paper, they declined to publish it. Arnold Knible of Faber explained to Pound on 22 September 1939, "I am afraid to disappoint you over the endpages map as this is regarded by the directors as one of those luxuries that must be, in the interest of wartime economies, eliminated from our book production." Laughlin also rejected the map, curiously explaining his decision not to use it "for fear of throwing people off. Tho, I dunno" (29 February 1940, Box 26, Folder 948). Pound defended the importance of the map to Laughlin in a letter of 12 March 1940, declaring that it "indicates the various invasions of China, and HELPS the meaning. inten'd as end-paper back & front inside the covers." In late August 1941 Laughlin, possibly feeling guilty at the exclusion and with the volume only a week away from its publication, told Pound of his confusion with the endpapers: "Re them chinese endpapers. hell, boss they didn't make no meaning to me at all, though I looked at them all four sides up, so we just left them out."[25]

The map itself, carefully drawn by Dorothy Pound, who also did the ideograms for the volume, illustrates those Chinese invaders who constantly threatened the stability of the dynasties: Turks, Tartars, Kalkas, Mongols, Manchus, and Mings (fig. 1). But the map is not so much a geographical record as a moral and historical account with dates and leaders noted from the Tang (618–907) to Manchu rule (1616–1912). The purpose of the map is manifold. Not only does it provide a record of origin for the various invaders and dates of action, but it is a moral summary of the change that occurred over centuries and the threats from outside China to its peace that the Chinese Cantos express, especially in Canto 54, which displays the Chinese ingenuity as well:

Tchang-siun fighting for SOU TSONG had need of arrows
and made then 1200 straw men which he set in dark
        under wall at Yong-kieu
and the tartars shot these full of arrows. And next night
Colonel Tchang set out real men, and the tartars withheld

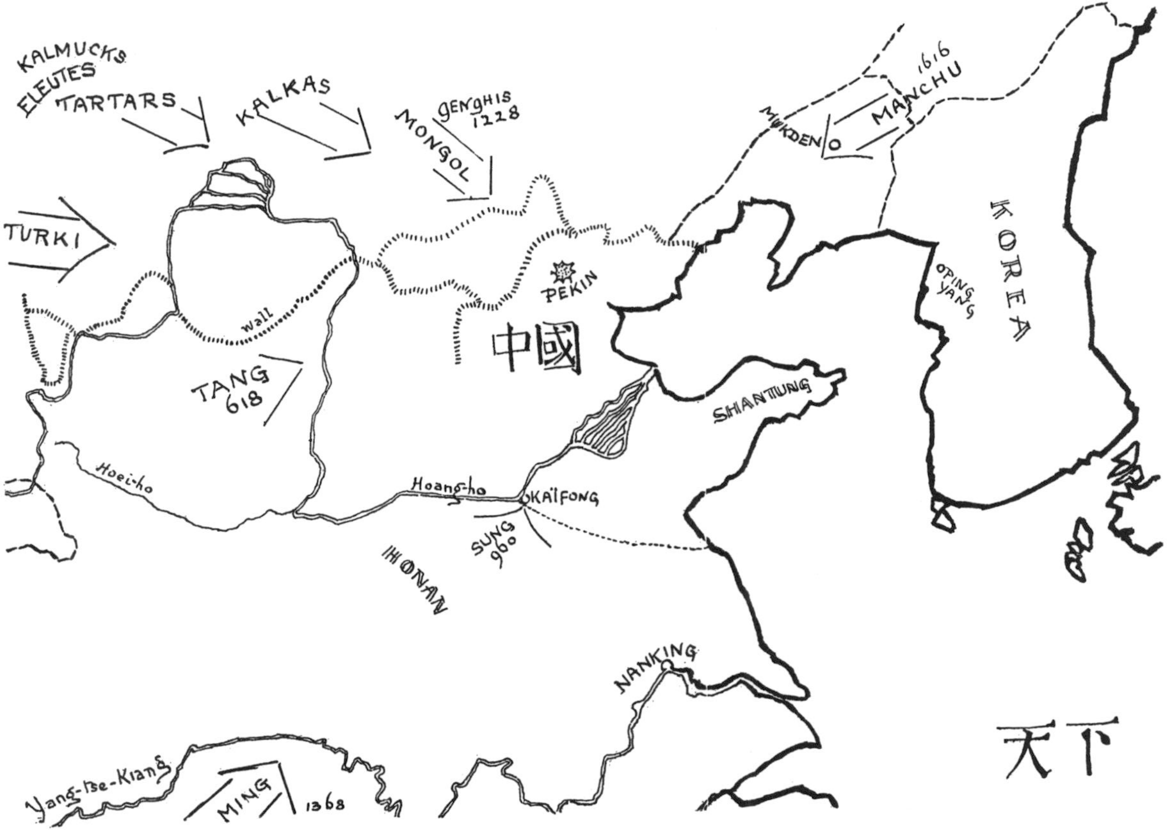
KALMUCKS
ELEUTES
TARTARS
KALKAS
GENGHIS
1228
MONGOL
1616
MANCHU
MUKDEN
TURKI
PEKIN
中國
KOREA
OPING
YANG
wall
TANG
618
SHANTUNG
Hoei-ho
Hoang-ho
KAÏFONG
SUNG
960
HONAN
NANKING
天下
Yang-Tse-Kiang
MING
1368

Fig. 1

their arrows

till Tchang's men were upon them.

(54.288)

The ideograms on the map are themselves telling. The central one below Pekin, "Chung Kuo," is Mandarin for China (Chung appears repeatedly in *The Cantos,* notably in 52, 56, 57, and 85). Its placement under Pekin in the center of the map visualizes China as the Middle Kingdom. H. A. Giles's comment on the ideogram in *A Chinese-English Dictionary* is clear:

> The Middle Kingdom—China, from a belief that it was situated at the centre of a vast square earth, surrounded by the Four Seas, beyond which lay islands inhabited by barbarians. . . . The term is also found in the sense of "the middle kingdom," the capital.[26]

The ideogram on the lower right of the map, "T'ien Hsia," combines the ideogram "heaven" with "ground" to mean "under the sky;—the earth; the empire of China," according to Giles (No. 11,208; 1388). The ideogram also looks surprisingly like the intials "E. P."

The source of the map is Pound's Triestine copy of de Mailla's *Historie generale de la Chine.* The author of the thirteen-volume history, who died in China in 1748, was himself a renowned cartographer of China, and of particular importance in the edition are the many charts, illustrations, tables, diagrams, and maps.[27] The majority of these illustrations are fold-out or full page, lending powerful corroborative detail and visual authority to de Mailla's narrative. They also provide a sense of exploration and discovery for the reader, who with the visual aids is better able to understand the confusing names and generations of dynasties and emperors cited in the eighteenth-century history. Significantly, following the half-title page but preceeding the full-title page in volume 1 is a tipped-in map of China dated 1777 and based on an original map drawn by de Mailla (fig. 2). The historian has himself illustrated his text, a feature Pound repeated with his ideograms and unpublished map for the Chinese Cantos.

A comparison of Pound's map with de Mailla's reveals few details in common other than the bold outline of the country and the similar shape of the territory. The lines of Pound's map are more freely drawn and less exact, while de Mailla follows precise lines of longitude and latitude, with many more cities and rivers identified and mountains drawn in. Relying on late-eighteenth-century terminology, de Mailla labels his four points

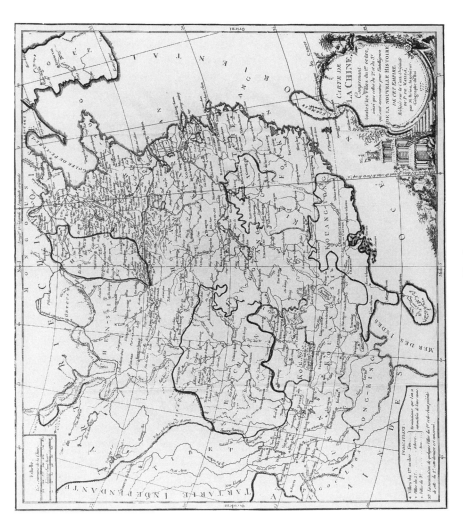

Fig. 2

"Nord," "Orient," "Midi," and "Occident." He also provides details of scale and indications of city size according to population. Provinces are also clearly marked by de Mailla in his elaborately drawn, scientifically rendered engraved map.

Pound's concern is with direction, movement, change. His map is fluid, de Mailla's static. Pound conveys a sense of flux, equal to the many movements of armies and people in the Chinese Cantos, as well as a sense of chronology, this section of *The Cantos* being in fact the longest stretch of continuous chronology in the entire poem, ranging from 3000 B.C. to the 1780s. By contrast, de Mailla emphasizes stability and permanence, a country established, settled, and undisturbed by either its past or its present. But for Pound, barriers like the Great Wall or major rivers are easily overrun; the emphasis of Pound's map is the struggle of Confucian order with invasion supported by the dates and names of leaders that catalog the energy of history. The map is a further effort to counter the resistance and ignorance of those uninformed about the Oriental past and its lessons for the West.

But Pound's map has a further value—that of visualizing history. Indeed, it is through the visualizing of Chinese history that Pound thought he could anchor the Chinese Cantos and elaborate through nonverbal means the detail he had compressed in Cantos 52 to 61. The failure of the map to appear in any later edition of the poem is, like the failure to reproduce certain ideograms, accidental, not intentional. Although the map was not included in either the Faber or New Directions editions, it does not reduce its importance or usefulness as a guide to understanding the Chinese Cantos. Pound firmly believed it would enhance his treatment of history and extend a technique he had already developed, that of visualizing history.

Essentially, visualizing history consists of Pound's use of nonverbal, pictorial elements to enhance his language, references, or allusions. The ideograms throughout *The Cantos,* from that for "sincerity" placed on the half-title page of the collected *Cantos* that he requested in 1953 (as well as the runner from Frobenius that appears in the tenth printing of 1986 but not in the eleventh of 1989 [nor the "Publisher's Note" that explains the source of the ideogram and runner]) to the final ideogram in Canto 114, demonstrate the importance of visual devices in the work. Pound wanted, in fact, the "single ideogram criterion" ("Ch 'eng") for the title page of *Cantos LII–LXXI*.[28] The dialectic between image and word dramatizes the difference of expression between Oriental and Occidental cultures, while establishing a literary exchange between the verbal and the visual as in Canto 55.290, Canto 56.308–09, or Canto 60.333.

Visualizing history enlarges *The Cantos,* whether through the ideograms, hieroglyphics, or drawings that constantly appear in the text. The following pictorial elements are the more prominent: the sign read by the narrator in Canto 52.103, the letters of Malatesta in Canto 9.37–39, the lettering on the pyramid of Canto 34.171, the inscription seen in the garden at Blaye in Canto 65.371, the John Adams for peace sign in 71.418, the musical score of Canto 75.464-65, the Arabic of Canto 77.488, the suite of cards at the end of Canto 88.603, the hieroglyphics in Cantos 93, 94, and 97 (637, 640, 641, 649, 691, 693, 695, 696), and the Greek, Latin, and Russian of Canto 10.43–44, 96.665, 672, 675ff. A specific example is the sign replicated in Canto 22.103 from the Calpe Club of Gibraltar:

> NO MEMBER OF THE MILITARY
> OF WHATEVER RANK
> IS PERMITTED WITHIN THE WALLS
> OF THIS CLUB

Here, history is literally a sign, although the interpretation of the signified undermines the signifier because few obeyed the words first seen by Pound during his 1908 trip to Gibraltar. But the unpublished Chinese map functions in a similar semiotic fashion as a sign of the Chinese past synchronically existing and uniting signifier with its signified. Visual history in the poem operates semiotically, establishing a code of reference that contains cultural, historical, and social meanings.

In Canto 63.352 Pound writes of Van Muyden's *editio terza,* the third edition of his *Short Treatise on the Institutions of Justinian,* lent to John Adams in a Latin version, that

design of the book is

exposition

of technical terms

The ideogram "Cheng" means "correct or true" and appears with the ideogram "Ming" at the end of Canto 51, which concludes *The Fifth*

Decad. The statement, taken as a critical demonstration of the role of visualized history in *The Cantos,* can be applied to the poem as a whole, since visual history clarifies and extends the meanings of language; in short, the physical design and pictorial elements of *The Cantos* contribute significantly to its understanding and comprehension. By using visual signs Pound is able to bring another dimension to the poem, one that compliments language and event by the visualization of experience. Whether a map, ideogram, inscription, signature, or photograph (Pound's portrait by Arnold Genthe continues as a frontispiece to *The Cantos,* sustaining the iconographic union of the poet with his poem), these elements transform the text into a living sign outlined by Fenollosa in his *Chinese Written Character,* which demonstrates the ideogram's ability to conflate expression and history. It fulfills the Confucian axiom that the transmission of knowledge can only occur through concrete manifestation. The "picture writing" of the Chinese ideogram gave Pound the model that enhanced the visibility not only of metaphor but of history. The map Pound provided for the Chinese Cantos is the extension of a technique he valued early and applied throughout the composition of the poem. And for the tangled references and allusions of the Chinese Cantos, he found it essential as he demonstrated in visual history what Fenollosa identified as the core of the Chinese language: the union of thing and action.

NOTES

The author wishes to acknowledge with thanks the assistance of Professor Richard Taylor and Mr. James Laughlin and the Trustees of the Ezra Pound Literary Property Trust for permission to quote from unpublished Pound documents and to reprint the China map, as well as to quote from unpublished letters by James Laughlin to Pound.

1. *Guide to Kulchur* (Norfolk, Conn.: New Directions, 1938), 274–77.
2. Pound to Lulu Cunningham of Hailey, Idaho, quoted in Charles Norman, *Ezra Pound,* rev. ed. (London: Macdonald, 1969), 375, 76.
3. Pound to Agnes Bedford, quoted in Humphrey Carpenter, *A Serious Character: The Life of Ezra Pound* (London: Faber, 1988), 569; Pound to F. V. Morley, quoted in Leon Surrete, *A Light from Eleusis: A Study of Ezra Pound's Cantos* (Oxford: Clarendon Press, 1979), 146–47.
4. *Selected Letters of Ezra Pound, 1907–1941,* ed. D. D. Paige (1950; New York: New Directions, 1971), 293.
5. Ezra Pound, *Cantos LII–LXXI* (London: Faber, 1940). Front jacket flap.

6. Quoted in Noel Stock, *The Life of Ezra Pound,* expanded ed. (San Francisco: North Point Press, 1982), 375–76.

7. Barbara Eastman, *Ezra Pound's Cantos: The Story of the Text, 1948–1975* (Orono, Maine: National Poetry Foundation, 1979), xii, xv, 80ff.

8. *Selected Letters,* 329.

9. For the upside-down "Kao Yao," see the Faber *Cantos LII–LXXI,* 18, and the New Directions edition (New York, 1940), 10; on Pound's noting the error, see Eastman, *Ezra Pound's Cantos,* 80.

10. Eastman, *Ezra Pound's Cantos,* xvii; John J. Nolde, *Blossoms from the East: The China Cantos of Ezra Pound* (Orono, Maine: National Poetry Foundation, 1983), 32 n. 1.

11. Eastman, *Ezra Pound's Cantos,* 83.

12. Ibid., 86, 82.

13. Ibid., 86.

14. Faber and Faber files, London.

15. Ibid.

16. 5 December 1939, in Ezra Pound and James Laughlin, *Selected Letters,* ed. David M. Gordon (New York: Norton, 1994), 110.

17. New Directions Archive, Norfolk, Connecticut.

18. Lilly Rare Book Library, Indiana University, Bloomington, Indiana, Pound MSS. 3.

19. Carpenter, *A Serious Character,* 570.

20. New Directions files, New York.

21. The blackened lines even mar the otherwise attractive bilingual edition prepared by Mary de Rachewiltz, *I Cantos* (Milan: Mondadori, 1985), Canto 52, 490–93.

22. This information is from Richard Taylor.

23. *Cantos LII–LXXI,* Faber edition, 8.

24. New Directions Archive, Norfolk, Connecticut.

25. Knible to Pound, Lilly Library, furnished by Richard Taylor; Pound to Laughlin and Laughlin to Pound, New Directions Archive, Norfolk, Connecticut.

26. H. A. Giles, *A Chinese-English Dictionary,* 2d ed. (Shanghai, 1912), No. 2875; 358.

27. Nolde, in his otherwise helpful study *Blossoms from the East,* fails to mention this aspect of de Mailla's history, although he does reprint Pound's rough map of the world from p. 4v of his *Notebook No. 33* showing the transmission of knowledge from China westward (429).

    Carroll F. Terrell in "History, de Mailla, and the Dynastic Cantos," *Paideuma* 5 (1976): 95–100, discusses de Mailla's history and reprints on pp. 100–122 sample illustrations from the work. In a letter quoted in the article, Eva Hesse reiterates that de Mailla's history was an eighteenth-century bestseller, but also "largely responsible for Europe's long fundamental misunderstanding of China" (96)

28. Pound to T. S. Eliot, 24 October 1939, quoted in Forrest Read, *'76, One World,* and *"The Cantos" of Ezra Pound* (Chapel Hill: University of North Carolina Press, 1981), 248 n. 1.

The Later Years

7

"Quiet, Not Scornful"? The Composition of *The Pisan Cantos*

Ronald Bush

A decade after their publication, Ezra Pound wrote Agnes Bedford that *The Pisan Cantos* were all composed at Pisa and that "not more than three lines" changed afterward. That is not, however, the story his manuscripts tell. I begin with his remark, not widely known and certainly not the first case of a poet rearranging old work in memory, for several reasons. The textual history of *The Pisan Cantos* is more interesting than Pound's recollection of it. And the implications of Pound's inaccuracy are anything but trivial. Pound's remark points to certain claims *The Pisan Cantos* make about their own value, to the way Pound and others reinforced those claims over the years, and to how the same claims have been used to justify or deride the authority of modernist verse. I have in mind here value judgments about poetic immediacy that Pound subtly reinforced by suggesting he had composed on the spot poems that themselves had dramatized a spontaneous epiphany of terror, natural beauty, and compassion. In an early review of the sequence, Robert Fitzgerald gave a name to Pound's achievement when he wrote that Pound had expressed "a personal desolation." Significantly, Fitzgerald went on to note "a kind of repentance that is enormously moving."[1] In the wake of this and similar responses, *The Pisan Cantos* casts a long shadow over the poetry of the next twenty years, whether it was the confessional verse of Fitzgerald's friend Robert Lowell or the less intimate meditations of Charles Olson, who had been Pound's first regular post-incarceration visitor in Washington. Anchoring Pound's influence was a general perception that the Pisan Cantos were confessions wrung out of a repentant fascist by a dark night of the soul and the healing force of nature. In other words, the spontaneousness of Pound's utterance combined with an apparent regression into natural simplicity had given his words a special authenticity. Critics have since questioned the sincerity of Pound's "repentance" as they recognized obvious strains of undiminished fascist loyalty in the poem. And recently they have begun to question more than that. For the question of Pound's contrition has been seen by post-structuralists as related to the way modernist poetry's "immediacy" authorizes factitious and perhaps inevitable mystifications of language and nature. The strong version of this position argues for a necessary connection between the modernist manner of *The Pisan Cantos,* its naturalization of experience, and the fascist politics of its author.

With so much at stake, questions about how *The Pisan Cantos* were written take on a special interest. To begin answering them, one might summarize the poem's textual history: although the bulk of the suite was written out longhand over the course of four stressful months, Pound built on drafts made before he was imprisoned, revised heavily when he typed his manuscript, and after Pisa made or allowed his editors to make a number of local changes (especially to Canto 81) that included removing an extensive series of Chinese characters along with their Confucian overtones.[2] After that brief statement of facts, however, the larger issues remain. As we shall see, the history just summarized suggests not one aesthetic and ideological context but several. Months before the end of the war, Pound began writing in his melancholy perch above Rapallo under the auspices of a visionary experience and what his recent critics would call a mystified belief in the conjunction of natural and political truth. His first efforts were symbolist in style and avowedly fascist. But after circumstances wrenched him out of his wartime retreat and into the circumstances of an army prison camp, his manner and his subject changed. The literary model of his first writing at Pisa was a realistic poetic diary in the manner of Villon, and his center of attention became the lives of the rough crew of soldiers around him. At the point when Pound first believed he had finished the poem, he had managed to effect an uneasy mixture of these very different perspectives, producing more than enough material to substantiate both his postwar supporters and detractors. Then things changed again. Jolted by a series of deaths (and by thoughts of his own execution), in a surge of defensiveness Pound imposed a polemical frame on the poem and gave it a force and coloring that in many ways contradicted what he had recently written. Interpreting *The Pisan Cantos* thus involves choosing among conflicting authorial signals and presents us with what may be an insoluble problem. On the other hand, the attempt may clarify some of our currently vexed interrogations of modernism.

A little background. In January 1940 Pound published the Chinese and Adams Cantos, bringing the number of cantos to 71. Cantos 52–71 had been written in a hurry—the Adams section in only five weeks—to propagandize a Confucius–John Adams–Mussolini ideogram of good government at a time when Europe was falling apart. The volume (like Pound's self-imposed 1939 mission to Washington) was a necessary detour in a crisis. In 1940 Pound wanted to get the poem out of "dead matter and negations." As he then told more than one friend, he planned only one more volume, and that was to be his *Paradiso*.[3] So he buttonholed George Santayana, also expatriated in Italy, and proceeded, as he put it, to "tackle philosophy,"[4] beginning from an already extensive reading of Scotus Erigena.

But Pound's new push seems to have lost its oomph in the confusions of the war. Between 1940 and 1944 he wrote a flurry of fragments, making two of them public[5] and putting others into his drawer to mine for phrases. (The shards that made it into *The Pisan Cantos* include "cat walks the rails," "the two halves of a talley stick," a lament for favorite restaurants, Frobenius's "der im Baluba," the Rothschild's plot against Mussolini, "Harriet Wilson's boy friend," the Confucian "the wise take delight in water," "what whiteness shall you add to this whiteness," and "affairs have their ends and beginnings," Aristotle's *ekasta* and *kutholou*, and Grosseteste's "lux enim.") The manuscripts of these fragments, like others I will mention, are preserved in the Beinecke Rare Book and Manuscript Library of Yale University. Their subject matter is miscellaneous. They touch on such things as the Battle of Marathon, Confucius, a conspiracy against Lincoln, how "Mr. Adams was bitched far the presidency," Pound's continuing preoccupation with usury, the history of Napoleon (the list goes on), but collectively they indicate more the pull of the moment than any clear direction.[6] Two of them, though, were more sustained: a typescript dated "Undici Dec. XX 1941" concerning the Confucian virtues of the governor (this is the fragment that includes the lines about ends and beginnings and *ekasta* and *katholou*, as well as "what candor"); and a sequence of fragments dating from 1943 that recalls Pound's flight from Rome to the Tyrol after the Italians, having deposed Mussolini on 25 July, surrendered to the allies on 8 September. Temporarily chaos reigned before the Germans took over Rome and three weeks later reinstated Mussolini as head of the Salò republic (the RSI). In hindsight, both of these sequences anticipated Pound's writing at Pisa, especially the second, which laments a world in ruins and seeks consolation in a landscape suffused with Greek and Confucian presences.[7]

As it turned out, though, there were still more significant bursts of activity, beginning with two cantos that Pound had never envisioned. By May 1944 the war had turned definitively against the Axis, and Pound and his wife Dorothy, forced to evacuate their flat in Rapallo, moved into the home of Pound's lifelong companion, Olga Rudge, up on the cliffs of Sant' Ambrogio. It was here, where he was subjected to running friction between the two women he loved, that he suffered the news that many of his sacred places had been blasted. The worst came on Sunday, 4 June, when he read in a Milanese newspaper that bombs had severely damaged his touchstone of Renaissance civilization, the Tempio Malatestiano in Rimini. From then on, if we are to judge by the poetry he wrote, Pound's state of mind, strained by his domestic relations, seems to have swung between phases of defiant denial and passivity bordering on the feeling of existence in an afterlife. The defiance we can see in the Italian Cantos 72 and 73, whispered about for years and now published both in the New Directions printings of the collected *Cantos* from 1986 on and in Mary de Rachewiltz's Mondadori *I Cantos*.[8] In late 1944, when the Allied push through Italy was stalled for the winter, Mussolini made what was to be his last public speech. It was a stirring appeal for a reversal of the Axis fortunes that had seemed doomed since Montgomery's victory in Africa, and it ended with a call for a *riscossa,* a counterattack. As it turned out, Mussolini delivered his speech on 16 December, days after the futurist poet and ardent fascist Tomaso Marinetti died, and the combination of the two events spurred Pound into writing. But, having since 1943 intermittently translated a selection of his earlier work into Italian in the company of his daughter Mary, he attempted his new cantos in a Dantescan Italian that incidentally enabled him to echo Mussolini's *riscossa* in Canto 73.[9]

I will not have much to say about the Salò cantos here, save to suggest how they are connected to the writing that followed them.[10] Canto 73 represents the exultation of Guido Cavalcanti, returned from the sphere of Venus to witness the heroism of a young girl who sacrificed her life for her country by leading Canadians who had raped her into a minefield. Canto 72 is longer and required more work. It depicts the appearance of Marinetti's spirit, who asks to appropriate Pound's body so that Marinetti can continue to fight in the war. Marinetti, though, is displaced first by Pound's friend Manlio Torquato Dazzi, and then by the ferocious figure of Ezzelino da Romano, the early-thirteenth-century Ghibillene whom Dante sees boiling among the tyrants of *Inferno* XII. It is in Ezzelino's suitably enraged voice that Pound calls for the damnation of treacherous Italian peacemakers and for the revenge of the monuments at Rimini.

Having drafted the two poems in a pencil notebook along with still more Italian Cantos (the notebook is now among the Olga Rudge Papers at Yale), in January and February of 1945 Pound published a fragment of Canto 72 and all of Canto 73 in *La Marina Repubblicana,* a newspaper associated with his friend Ubaldo degli Uberti, at this point undersecretary of state for the navy in the RSI.[11] Even before they saw print, he had gone on with Italian sequels on the back of his typescripts. These later efforts are in Italian, like Cantos 72 and 73, but unlike them, they are meditative, not martial. These were the drafts Pound had in mind when he wrote to his daughter at Easter 1945 that he had made numerous notes for more cantos but had decided not to use them. Yet, as Mary de Rachewiltz adds in her account of his letter, the drafts contain visionary moments her father was to draw upon that summer and fall.[12]

Pound's abandoned Italian work included manuscripts and multiple typescripts for a long series of cantos, beginning with a visionary meeting on the hillside near Sant' Ambrogio with a barefoot girl ("la scalza") and her companions, a visionary troupe including Sordello's lover, Cunizza da Romano. (One of the early autograph fragments of this meeting [reproduced in fig. 1] is from Feb[ruary, 1945].)

The draft cantos proceed to a complex textual dialogue between Sigismondo Malatesta, who boasts of making a renaissance out of his own resources, and Lorenzo de' Medici, contaminated by his family history of banking; a typescript concerning the great Renaissance figure Caterina Sforza, whose heroic resistance to adversity was clearly meant as a model of desperate courage; a typescript celebrating a kind of madonna of the cliffs, "Assunta"; a typescript about Scotus Erigena in which the medieval philosopher chides Dante in Irish brogue; an extended "Eliseo" or paradise proper; and a sequence on the great Roman builders Trajan and Hadrian.[13]

The most polished of these materials were two typescript drafts, apparently abandoned in midprocess so that Pound could rework their contents into still more cantos. An Italian Canto 74 survives in the form of four foolscap typescript pages marked 74-S (canceled), 74-2, 74-3, and 74-4, of which a great deal has been overwritten or marked for deletion. (See figs. 2–5.) More substantially, Pound produced six polished foolscap typescript pages of an Italian Canto 75, dated January 14. (See figs. 6–11.) The Italian 74 and 75 typescripts grew out of Canto 72 and absorbed the

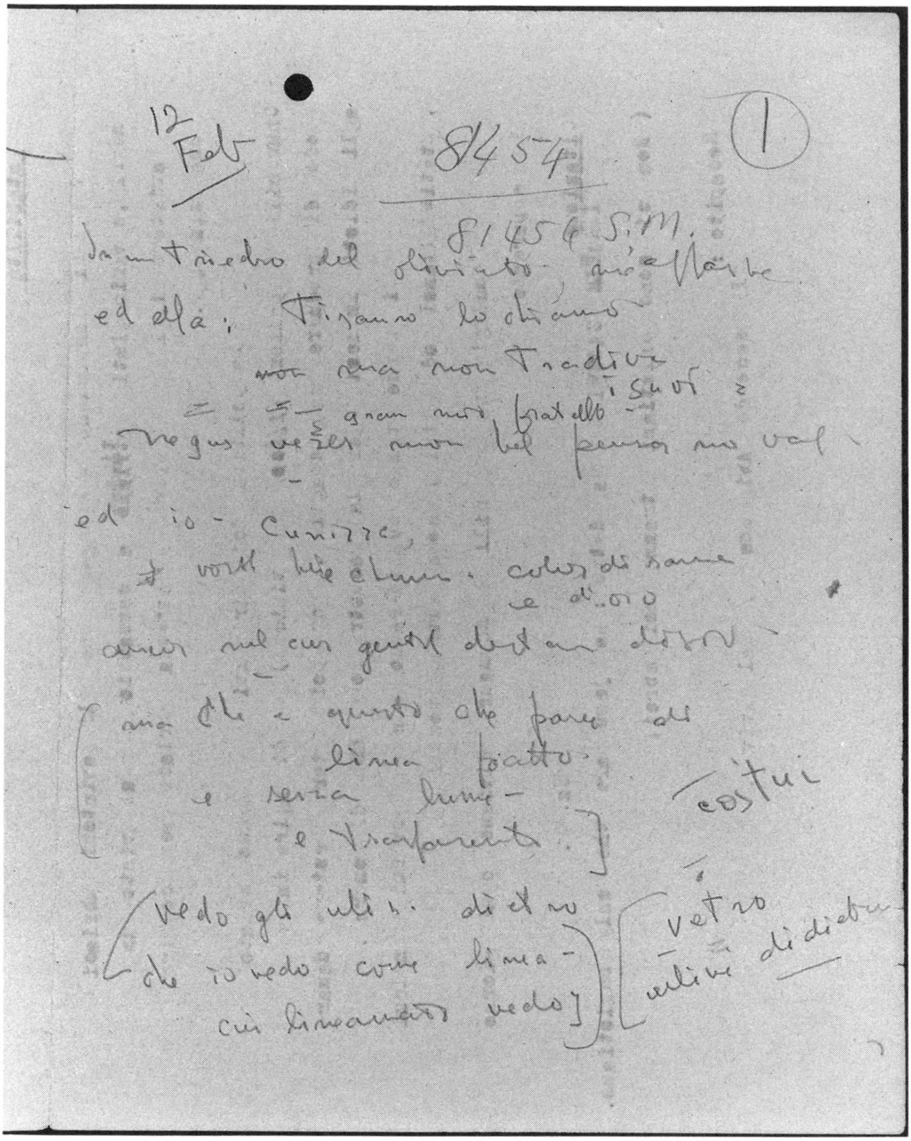

Fig. 1. Page [one] of an autograph sequence dated 12 Feb[ruary 1945]. The Yale Collection of American Literature, Beinecke Rare Book and Manuscript Library, Yale University.

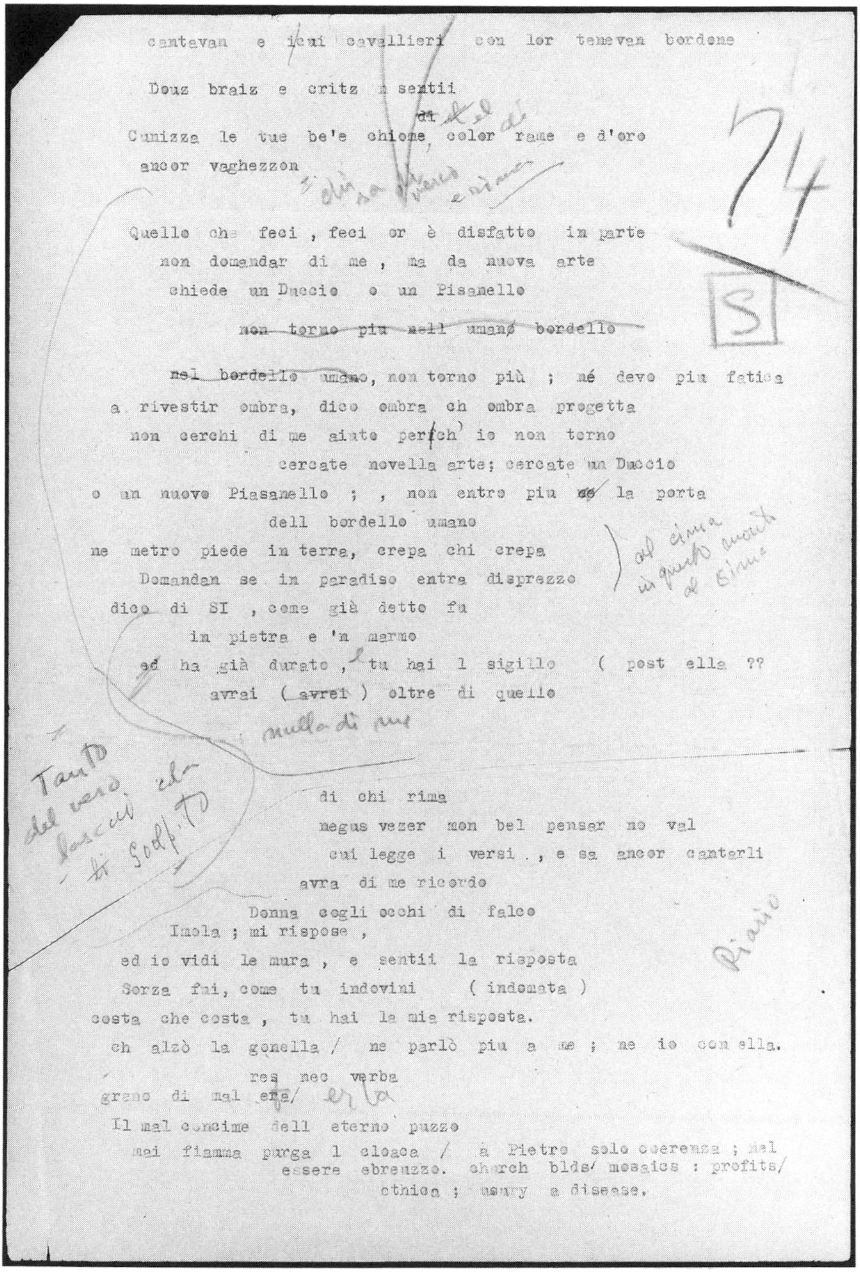

cantavan e icui cavallieri con lor temevan bordone

Douz braiz e critz 1 sentii

Cunizza le tue be'e chiome, color rame e d'oro

ancor vaghezzon

Quello che feci , feci or è disfatto in parte

non domandar di me , ma da nuova arte

chiede un Duccio o un Pisanello

non torno piu nell umang bordello

nel bordello umano, non torno più ; né devo piu fatica

a rivestir ombra, dico ombra ch ombra progetta

non cerchi di me aiuto perfch' io non torno

cercate novella arte; cercate un Duccio

o un nuovo Pisanello ; , non entro piu de la porta

dell bordello umano

ne metto piede in terra, crepa chi crepa

Domandan se in paradiso entra disprezzo

dico di SI , come già detto fu

in pietra e 'n marmo

ed ha già durato , tu hai l sigillo (post ella ??

avrei (avrei) oltre di quello

di chi rima

negus vezer mon bel penser no val

cui legge i versi , e sa ancor canterli

avra di me ricordo

Donna cogli occhi di falco

Imola ; mi rispose ,

ed io vidi le mura , e sentii la risposta

Sorza fui, come tu indovini (indomata)

costa che costa , tu hai la mia risposta.

ch alzò la gonella / ne parlò piu a me ; ne io con ella.

res nec verba

grano di mal era/

Il mal concime dell eterno puzzo

mai fiamma purga l cloaca / a Pietro solo coerenza ; nel

esser ebrezzo. chrch blds' mosaics : profits/

ethica ; usury a disease.

Fig. 2. Typescript draft for Canto 74 in Italian, page [1]; from January or February 1945. The Yale Collection of American Literature, Beinecke Rare Book and Manuscript Library, Yale University.

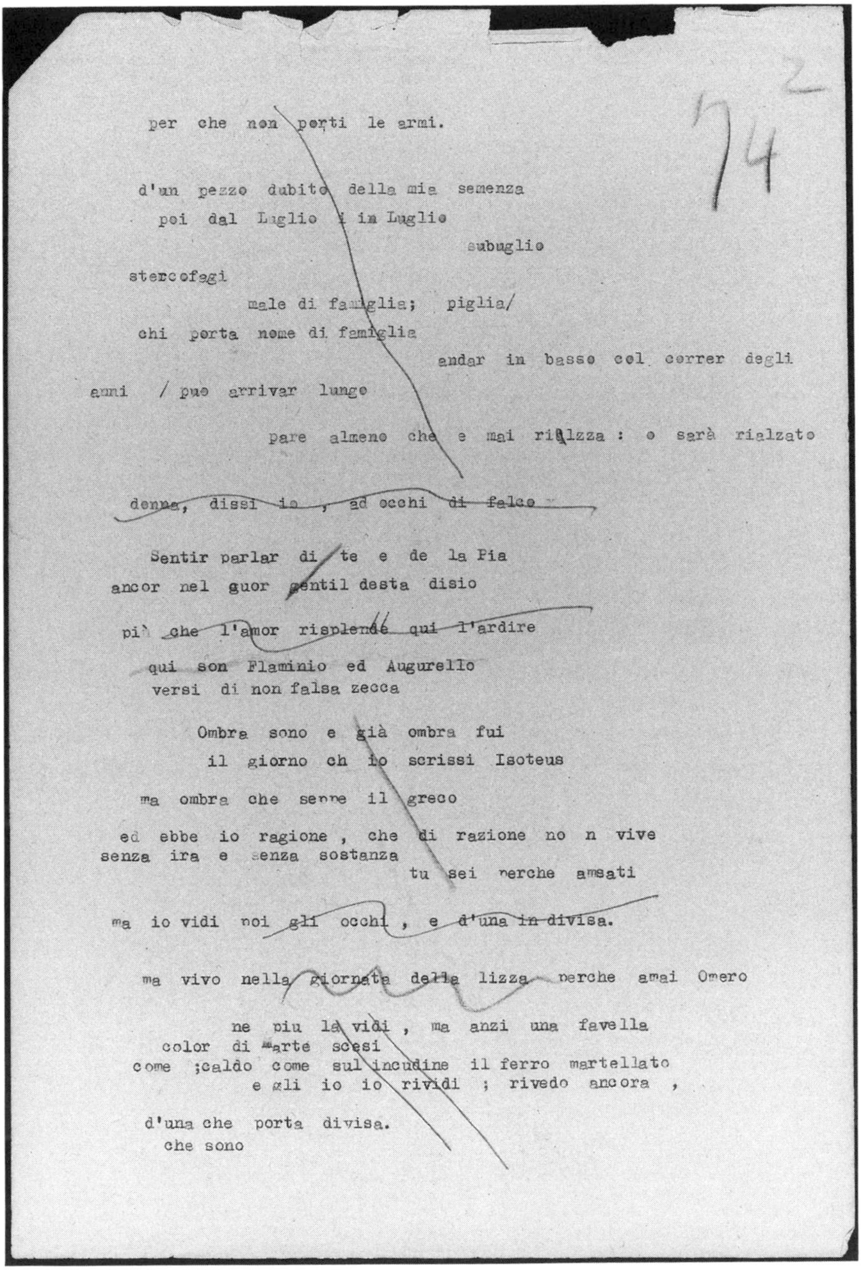

per che non porti le armi.

d'un pezzo dubito della mia semenza
   poi dal Luglio i in Luglio
                    subuglio
stercofagi
      male di famiglia; piglia/
chi porta nome di famiglia
             andar in basso col correr degli
anni / puo arrivar lungo
        pare almeno che e mai rialzza : o sarà rialzato

donna, dissi io , ad occhi di falco

Sentir parlar di te e de la Pia
ancor nel guor gentil desta disio
pi che l'amor risplende qui l'ardire
  qui son Flaminio ed Augurello
  versi di non falsa zecca
     Ombra sono e già ombra fui
      il giorno ch io scrissi Isoteus
  ma ombra che sepre il greco
  ed ebbe io ragione , che di razione no n vive
senza ira e senza sostanza
          tu sei perche amati
  ma io vidi noi gli occhi , e d'una in divisa.

  ma vivo nella giornata della lizza perche amai Omero

        ne piu là vidi , ma anzi una favella
  color di Marte scesi
come ;caldo come sul incudine il ferro martellato
      e gli io io rividi ; rivedo ancora ,
  d'una che porta divisa.
  che sono

Fig. 3. Typescript draft for Canto 74 in Italian, page [2]; from January or
February 1945. The Yale Collection of American Literature, Beinecke Rare
Book and Manuscript Library, Yale University.

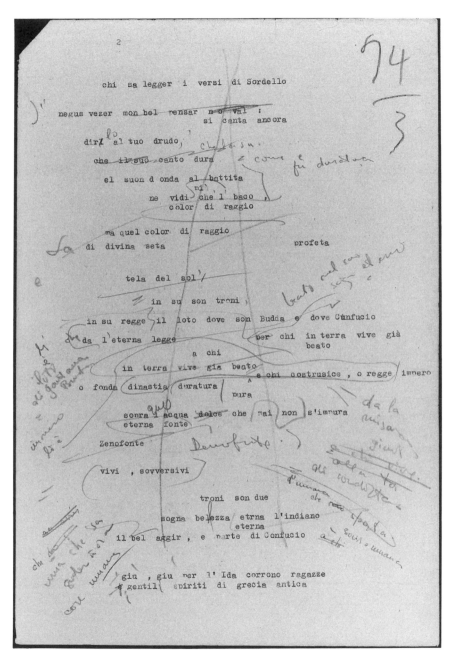

Fig. 4. Typescript draft for Canto 74 in Italian, page [3]; from January or February 1945. The Yale Collection of American Literature, Beinecke Rare Book and Manuscript Library, Yale University.

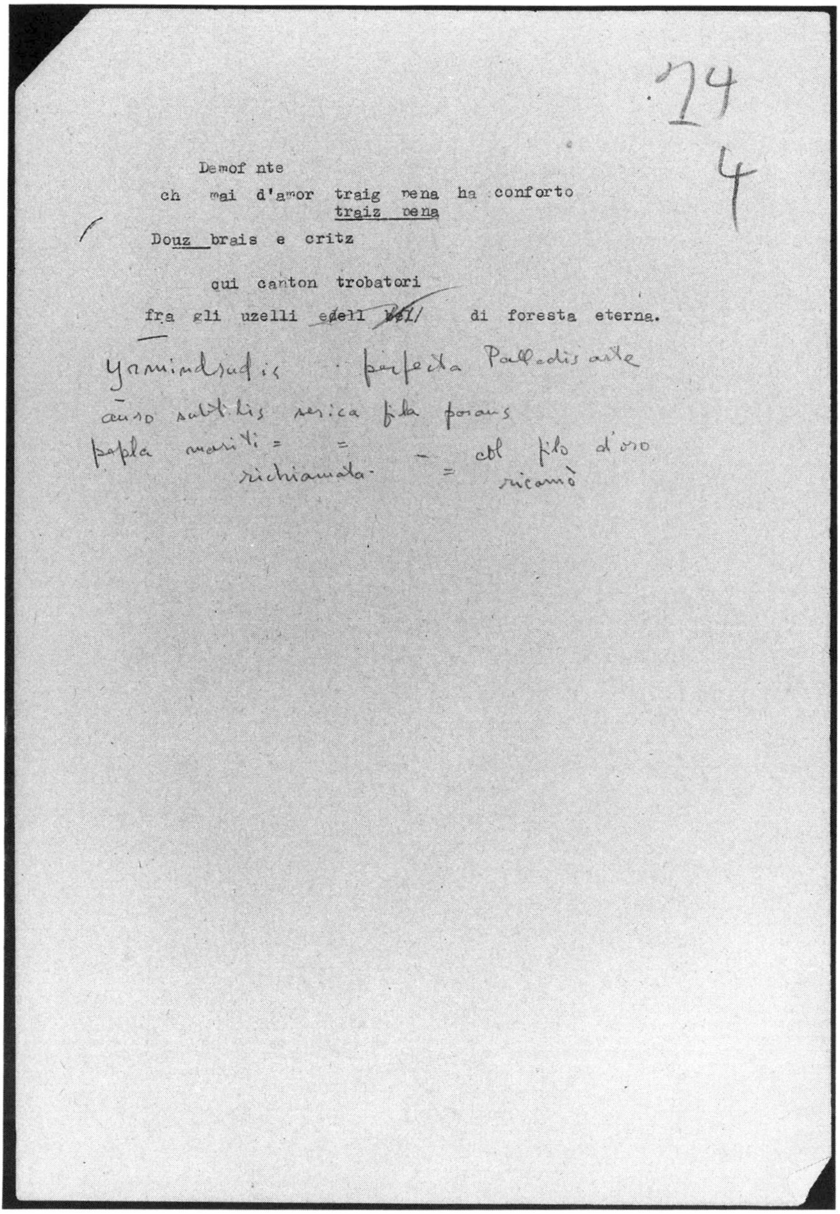

Demof nte

ch mai d'amor traig rena ha conforto
                traiz pena

Douz brais e critz

     qui canton trobatori

fra gli uzelli edell / di foresta eterna.

[handwritten notes:] yraminds ad is · perfecta Palladis arte
ceuso subtilis serica fila porans
papla marili = = = ctl filo d'oro
          richiamata· = richamò

Fig. 5. Typescript draft for Canto 75 in Italian, page 1, dated 14 January [1945]. The Yale Collection of American Literature, Beinecke Rare Book and Manuscript Library, Yale University.

extended preparations for a Paradiso that Pound had already made. One of their recurrent characters is Ezzelino da Romano's sister, Cunizza, whom the troubadour Sordello courted, and who (Pound believed) lived in her old age in the house of Guide Cavalcanti when Dante was a boy. Dante had placed much-married Cunizza in the sphere of Venus in the ninth canto of his *Paradiso*, and, twenty years before Pisa, Pound, then meditating on the mystical precisions of Guido Cavalcanti's "Donna mi pregha," began to imagine the reasons why. Some time between 1927 and 1930 he inserted Cunizza into a revised version of Canto 6, connecting her magnanimous liberation of family slaves with the quality of the love she shared with her troubadour suitor. He expanded the story in the contemporary Canto 29. Then, a few years later, in Canto 36, he insinuated Cunizza's remarks in the *Paradiso* about God's thrones into a constellation that included "Donna mi pregha," Erigena, Sordello, and a paean to the sacred light of coitus. All this would be explained in *Guide to Kulchur,* where he characterized Cunizza as the woman whose "charm and imperial bearing [and] grace" had been responsible for the last glow of Provençal song, for transmitting the culture of mystical philosophy and Romanesque architecture to the young Guido and the younger Dante.[14]

Pound wrote his winter 1945 drafts in an Italian idiom derived partly from Dante and Cavalcanti and partly from colloquial speech. They are set among the natural beauties of Sant' Ambrogio, from whose cliffs they register the disintegration of Italy. In the "Eliseo" typescript, Pound speaks of hearing "the ancient voices" [le vetuste voc(i)] louder than ever before ("più che mai prima"), "clear and more frequent" [chiare e più sovente]. As the world falls apart around him, he reassures himself that these ancient voices represent a paradisal bedrock in human experience that cannot be destroyed. And in the hillside meeting typescript, he portrays this ancient wisdom emanating from the figure of Cunizza, who appears at the *triedro,* the crossing of three paths near an olive grove. There, her hair shining with copper and gold, she defends her ferocious brother. Yet what she says is less important than the effect she makes, for in these texts Pound does his best to reproduce the atmospherics he admired in Dante's *Paradiso*. So Cunizza is followed by another apparition, Sigismondo Malatesta's lover Isotta, who reminds Sigismondo Malatesta's court poet Basinio of a chrysalis the color of light.

Cunizza appears prominently in the Canto 74 typescript fragments, but such moments are treated more fully in Canto 75, which elaborates them within a larger structure that, like the ninth canto of Dante's

```
                                    14 Jan
            é
   nel  periplo che fa l gran ammiraglio ;il sole
                         il vostro sole

   Il Sol gran ammiraglio conduce la sua flotta
        nel gran periplo                              triplo
   nel suo gran periplo                               triedro
conduce la flotta sotto i nostri scoglie
                   Anchise senti cosi cantar le donnine
che lamentarono Primavera Morta , che tu che accosta
questi nostri prati , senti le voce delle niffe liete
        rada la nostra bella pianura   ora le barche delle
pianeta ,                         a radere noste lite

            non cercate fra loro i vostri ,
lo sangue azzurro/ gli apporte a migliaia
       che canda fra nebbia e neve , a miglaia ,
       e i fiocchi giacon e fondon
       fondon e giaccion i fiocchi        sotto l ArAprile
Europòti//due questo Europto porta
              ch'      Euro        scorta
           ovvero Volturno   e Volturno
        come i latini dico / qualche volta.


                    li nell borgo altro , coi cristiani
                indugia un po sul suo grattacielo ,
            ned chiaccherar , e per sfogar rancori
            va anche li a cerca d argomento , e di sentir novelle
      da Fi/Firenze .    ( al piano dell orgoglio /


   a radere nostri liti , la pianura
          pieno di prati e di tanti fiorni
          di canti lieti, e ragionar d'amorá
                                                Sest Empirico /

                   Quintillia io mi chiamai ,   ( calvo e Gallo
                             Licoris )
            quest' è Licore


   radere queste lite/ e la pianura/


frutto maldetto dell eterno puzzo
       perversione d'ooghi buon istinto
          nel pozzo nero ogni luce muore
          indegna dell alto dono, e razza morta

                        é
       ma vio quel giorno nella lizza
       perch" amai Omero
```

Fig. 6. Typescript draft for Canto 75 in Italian, page 2, dated 14 January [1945]. The Yale Collection of American Literature, Beinecke Rare Book and Manuscript Library, Yale University.

misurando i miei/ versi contra i suoi
plasmando i miei/ sulla sua modella

75/2

//

quel ch io costrussi fu del mio stipendio e braccio   Sig/
Mise la crusca nel pane di Cristo / troppo misto /
mercia sul mercato/ compra al IO e vedne poi al cento/

Ne piu son vita e fiamma (gran ombra con poco f amma
pel benefiche"feci , ho questo perduto
d'io intenzion io non fu maligno   arcigno

non del tutto fiammo / condusse mia città alla rovina
pur combinando pace
(Napoli)

altrui errore /
strinse : e minaciando fame/ ch hanno appreso or
i gross giudei / goder dell indugio /

bel frutto fu , ma di si mala pianta
far del male per averne bene / eredita di bello e di brutto
Savanorola furibondo/ nell altro ecesso / . Paradiso
avvuso deciso riso
bel viso diviso ,
distrusse i liuti / arte di lana / per male del usura
Fiandra , raso: serge , rozzo perdendo il
produrre delle fabriche /
dei tellai /
ci fa profitto e perde il tellaio /
per pronto lucro perde il tellaio / albero nel zolfo /
se vuol entrare , cercate prima la porta/
a crear non s'arriva coll acquisto/ fiamma mista/

il mala erba/
fra tanta erba, trova un po' di verso
sta questo no ch è verso
frane dove non era gran mistero /
distruggere i simboli del bel pensiero/

Cos/ to Nic. d"Est
cambio della moneta/

Lo bons reis Carolus : nella cui corte
Erigena teneva bel discorso
filava e brodava la Regina
serviva il marito ; e li fece camicia

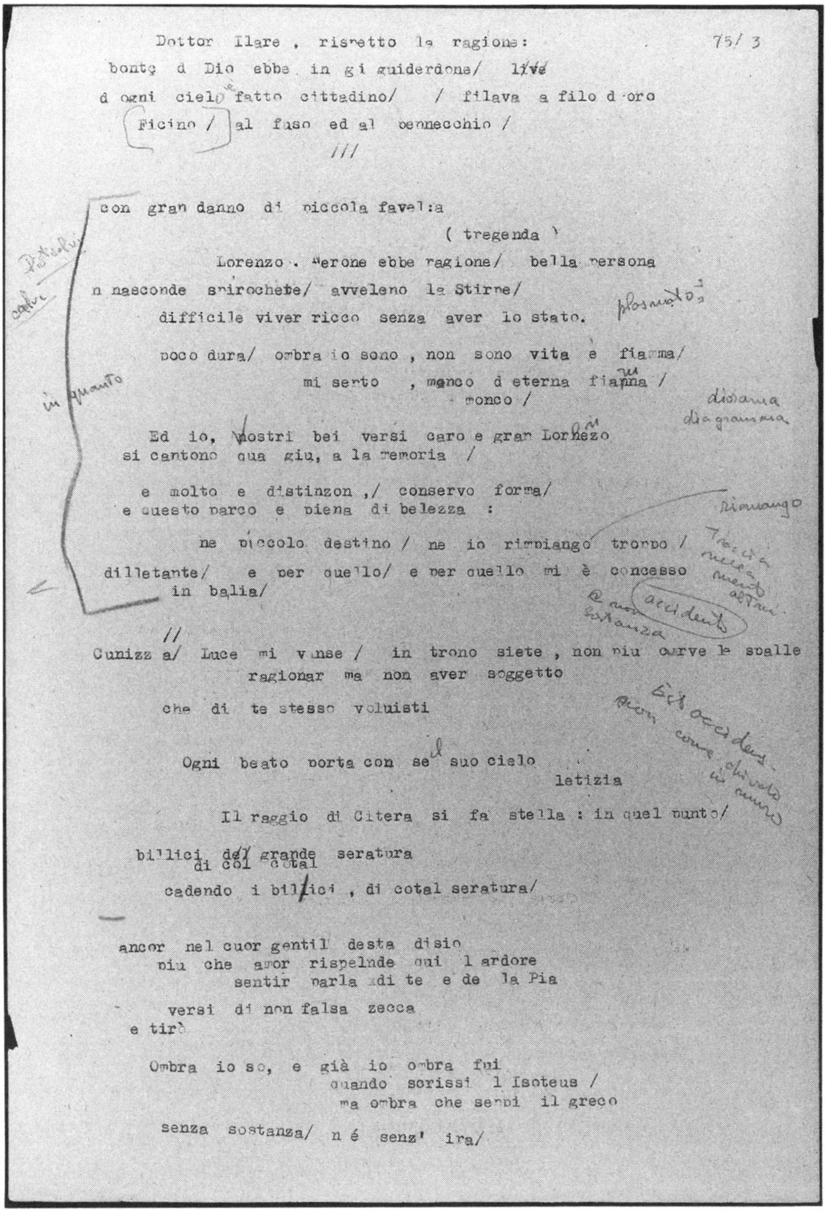

Dottor Ilare , rispetto la ragione:
bontq d Dio ebbe in gi guiderdone/ live
d ogni cielo fatto cittadino/ / filava a filo d oro
Ficino / al fuso ed al pennecchio /
///

con gran danno di piccola favella

(tregenda)

Lorenzo . Nerone ebbe ragione/ bella persona
n nasconde spirochete/ avveleno la Stirpe/
difficile viver ricco senza aver lo stato.

poco dura/ ombra io sono , non sono vita e fiamma/
mi serto , manco d eterna fiamma /
- monco /

Ed io, Nostri bei versi caro e gran Lorenzo
si cantono qua giu, a la memoria /

e molto e distinzon ,/ conservo forma/
e questo parco e piena di belezza :

ne piccolo destino / ne io rimpiango troppo /
dilletante/ e per quello/ e per quello mi è concesso
in balia/

//
Cunizz a/ Luce mi vinse / in trono siete , non piu curve le spalle
ragionar ma non aver soggetto

che di te stesso voluisti

Ogni beato porta con se suo cielo
letizia

Il raggio di Citera si fa stella : in quel punto/

billici del grande seratura
di col cotal
cadendo i billici , di cotal seratura/

ancor nel cuor gentil desta disio
piu che amor risplnde qui l ardore
sentir parla di te e de la Pia

versi di non falsa zecca
e tir?

Ombra io so, e già io ombra fui
quando scrissi l Isoteus /
ma ombra che seppi il greco

senza sostanza/ n é senz' ira/

Fig. 8. Typescript draft for Canto 75 in Italian, page 4, dated 14 January
[1945]. The Yale Collection of American Literature, Beinecke Rare Book
and Manuscript Library, Yale University.

```
tu sei, perche amasti

      ma gli occhi io vidi noi. Era in divisa/

   Cunizza io dissi , le tue bele chiome
   color di rame e d oro
   ancora chi legge i versi di del tuo drudo

      Negus vezer si cana ora fra noi .

dille a Sordello/ / ed ella noi sali , ne vivi solo il baco
      color di luce, e color di sole/

   qui son Flaminio e Augurello/    ( above with Pasinio
      versi di non falsa zecca/

   Gautama Buddha , nel suo sogno eterno /

quel e Confucio che da  la  legge . a chi costrusse un impero
e regge la dinastia  le dinaste durature/

                   //

Mai con codardi ( codini ) sarà l arte monda
ascia che i Dei tornan/  ritornana fra di voi /
      e conquesto
Ave Mar e Stelli mi suono all orecchio , per l aria seriale
   e col ramo di  . io la vidi

   come Kuanina, col ramo fi salce/  vidi l eterna dolcezza

   formata: di misericordia la madre, dei mar protettrice
         socorso in naufraggio /      manifesto/
      sempre rimista a Porto, e Monte Rosa    delle grazie

distrutta è la Fano / a Pantaleo mi Rifugio
               da
                  la dorata/  sm sempre caccita/
vaga, invicta ; Lucina dolentibus/   sono così lunare

      di bachi protettrice ; umile; duratura/

   Il pargoletto mi ama , ch io nutro / Io son la Luna/

non son la Sofia ; anzi la temo
ieratica/ mosaicata/

Sofia hecate ; nemmeno conosco / mai incoronta , d nell alta sfera
      hieratica/ stato lontano : daneggia. taglia ; terre.

   io son la cacciata. Io , da Giove amata : mesta,
errante. Europa mi chia chiamai / sotte le stelle d'rgo
      sotte gli ulivi , vi vista da te olir /
mio marito bexava la terra del //olivo   sul    Zallava
   il mio snoso novello                         ol olivo
col ramo pargoletto sedevo / tu m hai visto /    vangava
non son Sofia , anzi la temo
```

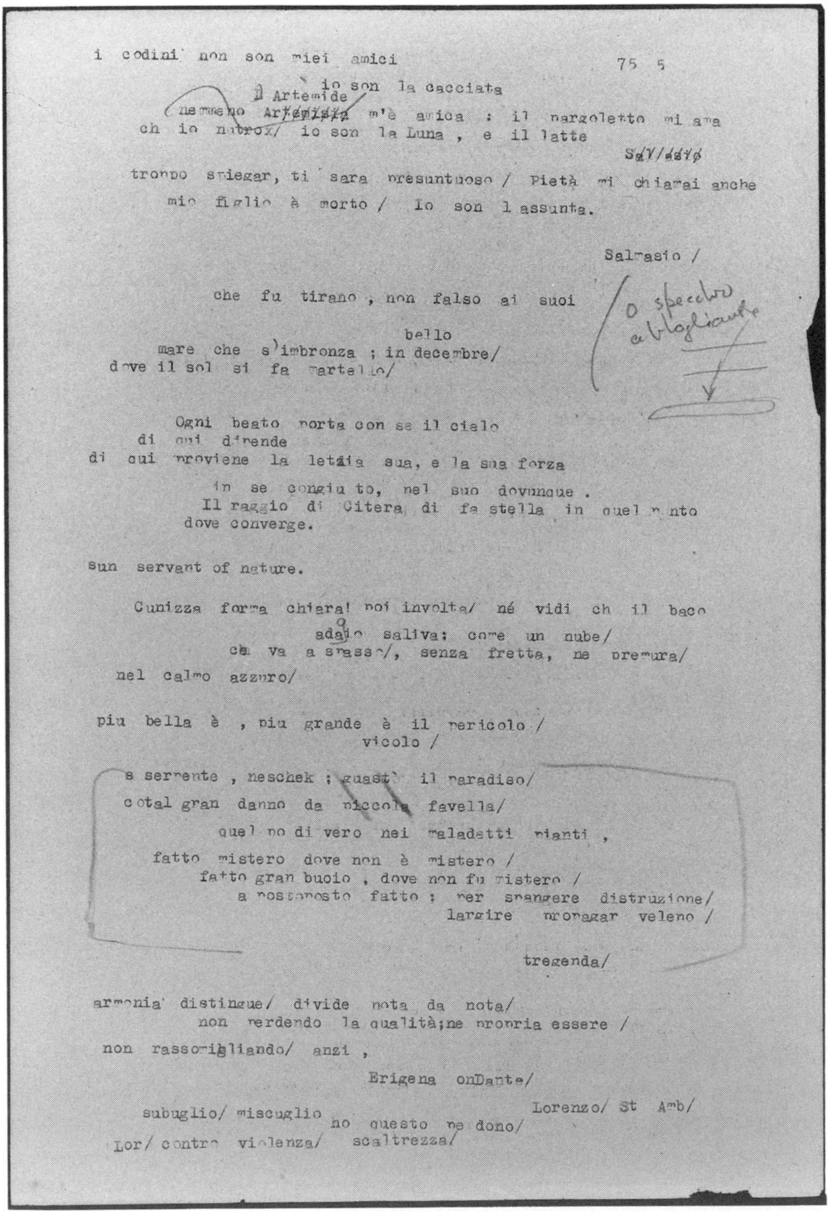
i codini non son miei amici 75 5
io son la cacciata
Il Artemide
nemmeno Artemisia m'è amica : il pargoletto mi ama
ch io nutrox/ io son la Luna , e il latte
Salasio
troppo spiegar, ti sara presuntuoso / Pietà mi chiamai anche
mio figlio à morto / Io son l assunta.
Salmasio /
che fu tirano , non falso ai suoi
o specchio abbagliante
bello
mare che s'imbronza ; in decembre/
dove il sol si fa martello/
Ogni beato porta con se il cielo
di cui dipende
di cui proviene la letizia sua, e la sua forza
in se congiu to, nel suo dovunque .
Il raggio di Citera di fa stella in quel punto
dove converge.
sun servant of nature.
Cunizza forma chiara! noi involta/ né vidi ch il baco
adagio saliva: come un nube/
che va a spasso/, senza fretta, ne premura/
nel calmo azzuro/
piu bella è , piu grande è il pericolo /
vicolo /
s serpente , neschek ; guastò il paradiso/
cotal gran danno da piccola favella/
quel po di vero nei maladetti pianti ,
fatto mistero dove non è mistero /
fatto gran buoio , dove non fu mistero /
a postoposto fatto : per spangere distruzione/
largire propagar veleno /
tregenda/
armonia distingue/ divide nota da nota/
non perdendo la qualità;ne propria essere /
non rassomigliando/ anzi ,
Erigena onDante/
Lorenzo/ St Amb/
subuglio/ miscuglio ho questo pe dono/
Lor/ contro violenza/ scaltrezza/

Fig. 10. Typescript draft for Canto 75 in Italian, page 6, dated 14 January [1945]. The Yale Collection of American Literature, Beinecke Rare Book and Manuscript Library, Yale University.

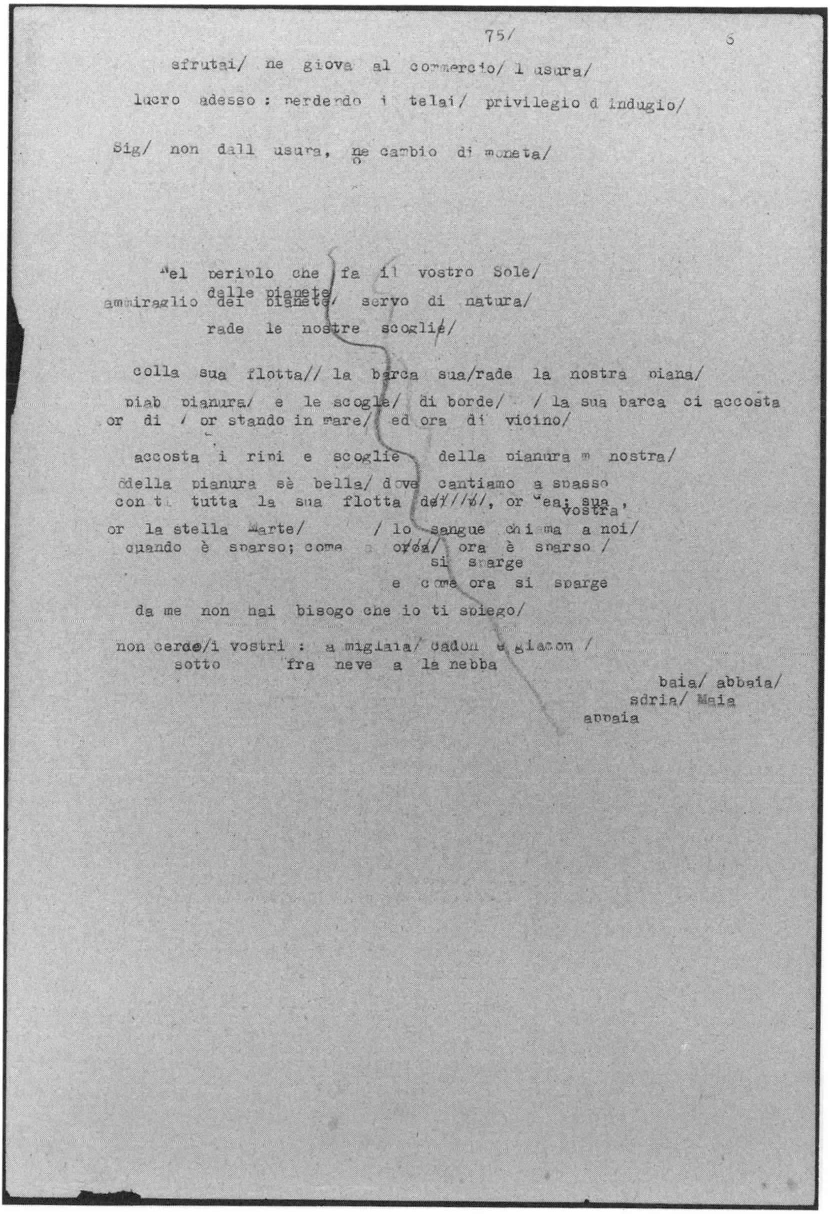

sfrutai/ ne giova al commercio/ l usura/

lucro adesso : perdendo i telai/ privilegio d indugio/

Sig/ non dall usura, ne cambio di moneta/

"el periplo che fa il vostro Sole/
ammiraglio delle pianete/ servo di natura/
    dei pianete
        rade le nostre scoglie/

colla sua flotta// la barca sua/rade la nostra piana/
    piab pianura/ e le scogla/ di borde/ / la sua barca ci accosta
or di / or stando in mare// ed ora di vicino/

    accosta i rivi e scoglie della pianura m nostra/
della pianura sè bella/ dove cantiamo a spasso
con ti tutta la sua flotta de////, or "ea; sua'
                                        vostra'
or la stella Marte/   / lo sangue chiama a noi/
    quando è sparso; come ored/ ora è sparso /
                            si sparge
                e come ora si sparge
    da me non hai bisogo che io ti spiego/

non cerde/i vostri : a migliaia/ cadon e giacon /
        sotto   fra neve a la nebba

                                    baia/ abbaia/
                                    sdria/ Maia
                                appaia

Fig. 11.   Typescript draft for Canto 75 in Italian, page [7], dated 14 January [1945]. The Yale Collection of American Literature, Beinecke Rare Book and Manuscript Library, Yale University.

Paradiso, contrasts the glory of Cunizza in the heaven of Love with the financial corruption of Florence. Loosely translated, the typescript begins (see fig. 6): "The sun, great admiral, gathers his fleet . . . / on his great periplum / gathers his fleet under our cliffs" [Il Sol gran ammiraglio conduce la sua flotta / nel gran periplo / nel suo gran periplo / conduce la flotta sotto i nostri scoglie]. Soon we find snow playing over the Ligurian landscape while the sun leads a procession of planets and spirits in the sky. Meanwhile we hear in fragments Cosimo de' Medici talking about money changing, and Basinio speaking of a Cunizza who, like the canto's other spirits, exists in several states. Basinio, we are told, can only see the "baco" (the silkworm or cocoon) of her butterfly before she fades into a constellation of similarly diaphanous women. This sequence continues (see fig. 9):

Ave Maris Stell[a] mi suono all' orecchio, per l'aria seriale
    e col ramo di   , io la vidi
  come Kuanina, col ramo di salce/ vidi l'eterna dolcezza
  formata: di misericordia la madre, dei mar' protettrice
    socorso in naufraggio /   manifesto
  sempre rivista a Prato, e Monte Rosa delle Grazie
distrutta è la Fano / a Pantaleo mi Rifugio
    da la dorata/ sempre cacci[a]ta/
vaga, invicta; Lucina dolentibus/   sono così lunare
    di bachi protettrice; umile; duratura/
    il par[go]letto mi ama, ch' io nutro/ Io son la Luna/
non son la Sofia; anzi la temo
ieratica/ mosaicata/
So[f]ia Hecate; nemmeno conosco / mai incoron[a]ta, nell' alta
                        sfera
    hieratica/ stato lontano: daneggia, taglia; terrore.
    io son la cacciata. Io, da Giove amata: mesta,
errante. Europa me chiamai / sotte le stelle d'Orgo
    sotto gli ulivi, vista da te olim/
mia marito ~~beccava~~ (la terra) ~~del~~ // sul clivo/
           ^zappava al ^il^ clivo
            vangava^
  il mio sposo novello
col pargoletto sedevo / tu m hai visto/

[Ave Maris Stella [Hail star of the seas], sounded in my ear
                                through the evening air
    and with a branch of   . I saw her
as Kuanon, with willow branch/ saw the eternal sweetness
created: of pity the mother, protectress of the seas
        succor in shipwreck/ manifest
always seen again, at Prato and Monte Rosa ^delle Grazie^
Fano destroyed and / at Pantaleo I take my Refuge
            from la (D)orata/ always driven out
vaga, invicta [wandering, unvanquished]; Lucina dolentibus/
                                and so I am lunar
of silkworms the protectress; humble, lasting
    the little boy loves me, whom I nourish/ I am the Moon
I am not la Sofia / in fact I dread her
hieratic/ mosaic'd
Sofia(,) Hecate, I don't know which/ never crowned in
                                the high sphere
    hieratic/ distant state: damages, cuts; terror.
    I am the one who is banished, Io, beloved of Jove,
        dismal,
wandering. Europa was I called, / under the stars of Argus
    under the olives, seen by you olim (in the past) /
my husband ~~broke~~ (the earth) // on the hillside
        ^hoed on the hillside, spaded^
    my new bridegroom
    I was sitting with the little boy / you saw me]

Pound in this passage transforms the moonlit landscape into a presence
both intercessor and spirit of place. Distressed by the destruction around
him, he conjures up a compassionate compound ghost. And yet he never
lets us forget that compassion is part of a stronger emotion. His epiphany,
suffused with eros, is at one with his vision of Cunizza, who just before
this passage has appeared with her eyes "in costume" (masked), reading
the verses of her lover. And if the wraith appears humanly vulnerable, she
is not. Her basis is pure spirit. Though she claims she has descended from
the ideal, the syntax makes it difficult for us to separate her from that
which is "hieratic" and "mosaic'd." An apparent embodiment of charity or
compassion, she is unthinkable apart from art and poetry, and she appeals

to us aesthetically rather than morally. This is hardly surprising in Pound, who ordinarily thinks of morality as an outgrowth of intense perception. But it does represent an extremely delicate, even precarious, experience on which to found the kind of judgments Pound soon found himself wanting to make.

The verses of these Italian Cantos 74 and 75 (figs. 2–5 and 6–11), written in January and February, were still in Pound's head when, four months later and the Allies in control of Italy, he endured three weeks of bureaucratic shuffle and was incarcerated on 24 May in a wire cage exposed to the elements in the U.S. Army Disciplinary Training Center outside Pisa. Three weeks after that, he was released from the cage and moved to the center's medical compound, where he occupied an officer's tent and acquired a packing-crate table, a pencil, and four or five inexpensive writing pads. In the tent he set about composing in longhand, at first on the pads turned sideways.

Pound's holograph manuscript comprises the first text of *The Pisan Cantos* proper, and at this point two things about it are worth noting. The first is that Pound's pencil manuscript, running to more than 300 pages, is a distinct version of the text, containing much that subsequent revisions do not. The second is that this version was in crucial ways conditioned by the earlier typescripts of the Italian Cantos 74 and 75 and their family of manuscripts. And here I mean more than what should be obvious to anyone familiar with the "Pisans" as published—that Pound borrowed freely from his earlier Italian verses. The Canto 74 he finally published, for example, returns several times to a visionary encounter with Cunizza "al Triedro," and with her companion, who whispers "Io son' la Luna." And the first page of Canto 76 as published retains a passage every element of which had been sketched out earlier in the year:

> But on the high cliff Alcmene,
>> Dryas, Hamadryas ac Heliades
>> flowered branch and sleeve moving
>> Dirce et Ixotta e che fu chiamata Primavera
>>> in the timeless air
>
> that they suddenly stand in my room here
> between me and the olive tree
>> or nel clivo ed al triedro?

> and answered : the sun in his great periplum
> leads in his fleet here
> > sotto le nostre scogli
> under our craggy cliffs
> > alevel their mast-tops
> > Sigismundo by the Aurelia to Genova
> > > by la vecchia sotto S. Pantaleone
> Cunizza qua al triedro,
> e la scalza, and she who said: I still have the mould

Beyond these linguistic holdovers, it is apparent that Pound's manuscript carries on the otherworldly mood of his Italian verses, and like them, aestheticizes his experience. Though she shades into the Virgin Mary, Pound's La Luna derives from his thinking about the troubadours and Cavalcanti. As in the translation of "Donna mi pregha" he published in Canto 36, he celebrates a love that does not take "delight" in its object but "in the being aware." He understands, he tells us elsewhere, the true "matter of Dante's *paradiso*" not to be moral philosophy but rather "the glass under water, the form that seems a form seen in a mirror," and similar "realities perceptible to [heightened] sense." And, he says, he admires Cavalcanti in some ways more than Dante, because, being a "natural" rather than a "moral" philosopher—a thinker more like Erigena than Virgil—Cavalcanti treats this "matter" more intensely.[15]

Certainly it is in the spirit of these remarks, working with and through a recent reading of Confucius, that the manuscript text of *The Pisan Cantos* begins. For (probably the most striking thing about them) Pound's longhand pages start with the verses that now appear at lines 10 and 11—"The suave eyes, quiet, not scornful, / rain also is of the process." In these opening lines Pound telescopes a vision of the *stilnovisti* beloved with a mystical reading of Confucius very like the one that concludes his contemporary translation of *The Unwobbling Pivot*: "The *unmixed* functions (in time and space) without bourne. This unmixed is the tensile light, the Immaculata. There is no end to its action."[16] "The suave eyes," then, initiate a poem whose theme involves the redeeming energies of light and reason, and whose essential shape unfolds in intuitions of Aphrodite that prepare us for the appearance of "pale eyes as if without fire" in Canto 80 and then for the subtle eyes of Canto 81. The latter manifest themselves in blindfold, as Cunizza's eyes in the Canto 75 typescript are "in costume," and like those eyes they are "senz' ira"—

"without anger." They prepare us for Canto 83, in which other eyes, he exults, "pass and look *from* mine."

Which is to say that in its thematic contours the longhand text of the Pisan Cantos is not radically different from the published text, at least as it has been interpreted ever since Forrest Read's analysis of 1957.[17] And yet, how different the schema looks in the light of the Italian Cantos 74 and 75. Pound, we can now see, did not discover the eyes that *The Pisan Cantos* celebrates in the Pisan landscape, nor were they forced upon his consciousness by either his bitter incarceration or the circumstances of his fellow inmates. He had them already in mind, and he used them to filter his experience. This helps explain a nagging dissonance in the poem. The goddesses of *The Pisan Cantos* are disconcertingly slight in relation to the depth of experience we find in Pound's more genuine moments. And they are oddly disengaged from it. When they appear, it tends to be in histrionic, even sentimental, passages. These passages speak of ecstasy, the poem's great moments of sympathy with his fellow inmates. Yet Pound invokes the force and the counsel of his divinities to justify a jeremiad against his accusers and the modern world.

All of which, I think, corresponds to another off note—the fact that the sequence goes out of its way to emphasize endearing glimpses of nature. Pound's disciplined concentration on the natural object made his reputation, of course, and *The Pisan Cantos,* in manuscript as in publication, boasts a number of celebrated examples. Pound himself, moreover, calls attention to their importance when near the end of Canto 78 he remarks, "as for the solidity of the white oxen in all this / perhaps only Dr Williams (Bill Carlos) / will understand its importance, / its benediction. He wd/ have put in the cart."

But Pound's use of the word "benediction" should make us pause. The white oxen here, along with the katydid and Madame Vespa the wasp and the green midge half an ant-size in the rest of the sequence, are agents of that same force that flows through Kuanon and Cunizza—a force that has more to do with beauty than with human fellowship or suffering. So in *The Pisan Cantos,* the resurgent power of nature that in Canto 83 insures that the "mint springs up again / in spite of Jones's rodents" is directly related to what in Pound's winter manuscripts transcended the rubble of the war and whispered "ancient voices / clear and more frequent." The small creatures, on which so much of the poem's message depends, belong to a force as preliminary to Pound's Pisan experience as *la luna*. Instead of instancing unbidden interruptions of the untainted here and now, they manifest power that Pound equates with "ancient" discourse and characterizes in terms of a Confucian "process" that he unself-consciously turns to political purposes. No less than in Emerson or Thoreau, nature in *The Pisan Cantos* confronts an isolated man that he may teach a timeless lesson. And as in especially Thoreau, whom Pound reread and praised in the early 1940s, the timeless lesson bears an undercurrent of very timely politics. In the writing of Thoreau and Emerson, nature appears as a polemical counter in a campaign of cultural resistance to the exchange relationships of modern industrial life. In the "Baker Farm" section of Thoreau's *Walden,* Thoreau throws in relief both the natural world and "the only true America" by means of an ugly portrait of an Irish family identified with life in the marketplace. At Pisa, Pound replicates the same discourse, substituting Jews for Thoreau's Irish. What nature tells him has the force of a political jeremiad, only it now resonates not only with the politics of American nativism, but with the politics of fascism, which sees marketplace capitalism as the primary hindrance to the emergence of a revolutionary new society. And no less than in *Walden*'s nostalgia for an America that has passed, Pound's elegy frequently turns sour.

Along with the unexpectedness of the opening lines (of which more in a moment), a number of other features in Pound's holograph manuscript help explain the interpretive difficulties of his final text. The most striking of these suggest not harmony but departure from the *stilnovisti* tone of the 1945 Italian Cantos and the emergence of a second poetic idiom.

Begin with the substantial and sometimes quite impressive passages Pound chose later to omit from Canto 74. One—MS pages 88ff.—touching on T. S. Eliot and Nancy Cunard, seems to have been excised in part because Pound refashioned a section of it for the Wilfred Scowen Blunt lines of Canto 81 and in part because it would have embarrassed Eliot.[18] I give the beginning of it here:

> & the rain @ Ussel beat all
>
> the night in blind fury
> Nancy out of the 90'[s] at
>   Perigeux e ad Arle
> in that room Napoleon the bis
> in this other room no man.
>   ou Tis

so his eminence, the eminent Possum
    visited the Dordogne cavernes—
& our eminent confrere mistrusted
    the authorship & antiquity
of the designs on post cards. — but if not Picasso -
who faked 'em[?] & old Ionides
had taken extreme dislike to
                    Napoleon barbiche.
near him @ a reception — remembering
    Swinburne and Howells the pirate
Violet's garden Natalie's garden
      with the old trees propped up/
Harriet's lawn once seen —
        as subaqueus —
the Tower at Leacock   ou tis
    "A L'Amitié" (Voltaire Louis XIV)
a Mme du Châtelet. Le Couvreur
cherry & apple wood. or
       scent of the fig branch burning.
I have always sd. old Blunt
from his four-poster. 'always gone on
    the principle — when in doubt —
do it —'
    a long life & a, on the whole,
              happy one —

Among the other interesting notes and excisions in the holograph text, one finds a brief plan that describes the subject of Canto 74 as a Nekuia or descent followed by action and associates Canto 75 with Tai-shan and Canto 76 with Venus (MS p. 46); an excised line at the very end of Canto 74 that follows the words "we who have passed over Lethe" with the words "seeking Eunoe" (MS p. 119; see fig. 12); and the specification of "six pair" of eyes in a tentative working out of a Canto 81 much fuller than the one the published version gives us (MS p. 249; see fig. 13).

More interesting than any one fragment, though, is the collective evidence of a major change in practice—evidence that runs counter to the Italian drafts' symbolist treatment of natural process and suggests something about the final sequence's authentic strengths. When he started writing in the medical compound, Pound, it is clear, proceeded as if he were

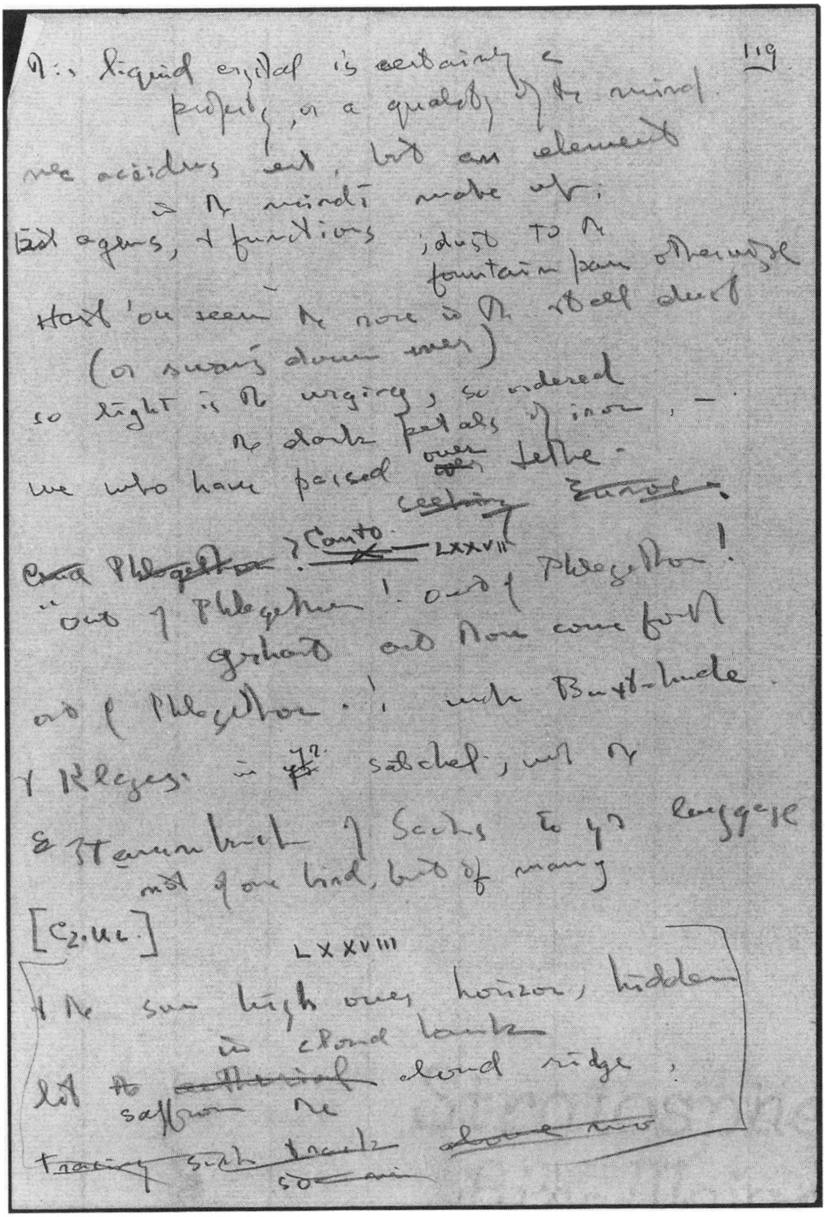

Fig. 12. Autograph draft for Canto 74, composed in June 1945 in the detention camp at Pisa, page 119. (See also fig. 13.) The Yale Collection of American Literature, Beinecke Rare Book and Manuscript Library, Yale University.

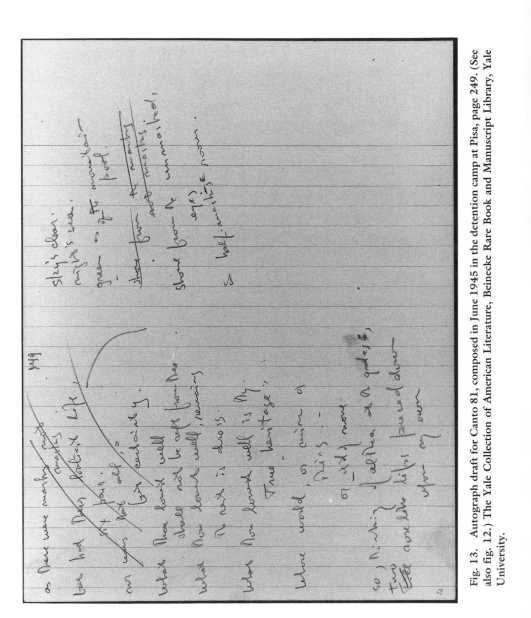

Fig. 13. Autograph draft for Canto 81, composed in June 1945 in the detention camp at Pisa, page 249. (See also fig. 12.) The Yale Collection of American Literature, Beinecke Rare Book and Manuscript Library, Yale University.

keeping a poetic notebook and seemed to have been launched by the presence of death. Not only did he record the dates of key occasions in his text, for example, but the earliest event he identifies was the hanging, on 2 July 1945, of Louis Till. (Till, as it turned out, was the father of Emmet Till, whose murder years later would help instigate the civil-rights movement in America.) Near the beginning of Canto 74 Pound records that "Till was hung yesterday," and in another manuscript passage a few pages later he inserts "July 6th" (MS p. 36), a date only three weeks after he left the cage.

Reinforcing the material's diary-like texture is the first use Pound made of it. When he was at last permitted to write to his wife, Dorothy, he sent her fragments of his work in place of substantive communications. The first of these enclosures consisted of what would later become his suite's most famous lines ("Pull down thy vanity"). In his accompanying note, dated 23 September, Pound said that he was sure the lines would be "more human than a dull letter" and added that they were "mild" enough for his mother to see.[19] Such was the first context of Canto 81. As we shall see, it would not be the last.

Pound assumed he would preface to the sequence an already drafted Cantos 74 and 75, for the manuscript refers to what is now Canto 75 as "Canto LXXVII" and what is now Canto 76 as "Canto LXXVIII" (MS p. 119; see fig. 12). By 2 October, though, he tentatively decided to forget about the Italian manuscripts, and he wrote Dorothy, "I have done a Decad 74 / 83, which don't seem any worse than the first 70." He also seems to have been quite definite that Canto 83 would be the last, because on 4 October he instructs her to sound out Eliot about publishing "cantos 72 or 74 to 83."

By the onset of his composition at Pisa, then, and lasting until a point when the bulk of the Pisan Cantos as we know them had reached an advanced state, Pound was less concerned with goddesses and katydids than with the fate of the people he knew and the affections of the family he was writing for. He was also less certain of where he would start and where he would end than his visionary structure suggests—which speaks, I believe, of the truest sources of his poetry and helps put the importance of the Pisan landscape in a context very different from the one in which it has traditionally been construed. A note from Dorothy to Pound before she had read any of the Pisan Cantos also helps. On 25 September, Dorothy, unsure that Pound would ever receive her message, wrote that "Should this reach you.—You may imagine that I am thinking of you all the time: but I do not worry all that time. I only hope captivity is not proving bad for your health, & that you are able to work at some writing or other. The moment perhaps for those ~~Memoirs~~ 'Memories'?"

The word "Memories" here has Dorothy's quotes around it, and points to the fact that the two of them have already discussed the possibility of a serious work about Pound's life. That explains why, on 13 October, having seen parts of Cantos 74, 76, 80, and 81, she writes with the delight of a prophet confirmed (and then with a nagging uneasiness about private experience): "Of course," she exclaims, "all these last, apparently, scraps, of cantos, are your self, the memories that make up yr. person." But she adds: "Is one then only a bunch of memories? i.e. a bunch of remains of contacts with the other people?"

Considering how charged issues of memory had become for Pound, Dorothy's questions would have been haunting. In the account of his American lawyer, Julien Cornell, "after a week or so of the mental and physical torment of confinement in the cage, Pound's mind gave way. He says that he can now recall only the sensation that the top of his head was empty; also that his eyebrows were constantly taut in a raised position, due to the heat and glare. . . . he was stricken with violent terror and hysteria, and also affected with amnesia." The amnesia, it seems, was most terrifying of all. As he told Jerome Kavka, the young therapist assigned to his case in his early days at St. Elizabeths, he felt he had "burst a mainspring at Pisa." And although, as Kavka noted, it seems that Pound had "deplored the psychoanalytic method" partially because "it would bring up too many painful memories," when his mind went at Pisa, Pound was desperate to remember so that he could maintain his self-esteem. (As late as February 1946 he would movingly complain to James Laughlin from St. Elizabeths that as he was no longer required to "THINK anymore [I] shalt be happy when I begin (i.e. IF) to remember.")[20]

Whatever his conflicted feelings about them, at Pisa Pound did write his "Memories," and in them he resurrected persons young and old, famous and obscure, artistic and not. And it is the premeditated exercise of this remembering, it seems to me, rather than an inspired response to the landscape, that assures these cantos a place on our shelves. Although there are ugly blinkers on Pound's sympathy, in my experience we tend to forgive them because of the generous way he remembers the dead.

Nor did his exercise lack an appropriate literary frame. As Achilles Fang observed in the late 1950s, Pound's rememberings derive precedent and structure from a work he had for many years praised and imitated.[21]

In 1921, Pound had used François Villon's "Grand Testament" for an opera. Now, fearing he might succeed Till on the gallows, he imagines himself with Villon "under *les six potences.*" Hence a great deal of *The Pisan Cantos* can be construed as an elaboration of the "Testament"'s stanza 29: "Where are those laughing comrades / that I was with in former days, / who sang so well, talked so well / and so excelled in word and deed? / Some are dead and stiff— / nothing now remains of them: / may they find peace in Paradise, / and may God save the rest."[22]

Pound, though, did not simply reproduce Villon's recitation of legacies. Concentrating on those cries in the last extremity that punctuate Villon's tough humor,[23] the Pisan Cantos throughout associate memory with broken pride, forgiveness, unconscious intensity, and tears. And though it may be argued that Pound's tears started out in self-pity, very early in the composition they become fused with the kind of compassion that (like the sunset in *Purgatorio* VIII that Canto 74 quotes) "softens" [ch'intenerisce] the heart. Like a mantra that sidesteps psychic resistance and discovers sympathetic powers beyond the ego, Pound's mnemonic exercise, he tells us, restored his power to feel. In his words it bathed the "dust and glare evil" of his confinement with a fountain of self-forgetful reminiscence. And he recorded the experience with gratitude. So in Canto 74, shortly after the echo of Dante's sunset, "the tides [that] follow Lucina" remind him "that [he] had been a hard man in some ways / a day as a thousand years." And in Canto 80, Villon's plea, "repos donnez a cils," unleashes Pound's answering French: "Les larmes que j'ai creées m'indondent / Tard, très tard je t'ai connue, la Tristesse, / I have been hard as youth sixty years."

This confession, validated by Pound's frequent testimonials to the dead, acquires increasing poignancy in the text preserved in the holograph manuscript, and, parallel with the orchestrations of nature and Aphrodite, culminates in Pound's intended conclusion. Canto 83 starts with Eregina and light but finds its completion in *hudor*—water in the form of mist, rain, and tears. It is perhaps most poignant in Pound's memory of H. D., the dryad "whose eyes are like the clouds over Taishan / When some of the rain has fallen / and half remains yet to fall." But it is almost as moving in its filial close, where Pound gives voice to his elderly mother and his late Aunt Frank. Their recollections reach back "40 years, 60 years?" to another era.[24]

It is worth repeating that as late as 4 October 1945 Pound still intended to make Canto 83 the last poem in his new sequence. (As already mentioned, he had instructed Dorothy in a letter of that day to ask T. S. Eliot his opinion of "cantos 72 or 74 to 83.") That date marks the terminus of what we might call the second of the three distinct phases of *The Pisan Cantos* text. (The Italian poems written at Sant' Ambrogio represent the first.) By 4 October, Pound's manuscripts and his correspondence tell us that he had completed longhand drafts of Cantos 74–83 and had begun to retype and revise much of them. Letters to Dorothy at the Lilly Library at Indiana University, for example, show that by 2 October Pound had sent (and by 31 October Dorothy had received) carbons of scattered typescript pages subsequent to the pages Pound sent on 23 and 25 September and that Dorothy received on 13 October. The latter included the lynx passage destined for Canto 79, intended for her birthday. Then on 8 October Pound wrote her that ten cantos (74–83) were "I think in shape." All this time, Pound was directing Dorothy to send the carbons up the hill to Olga and Mary so they could retype them neatly, and then to insert proper Chinese ideograms in place of the ones he had sketched. Dorothy (and Mary) would do as they were told, but their fresh copies would never be used. Pound took his own original typescript to America, where it was used as the basis for a new typing by Herbert Creekmore at New Directions.

Just after 4 October something occurred that would once again wrench the Pisans out of their course. Dorothy wrote that the poet J. P. Angold had died, and as Pound wrote back on 8 October, he was heart-broken. Angold, he said, was the "best granite" of his poetic genera-tion. On 8 October Pound began an unforeseen Canto 84 with a cry of grief. He continued in the same vein after 17 October with farewells to the collaborators Laval and Quisling, who had been condemned in the interim. Pound was unsure about the appropriateness of all of Canto 84, though, and both his manuscript and typescript contain several pages dated 11 November that he finally removed.[25] And only his departure from the DTC seems to have ended his postscripts. He was removed for transfer to Washington at 8:30 in the evening on 16 November 1945, and on 4 December Dorothy received the rest of his typescript and sent it (as it turned out, pointlessly) on its way to Mary to retype.[26]

Parts, it should be said, of Canto 84 were of a piece with what he had just written. Its finale, for instance, was, though off balance, genuinely moving. In lines he later excised, he laments (as one critic has said he does in *The Pisan Cantos* as a whole) "the errors [if not of his political then at least] of his personal life,"[27] and he uncomfortably recalls the two women his domestic arrangements had grieved. Not counting the Olga fragment inserted in the tenth New Directions printing of the collected *Cantos*, it is the only time in his composition that he called Olga Rudge by name:

So the old Emperor sd to Shun
"If you can keep the peace between
        those two hell-cats
you will have no trouble in running the Empire"
Magnanimity / magnanimity /
      I know I ask a great deal
Gaudier, Hulme gone in that one
Young Dolmetch and Angold in this one
and the Italians
      "are not interested
in fighting foreigners,
they are only interested in fighting each other"
Olga Rudge dixit, who knows 'em[28]

Yet this conclusion (as suggested by Pound's decision to scrap it) was not what his heartsick anger wanted to say. After 8 October when he had written Dorothy that the cantos typescript was finished, and before 17 October, he composed his angry lament for the fascist "martyrs." Then sometime after the 17th he inserted the keynote of the third distinct stage of *The Pisan Cantos* text—a fitting counterpart to the Canto 84 he had just composed. Hard as it may be to believe, the famous opening elegy to Mussolini, which seems to give *The Pisan Cantos* so much of their characteristic tone, was an afterthought. I give the passage as it appears on Pound's first typescript (see fig. 14).

    The enormous tragedy of the dream in the peasant's bent
  shoulders
    Manes / Manes was tanned and stuffed
thus
  B[enito], and la C[lara], a Milano
      by the heels at Milano
    that magots shd/ ead the dead bullock
  DIGENES , but the twice crucified
         where in history will you find it

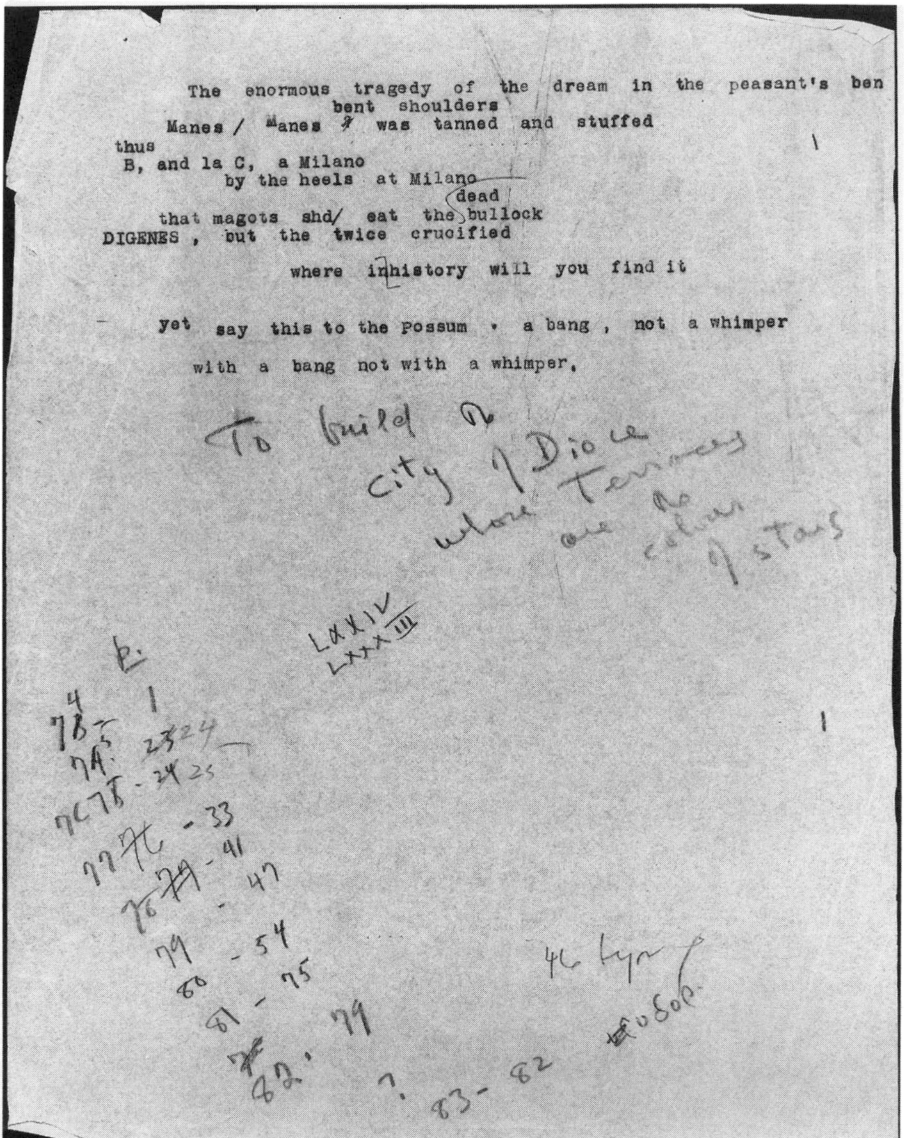

The enormous tragedy of the dream in the peasant's ben
                bent shoulders
        Manes / Manes # was tanned and stuffed
thus
   B, and la C, a Milano
          by the heels at Milano
                        (dead
        that magots shd/ eat the bullock
DIGENES , but the twice crucified

            where in history will you find it

    yet say this to the Possum · a bang , not a whimper

    with a bang not with a whimper,

Fig. 14. Typescript draft incorporated as the beginning of Canto 74 sometime in early November 1945, when Pound adds the penciled "1" in the top right corner, making it page 1 of a three-page sequence that resembles the poem's final version. The Yale Collection of American Literature, Beinecke Rare Book and Manuscript Library, Yale University.

yet say this to the Possum, a bang, not a whimper
with a bang not with a whimper
To build the city of Dioce whose terraces are the colour
of stars

These lines, far from being the originating kernal of the suite, in fact surfaced slowly. Pound made longhand notes for the verses about Manes and the city of Dioce[29] on a still empty manuscript notebook he would later use for the last part of Canto 80. Then, on two pieces of toilet paper he wrote out a version without Dioce but including the dream,[30] Benito, and La Clara. Some time afterward he recopied the lines on a leaf between pages 91 and 92 of the Canto 74 manuscript and typed them, still without Dioce, onto a separate sheet. We know that he did not insert them into the text even then, because of the typewriters. Having retyped the first two-thirds of Canto 74 on an elite machine, the Mussolini lines, already extant as a separate fragment on the pica typewriter, had not yet been inserted. Pound in fact had written an "incipit" next to the "Canto ?74" above the first lines of his elite text, lines that still began, "The suave eyes, quiet, not scornful" (see fig. 15). It was likely among his last decisions at Pisa to affix the page he had typed on the pica machine, beginning, "The enormous tragedy of the dream," and add in longhand "To build the city of Dioce . . ." Then and only then did he boldly pencil in (p.) "1" and with the same pencil renumber pages 1–9. (For a reproduction of the first three pages of the typescript, see figs. 14–16.)

But however belated, or rather precisely because belated, Pound's new opening pointed to the emergence of a distinctive version of the text, by which I mean not that he rewrote his poem, but rather that he changed enough cues to make what remained vibrate in a different way. Along with the remembrances of personal friends he excised from Canto 74, the political Canto 84 he added in October and November, his decision to cut the personal ending of that canto, and various small changes he made throughout, the new opening lines transformed what had started as a visionary sequence into a political statement.

Not that the holograph manuscript and its associated early typescript had flinched from politics. On the contrary, they contained enough to regard it at moments simply as an elegy for Fascist Italy. To take a rather subtle example, recall the line from Canto 77 that goes "Missing the bull's eye seeks the cause in himself" (77/468). Pound had plucked it from Confucius's The Unwobbling Pivot, where in Pound's 1945 translation a

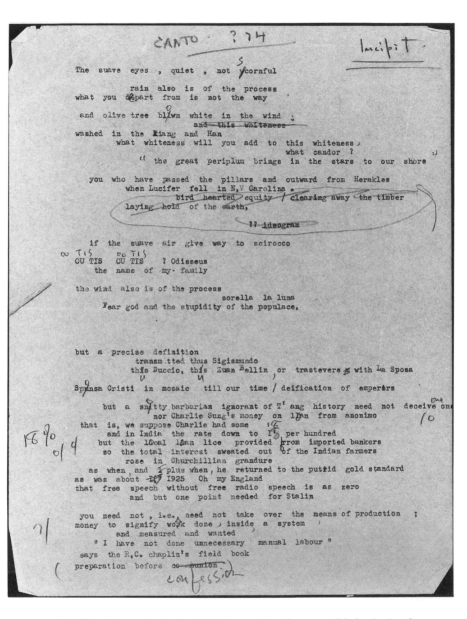

Fig. 15. Typescript draft originally considered as a possible beginning for Canto 74, prior to Pound's adding the typescript fragment shown in fig. 14. The Yale Collection of American Literature, Beinecke Rare Book and Manuscript Library, Yale University.

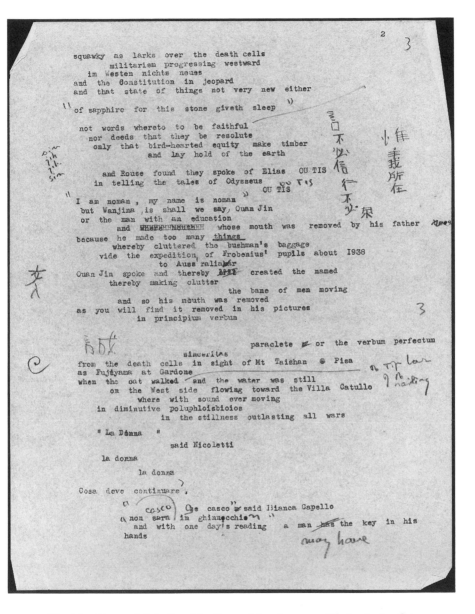

```
        squawky as larks over the death cells
              militarism progressing westward
        im Westen nichts neues
and the Constitution in jeopard
and that state of things not very new either

"  of sapphire for this stone giveth sleep


    not words whereto to be faithful
      nor deeds that they be resolute
        only that bird-hearted equity make timber
                and lay hold of the earth


        and Rouse found they spoke of Elias   OU TIS
        in telling the tales of Odysseus
                                    OU TIS
"  I am noman , my name is noman
    but Wanjina  is shall we say, Ouan Jin
    or the man with an education
               and WHERE UMOUTHH  whose mouth was  removed  by his father
because he made too many things
        whereby cluttered the bushman's baggage
        vide the expedition, of Frobenius' pupils about 1938
                to Auss raliabar
Ouan Jin spoke and thereby ATTT created the named
        thereby making clutter
                        the bane of men moving
        and so his mouth was removed
as you will find it removed in his pictures
            in principium verbum


                        paraclete g or the verbum perfectum
                 sincerites
from the death cells in sight of Mt  Taishan  @  Pisa
as Fujiyama at Gardone
when the oat walked and the water was still
        on the West side  flowing toward  the Villa Catullo
            where with sound ever moving
in diminutive poluphloisbioios
                in the stillness outlasting all wars

" La Donna  "
                said Nicoletti
    la donna

        la donna

Cosa deve continuare ,

        "  casco " Oge casco " said Bianca Capello
(  non sara  in ghianocchio "
        and with one day's reading  a man  has the key in his
hands
```

section reads, "there is an analogy between the man of breed and the archer. The archer who misses the bulls-eye turns and seeks the cause of his failure in himself."[31] To an uninformed reader, the line in Canto 77 suggests a confession of moral failure. On the contrary, Pound posted walls with the maxim during the war,[32] using it to suggest that the Fascists' blunders had more to do with a weakness of will (or with the deficiencies of Mussolini's advisors) than with faulty principles.

After Pound completed his typescript, though, it became difficult not to read even ambiguous passages along similar lines. Thus the Confucian references on the first pages of Canto 74 that Pound had flavored with Cavalcanti now seem primarily political, as were the Confucian Cantos 52–61. Think of "what whiteness will you add to this whiteness, / what candor?" Pound found the question in Mencius, where it is asked by a disciple after Confucius's death,[33] and he quoted it in a 1941 fragment. But in its new surroundings, the question is hard to dissociate from the death of Mussolini, which took place on 28 April 1945.

Or consider, one line before it, "What you depart from is not the way," which was suggested by a discussion of process in *The Unwobbling Pivot*. We can read the words as a self-accusation, meaning roughly: "adversity has shown me problems in my way of living; and so my old life could not have been the way." And in fact Pound had first written on his manuscript, "what is left is not the way." With Canto 74's new opening, though, the line all but shouts: "I know the way, and I am not going to leave it."

Also, think about Pound's tone. The Mussolini lines send *The Pisan Cantos* in this third version on its way bristling with self-protective hostility. Reading quickly, we are likely to remember not Pound's openness or his generosity, but a "proud and intransigent . . . stoicism" that allows him "to control and order" chaos and despair.[34] In this mood nature sounds less like an unpredictable series of quotidian miracles than like a force allied with Pound and eager to rebuke their common enemies. Nor can he in this version of the poem afford to sympathize with America. And so, in a truncated Canto 81 his emphasis now shifts from vision to admonition, and Pound's possessed voice cries out, in Peter D'Epiro's words, against "the empty pride of his victorious captors (and the nation they serve, along with its self-righteous artists)."[35]

> "Master thyself, then others shall thee beare"
>   Pull down thy vanity

Thou art a beaten dog beneath the hail,
A swollen magpie in a fitful sun,
Half black half white
Nor knowst'ou wing from tail
Pull down thy vanity
        How mean thy hates
Fostered in falsity,
        Pull down thy vanity,
Rathe to destroy, niggard in charity,
Pull down thy vanity,
        I say pull down.

I wish to conclude, however, not by emphasizing the *ressentiment* of this outcry, but with a plea not to judge it too quickly. Because of the succeeding frames Pound incorporated into the manuscript and typescript texts of *The Pisan Cantos,* it seems to me George Kearns is as justified arguing that Canto 81 is a "confession of [Pound's own] failure and vanity"[36] as Peter D'Epiro is when he holds it confesses nothing. Pound provided encoded instructions for both, with the result that neither reading by itself suffices. To appropriate Jerome McGann, in *The Pisan Cantos* as in *The Cantos* as a whole, Pound left the telos of his writing indeterminate as he composed, and he thus opened himself to contradictory interpretations. In McGann's words, as the poem's images, each detached from narrative support, succeed one another, Pound's "discourse accumulates a structure that grows increasingly overdetermined." The result is that "every part becomes open to invasion from every other part."[37] What a given image signifies then may change dramatically from year to year or, as in this case, from month to month. Or to put it in simpler language, we may never know for certain whether the eyes in *The Pisan Cantos* are "quiet, not scornful" after all.

Nor is this situation aberrant, either in Pound's work or in modernist literature in general. Far from being an accident of Pound's unusual circumstances at Pisa, the opposition of aesthetic ideals in the poem between symbolist closure and diary-like openness, or Pound's ideological opposition between mandarin values (Confucius and Mussolini) and bohemian-anarchist ones (Villon), recurs in the *Cantos* from the beginning. As I have argued in an essay entitled "Excavating the Faultlines of Modernism: Editing Ezra Pound's *Cantos*," the same oppositions characterize Pound's creative and editorial practices from the teens to the

1960s. (To cite a dramatic example, the text of Canto 6 as revised for *A Draft of XXX Cantos* [1930], which contributed an important predecessor [Cunizza] to the goddesses of *The Pisan Cantos,* was when originally published in 1919 a *feminist* document, related to Pound's work on the *New Freewoman.*)[38]

More, what is true for the *Cantos,* a poem that Pound thought of in the depths of his passion for Mussolini as a fascist text, is no less true for the other classics of modernist literature. Yeats, Eliot, Joyce, Henry James, and others have been taken to task for formalist elitism and for conditioning "bourgeois ideology's growing dependence on 'organicist' concepts of society," and modernist literature itself has been condemned by onetime supporters such as Richard Poirier as a "snob's game."[39] Yet honestly considered, the major works of these authors *(The Tower, The Waste Land, Ulysses, The Golden Bowl)* resist organicism and aestheticism as much as they are drawn to them. What Frank Kermode has called modernist literature's characteristic and pervasive "skepticism,"[40] a quality no less evident in the diary-like openness of *The Pisan Cantos* than in the self-conscious forms of *Ulysses,* is inscribed in modernist forms even when their subjects are repellent. Hence the literature inevitably reverts to an implicit or explicit critique of both organicism and aestheticism. To enlist Theodor Adorno on Beckett, all modernist work implies that "art is most valid" not when it naively mimes populist energies but "when it proves itself intransigent to the deception of realism, refusing to put up with all that is innocent and harmless. If it is to live on, it must elevate social criticism to the level of form, de-emphasizing manifestly social content accordingly."[41] One could even insist that it is in modern literature's politically most unpleasant expressions that one best sees this principle operating: amid the fascist laments of *The Pisan Cantos,* for example, or within the dark eugenicist fantasies of Yeats's *Purgatory.*[42]

Finally I wish to suggest that criticism that stays close to textual study may be the most effective way to resist easy generalizations about the perniciousness of modernist form. Just as Hans Gabler through his edition of *Ulysses* has uncovered patterns of revisions that associate Joyce as easily with postmodernism as with modernism,[43] so other recent efforts of textual scholars have raised complex questions about the aesthetic and ideological premises of H. D. and Virginia Woolf, Lawrence and Faulkner.[44] No less than the foregoing examination of *The Pisan Cantos,* these essays attempt through a combination of historical and editorial attention to tell not the story but the stories of a text.

NOTES

1. Ezra Pound to Agnes Bedford, 8 April 1957, as quoted in Ben D. Kimpel and
   T. C. Duncan Eaves, "More on Pound's Prison Experience," *American Liter-
   ature* 53, no. 3 (Nov. 1981): 474. Pound added, "and I can only recall one
   [emendation]."
   Fitgerald's review ("'What Thou Lovest Well Remains'") was published in
   the *New Republic* for August 1948 and is reprinted in *Ezra Pound: The Criti-
   cal Heritage,* ed. Eric Homberger (London: Routledge, 1972), 359–63. See
   p. 363.
2. There are, for example, more than sixteen lines substantially altered in Canto
   81 alone in Pound's Washington revisions of a new typescript New Directions
   prepared. Pound also dropped a five-line proem to Canto 84.
   About the Chinese characters, there is no written evidence that Pound
   authorized their omission. On the contrary, in letters whose photocopies are
   in the Beinecke, he badgered James Laughlin to put them all in and to do
   them well. Finally, however, New Directions' delays in publication drove
   Pound wild and seem to have worn him down. At least in a letter to Laughlin
   of 21 [February? 1947?] he has been reduced to asking that one key ideogram
   be allowed to remain on page 6 of the *Yale Poetry Review* proofs of Canto 83
   in lieu of the "more" he remembers being there originally.
   Still, in the instructions Pound scrawled on the first page of the typescript
   copy that was sent to Faber and Faber, he urged the English firm to include
   the characters even though New Directions had not (MS in the Butler Library,
   Columbia University).
   A letter from James Laughlin to T. S. Eliot at the Lilly Library, Indiana Uni-
   versity, dated 23 December 1945, indicates Laughlin was already worried
   about the expense of printing the Chinese characters (he asks Eliot to share the
   burden).
3. Pound's comment about "dead matter" comes from a letter of 3 November
   1939 to Douglas McPherson. See *Selected Letters of Ezra Pound, 1907–1941,*
   ed. D. D. Paige (1950; rpt. New York: New Directions, 1971), 328. Pound
   wrote of his plans for one more volume to Lulu Cunningham in 1939 in a let-
   ter quoted by Charles Norman in *Ezra Pound* (New York: Macmillan, 1960),
   376. Both letters are cited by Humphrey Carpenter in *A Serious Character:
   The Life of Ezra Pound* (London: Faber and Faber, 1988), 575.
4. Letter to Santayana in December 1939, cited in Carpenter's *A Serious Char-
   acter,* 576. Pound had featured Erigena prominently in Canto 36, and in the
   late 1930s had worked through some of the Erigena in the *Patralogia Latina.*
   His notes (Box 69, Folder 2681) can be dated from a provisional sketch of the
   Chinese Cantos they include. For a discussion of the significance of Erigena in
   Pound, see Peter Makin, "Ezra Pound and Scotus Erigena," *Comparative Lit-
   erature Studies* 10, no. 1 (March 1973): 60–83; and Carpenter's *A Serious
   Character,* 578.
5. He published, for instance, a fragment entitled "Canto Proceeding (72 circa)"

in *Vice Versa* 1, nos. 3–5 (January 1942), 1–2, and included another fragment, called "Lines to go into Canto 72 or somewhere," in a letter of 12 March 1941 to Katue Kitasono. (See *Selected Letters*, 348.)

6. Carpenter, *A Serious Character*, 581, also mentions a 1940 letter to Eliot in which Pound announces material about silver mines and Erigena.

7. A page of this last was transcribed and published by Christine Froula in *Yale Review* 71, no. 2 (1982): 161–64.

8. See Ezra Pound, *I Cantos*, trans. Mary de Rachewiltz (Milan: Mondadori, 1985), 825–35. On the news of the Tempio's destruction, see Lawrence S. Rainey, *Ezra Pound and the Monument of Culture* (Chicago: University of Chicago Press, 1991), 212–13, 329–31.

9. See *I Cantos*, 1566. On Mussolini's speech, see Rainey, *Monument of Culture*, 331–32.

10. For commentary on Cantos 72 and 73 (some of it preliminary), see Massimo Bacigalupo, "The Poet at War: Ezra Pound's Supressed Italian Cantos," *South Atlantic Quarterly* 83, no.1 (winter 1984): 69–79; Barbara C. Eastman, "The Gap in the *Cantos:* 72 and 73," *Paideuma* 8, no. 3 (1979): 415–27; and Carpenter's *A Serious Character*, 637–40. (Carpenter provides a translation of a number of passages.) See also Rainey, *Monument of Culture*, 209–16; Eva Hesse, *Ezra Pound: Die Ausgefallenen Cantos 72 Und 73* (Zurich: Arche, 1991); and Robert Casillo, "Fascists of the Final Hour: Pound's Italian Cantos," in *Fascism, Aesthetics, and Culture*, ed. Richard J. Golsan (Hanover, N.H.: University Press of New England, 1992), 98–127.

11. Lines 9–35 of Canto 72 were published with editorial help by Uberti as "Presenza di F. T. Marinetti" in *La Marina Repubblicana* for 15 January 1945. Canto 73 appeared in the same journal as "Cavalcanti—corrispondenza repubblicana," 1 February 1945. (The young girl's story came from a newspaper article in the *Corriere della Sera*, 1 October 1944. See Rainey, *Monument of Culture*, 243–47.)

12. See *I Cantos*, 1569. Translations of Pound's typescripts of the Italian Cantos 74 and 75 have been now published by Massimo Bacigalupo. See *Paideuma* 20, nos. 1–2 (spring–fall 1991): 30–40.

13. This rather large collection of manuscript and typescript material can be found in the Ezra Pound and Olga Rudge collections at the Beinecke Rare Book Library of Yale University. The author is currently editing this material as part of a larger project on the composition of the Pisan Cantos.

14. See Ezra Pound, *Guide to Kulchur* (1938; rpt. New York: New Directions, 1970), 107ff., and for commentary, Peter Makin, *Provence and Pound* (Berkeley and Los Angeles: University of California Press), 199ff.

15. Citations are from Pound's "Cavalcanti" essay, circa 1927–28. See *The Literary Essays of Ezra Pound* (1954; rpt. New York: New Directions, 1968), 154, 158.

16. Ezra Pound, *Confucius* (New York: New Directions, 1969), 187.

17. See Forrest Read, "The Pattern of the Pisan Cantos," *Sewanee Review* 65, no. 3 (summer 1957): 400–419.

18. A reminiscence of Louis Dudek casts some light on what Eliot had to do with Pound's deletions. When they were speaking about cancellations in *The Pisan Cantos,* Dudek remembered, Pound mentioned a case "about T. S. Eliot in Spain and a young woman who tried to seduce him but found him too 'clerical.' Eliot had asked that this should not be printed. I couldn't catch whether this was a passage left out in the final version, or a part censored by the publisher, or something else again. Pound doesn't always make the connections clear." See *Dk / Some Letters of Ezra Pound,* ed. Louis Dudek (Montreal: DC Books, 1974), 30.

19. These and the other letters to and from Dorothy Pound quoted below are preserved in the Lilly Library at Indiana University, Pound Manuscripts III.

20. Cornell's statement occurs in a letter to the psychiatrist Wendell Muncie. See Julien Cornell, *The Trial of Ezra Pound: A Documented Account of the Treason Case by the Defendant's Lawyer* (London: Faber and Faber, 1966), 30–31. Jerome Kavka's notes and comments are taken from "Ezra Pound's Personal History: A Transcript, 1946)," *Paideuma* 20, nos. 1–2 (spring–fall 1991): 150, 171. Kavka's intuitions about Pound's unease with directed recollection are confirmed by Charles Olson, who talked to Pound in between the sessions with Kavka. Olson particularly recalls Pound's panic when Kavka forced him to write a life history. See *Charles Olson and Ezra Pound: An Encounter at St. Elizabeths,* ed. Catherine Seelye (New York: Viking, 1975), 54.

Pound's words to James Laughlin are in a letter of 26 or 27 February 1946.

21. See Achilles Fang's Harvard dissertation, "Materials for the Study of Pound's Cantos," 1958, 2:5–10. Fang was also the first to remark on the identity of Emmet Till.

22. As translated by Anthony Bonner in *The Complete Works of François Villon* (New York: Bantam, 1960), 33.

23. See, in Canto 74, "the name of my family," from Villon, 36; "Absouldre. . . ," from Villon's "Epitaphe," 162; "puvrette et ancienne" and "painted paradise," from "Ballade pur prier," 68. And in Canto 80, "repos donnez . . . cils," from Rondeau, 122.

24. For the connection between Aunt Frank and this passage, see Carpenter's *A Serious Character,* 4.

25. The missing typescript pages of Canto 84 were published by Matthew Jennet in the first number of *Sulfur* magazine in 1981, pp. 4–10.

26. The files at the Lilly Library record their arrival, which Dorothy acknowledges in a letter dated 13 December. See also Carpenter's *A Serious Character,* 694.

27. Peter Nicholls, *Ezra Pound: Politics, Economics, and Writing* (Atlantic Highlands, N.J.: Humanities Press, 1984), 170, commenting about the figure of Dorothy / Cassandra in Canto 68.

28. The typescript's final lines are:

> and it might have been avoided if
> Joe Davies had gone to Berlin instead of to Moscow

> "in our time
> Give us peace."

> If the hoar frost grip thy tent
> Thou wilt give thanks when the night is spente
> Italy, my Italy, my God, my Italy
> Ti abbraccio la terra santa

Pound's last important revision, made after the ones discussed in the fourth section, was to type the penultimate couplet onto the typescript of an earlier page.

29. The latter he remembered from what he had inscribed in 1940 onto the title page of Dorothy's copy of the freshly issued *Cantos LII–LXXI*—see Massimo Bacigalupo, *The Formèd Trace: The Later Poetry of Ezra Pound* (New York: Columbia University Press, 1980), 101.

30. There is a photocopy of this fragment at Yale, but the original is apparently owned by Kimpel and Eaves—see their "More on Pound's Prison Experience," 474. A near-finished version of these lines is scribbled on the inside endpaper in the small volume of Legge's *Four Books of Confucius* (now at Hamilton College) Pound took with him to Pisa.

31. *Confucius,* 127.

32. See Carpenter's *A Serious Character,* 635.

33. See *Confucius,* 194.

34. Nicholls, *Ezra Pound,* 166.

35. Peter D'Epiro, "Whose Vanity Must be Pulled Down," *Paideuma* 13, no. 2 (fall 1984): 252. D'Epiro's article capped a decade-long controversy over whether or not *The Pisan Cantos* should be read, as in most of the commentaries since Forrest Read's ("Pattern of Pisan Cantos"), as a statement of self-accusation and contrition. Summarizing both sides of the debate, D'Epiro made a persuasive case that it shouldn't, and he has since been joined by Peter Nicholls, *Ezra Pound,* 161ff., and Jerome McGann, *Towards a Literature of Knowledge* (Chicago: University of Chicago Press, 1989), 112ff.

36. George Kearns, *Guide to Ezra Pound's Selected Cantos* (New Brunswick, N.J.: Rutgers University Press, 1980), 167.

37. McGann, *Literature of Knowledge,* 119.

38. See Ronald Bush, "Excavating the Ideological Faultlines of Modernism: Editing Ezra Pound's *Cantos,*" in *Representing Modernist Texts: Editing as Interpretation,* ed. George Bornstein (Ann Arbor: University of Michigan Press, 1991), 67–98.

39. See Terry Eagleton, *Criticism and Ideology* (1976; rpt. London: Verso, 1985), 103; and Richard Poirier, *The Renewal of Literature: Emersonian Reflections* (New York: Random House, 1987), 98–99.

40. Frank Kermode, *The Sense of an Ending: Studies in the Theory of Fiction* (1966; rpt. New York: Oxford University Press, 1968), 104.

41. T. W. Adorno, *Aesthetic Theory,* trans. C. Lenhardt (London: Routledge and Kegan Paul, 1984), 354.

42. For a discussion of *Purgatory* in these terms, see Ronald Bush, "Modernism under Siege," *Yeats: An Annual of Critical and Textual Studies* 6 (1988): 3–11.
43. Gabler draws out the critical implications of his edition of *Ulysses* in "The Synchrony and Diachrony of Text: Practice and Theory of the Critical Edition of James Joyce's *Ulysses*," *Text* 1 (for 1981, but 1984): 305–27.
44. See, for examples, the essays by Lawrence S. Rainey, Brenda R. Silver, Eugene Goodheart, and Noel Polk in Bornstein, *Representing Modernist Texts*.

8

The Interwoven Authority of a
Drafts & Fragments Text

Peter Stoicheff

The problem of entrusting any edition of *The Cantos* with the authority necessary to bear the weight of interpretation is an enormous one and may be in evidence no more spectacularly than in the so-called *Drafts & Fragments,* which apparently ends the poem. That terminal and fractured shore has beckoned many readers, lured there in the certainty that their vision of the poem and Pound's will harmonize in a moment of suspended closure, dedicated to encountering the text of their desire. Not so miraculously, they do, because the *Drafts & Fragments* text is as much theirs as Pound's, a socially constructed text pushed and pulled by various requests for *The Cantos'* close that Pound either refused to, or could not, accommodate.

For a number of reasons, the *Drafts & Fragments* volume is the least authorially sanctioned of any in the poem, and as much the product of readerly and editorial wishes as of Pound's. As we have seen in other essays here, textual authority in *The Cantos* scatters far beyond Pound himself; the history of *Drafts & Fragments* shows even more vividly than the other volumes that this is so. By this I mean that its title was not Pound's creation, its material was not wholly his choice, and its sequence was, at least at two critical locations, decided by others. More importantly, its status as the termination to *The Cantos* was occasioned neither by Pound's sense of the volume's finishedness nor even by his desire to print it as a record of *The Cantos'* provisional evolution beyond Canto 109. Instead, its first authorized appearance as a volume in 1968 was generated by external circumstances—it was the desperate but necessary counterattack on a 1967 pirated edition of poems (crudely printed by the crudely named Fuck You Press) whose preemption of Pound's control of publication will forever stop us from knowing whether he would otherwise have made his last cantos public, and in what form.

The facts concerning the piracy are essentially these: the writer Donald Hall interviewed Pound in Rome early in 1960 for the *Paris Review* Writers at Work series. Pound had requested that he be paid for the session, and George Plimpton and Hall (editor and poetry editor of the *Paris Review* respectively), never having paid an interview subject before, decided to purchase some of Pound's new post-*Thrones* material for publication in the same issue in lieu of changing their policy. Pound gave Hall a collection of cantos numbered 110 to 116, which he had written in 1959, from which Hall was to select those that "particularly relate to the interview."[1] Hall retyped and returned this collection of cantos; Pound edited from that clean version, and sent a modified second collection to Hall a short time later.

During the process of typing clean copies of these two collections that he received from Pound in the spring of 1960, Hall made two carbons of each page.[2] Shortly thereafter, Hall lent a student (Tom Clark, who was writing an honors thesis on *The Cantos'* structure) his own copies of the second set of typescripts, which were then retyped by a friend of Clark's, Robert Howell, and a carbon made, which remained in Clark's possession. From 1963 to 1967 Clark lived in England, studying Pound's poetry at Cambridge. He returned to the United States in 1967 and while in New York City "bumped into Ed Sanders while walking down St. Marks Place, between 2nd and 3rd Aves. . . . Sanders said, as I recall, 'Got any manuscripts we can instantly freak into print?' It was a fairly casual question. Sanders was a zealous and aggressive underground publisher; I was poetry editor of the 'Paris Review,' and as such, usually had various manuscripts in hand."[3]

The Howell version of the second set of Hall typescripts was retyped on Gestetner paper, mimeographed on a machine in Sanders's apartment on Avenue A (the "secret location in the lower east side" of the edition's cover), with three hundred copies produced. Sanders, a student of classical languages, added the Greek words in longhand, as well as those Chinese ideograms that he could decipher and reproduce. The complete process of publication took only a few days: most of the copies were sold ("at a high price" recalls Laughlin) to Bob Wilson of the Phoenix Bookshop in New York, while the rest were shared by Sanders and Clark and distributed to friends. Hence the resulting edition, *Cantos 110–116: Ezra Pound,* is a copy of a copy of the second correspondence with Hall. Accidental changes do exist between the Hall text and the pirated volume, but, except for a couple of visual misreadings in Canto 110,[4] no substantive errors were introduced into the edition.

Laughlin first saw it a short time after its release in the fall of that year and immediately invited Sanders to the Russian Tea Room, where he treated his guest to a piece of his mind and a bit of lunch. Laughlin reasoned that the pirated edition demanded a quick rebuttal from New Directions "to get some copyright protection." He wrote to Pound about the Sanders edition and requested that Pound arrange what he would like to see in the volume. As he told an interested party in September 1968: "One reason for putting this New Directions *Drafts & Fragments* out fast, is to try to stop some more piracies of the Ed Sanders kind, his disgusting mimeographed version which he had made up from typescripts which he must have gotten from one of the poets to whom Ezra had sent them. . . . Pound's lawyers have gotten after Sanders, and he says he won't do it again, but with an anarchist like that you never know. It was on the basis of this piracy that I was able to persuade Ezra to do some work in putting these *Drafts & Fragments* into shape and let us bring them out now." [5] In the summer of 1968 Laughlin described Pound's situation and the likely outcome of the pressure he exerted on Pound to fashion the material for publication: "I now hear from him in Venice that the work is proceeding, though it is slow, because his eyes are in bad shape. It sounds as though what we will get will be about 20 to 30 pages of the portions of Cantos 110 to 117 which he has completed. So I think we will have to have some title such as 'Draft of Cantos 110 to 117.' There is precedent for this title as the first 30, when they were first done here, were titled 'A Draft of Thirty Cantos.'" A few months later, Laughlin would revise this provisional title to its present one (probably because he received the unprecedented incomplete versions of three cantos—111, 112, and 115—which were not in shape in the usual sense). During the spring and summer of 1968 Laughlin was in contact with Pound concerning the proofreading of the typescripts Pound had mailed him, and he offered suggestions for changes. Pound's replies were often no longer than one or two words, implying not only ill health and poor vision, but a weariness with the whole procedure.[6]

In preparing the material for Laughlin, Pound worked from the second set of typescripts he received from Hall in 1960; he probably emended in his own hand, according to his daughter Mary de Rachewiltz, and had his companion Olga Rudge type the edited copy. There are minor substantive changes between the second 1960 Hall version of the poem group and the version Pound sent Laughlin in 1968 (the 1960 canto 116 retained the Heraklean voice from Pound's translation *Women of Trachis:* "And I am not a demigod / the damn stuff will not cohere," which is softened to the present "And I am not a demigod / I cannot make it cohere"; thus the present version significantly locates the inability to cohere more in Pound than in his poem). The major difference, though, was Pound's inclusion of the three fragments that would become "Notes for CXVII et seq." The first fragment is from a 1959 version of Canto 115; part of the second fragment is also from that poem, and part was written out in longhand by Pound in 1968; the third fragment is from a 1959 version of Canto 113. In the proofs, signed in Venice by Pound on 23 August 1968, these fragments are not given a number; they are included under the heading "Fragments of CANTOS" and are preceded under that heading by what are now the two "Addendum for C" fragments. Pound may have dictated the specific title ("Notes for CXVII et seq.") for these fragments later; the Latin, Laughlin speculates, suggests Pound's authorship. However, Eva Hesse told Laughlin that she was "most suspicious about the heading. . . . Did Ezra really think that one up? . . . [It] implies that he proposes to go on beyond 116, which I am sure was really intended to be THE END. This gives critics an opportunity to claim that he's now stuck and can't finish the job . . . [It] helps to sustain Olga's myth that he's still 'working on the Cantos,' but it places the whole status of the Cantos in serious jeopardy, don't you think?"[7] Evidently Laughlin did not, and there were reasons for his decision to include the fragments of cantos after 116. His role, he believed, was twofold: to make available to the reading public what Pound had written to that point, and in the process to get copyright protection over the potentially uncontrollable dispersal of fragments into unauthorized hands. Hesse's response astutely foresaw how editorial decisions concerning *Drafts & Fragments'* content had the potential (fulfilled later, as we will see) to affect readings not only of the isolated volume, but of the entire *Cantos*. In its conviction that Canto 116 was to be "THE END," though, the response also reflected the readerly usurpation of such crucial decisions.[8] In this case there were no consequences, largely because of Laughlin's understandable desperation to get copyright for anything he could, but in the later case of the ephemeral "CXX," whose mere existence as a published text may in fact be the result of readerly intervention, the effects are still being felt.

A similar editorial problem faced Laughlin concerning "Addendum for C," the two fragments that Pound included ("as an afterthought," grumbled Laughlin to his confused printer)[9] in the 1968 typescripts under the title "From Canto C." The first originally appeared in *Vice Versa* in 1941 with the title "Canto proceeding (circa 72)," the second in a letter of 12 March 1941 to Pound's friend Katue Kitasono, headed "Lines to go into Canto 72 or somewhere." The problem Laughlin faced was dizzying: to integrate into a 1968 volume two 1941 fragments originally intended for the territory around Canto 72 (a poem that had not been printed with *The Cantos* by that time) but now given the number 100 by their author for a volume beginning with Canto 110. Laughlin first wrote Pound asking, somewhat incredulously, "Am I right that you now want it [the first fragment] to be hitched evnetually [*sic*] onto, or into, # 100?" and suggested to Pound that it be "put at the end of the book, with the fragments. Would that be OK?" Pound's response was an ambiguous "yes," which left Laughlin with the problem of whether it was to the first or second of his questions and, if to the second, precisely where at "the end of the book" the fragment should go.[10] The next day, Laughlin wrote his printer to say that he hoped "we can persuade [Pound] just to have it at the back, among the fragments, with some indication that it eventually belongs with Canto 100, so that we won't foul up our title [*Drafts & Fragments of Cantos CX–CXVIII*]."[11] Two months later, Laughlin wrote to Douglas Paige, the editor of *The Selected Letters of Ezra Pound,* which first published the 1941 letter to Katue Kitasono, for permission to use the fragment from it. There he claimed that Pound "doesn't seem yet to have decided which Canto they [the lines] are finally to reside in, but just wants them put at the end of this collection."[12] Thus, in the absence of much authorial guidance, Laughlin had to place them himself between Canto 116 and the "Notes for CXVII et seq." fragments. In making the decision, Laughlin may have reasoned that all fragments appearing after Canto 116 should assume a historical order, and thus the 1941 fragments should lead.

By the time Laughlin saw the Sanders piracy and started the process of creating *Drafts & Fragments*, New Directions' upcoming 1970 *Cantos I–CIX* was still two years away; therefore publication of a separate volume seemed more likely to "get the special attention . . . to head off piracy." This decision resulted in the first authorized text of 1968, and a limited edition of 310 copies hand-printed by the Stone Wall Press in Iowa City under the direction of Kim Merker in 1969 (of which 100 were for Faber and Faber in London, 200 for New Directions, and 10 for the Stone Wall

Press). Laughlin anticipated receiving one hundred dollars per copy for the Stone Wall edition and declined to advertise it, rightly assuming that it would "sell itself by word of mouth."

One of the more interesting questions concerning the authorship of the end of *The Cantos* involves the appearance of "CXX" in the 1972 New Directions edition and its four printings, its subsequent disappearance, and its latest role as the penultimate fragment in "Notes for CXVII et seq." These eight lines, as it turns out, followed a curious route in their journey from a 1959 prototype of Canto 115 forward into "CXX" in the 1972 New Directions *Drafts & Fragments,* and then back a bit into the "Notes for CXVII et seq." fragments in printings eight (1981) through twelve (1991). Laughlin included the "CXX" lines for copyright protection, because they were printed without Pound's authorization in a journal out of Buffalo, New York, called *Anonym* in 1969 under the title "Canto 120," excerpted by someone using the pseudonym "The Fox" from a 1962 fragment (published in *Threshold*) of the 1959 unpublished typescript version of canto 115—a fragment that was deleted in the 1960 collections sent to Hall. The *Anonym* poem is in many respects that phantom reader's composition, for it extracts lines 16–18, 23, and 24–25 from the *Threshold* "Fragment from Canto 115" and reassembles them into a different order (23, 16–18, 24–25).[13] The title "CXX" seems to consider the three "Notes for CXVII et seq." fragments to be sequential separate cantos, producing numbers 117, 118, and 119 (one type of misreading that the specific numbering of those fragments permits). The recomposer was also likely aware, as Charles Norman was (and he might have been the source) that Pound had written in 1959 of how he still "hoped to make it to 120."[14] The act of placing them in that terminal position reflects a particular reading of *The Cantos* that insists on an organic unity to the poem (so definitively as actually to rearrange lines from a differently numbered, and apparently abandoned, canto). Equally important, it sympathetically privileges a narrative of Pound's ideological self-awareness and remorse and demands the cathartic close that will exonerate the poem and its poet. The author of the canto may be Pound; at the moment we cannot tell. Certainly, if it is, he invested a great deal of energy in covering his tracks: energy matched only by those who want to uncover them.

A case of such posthumous resurrection of authorship occurred in 1986, when the Denver *Bloomsbury Review* carried an article that argues that "allowing considerations other than artistic merit to influence our thinking about Pound's *oeuvre* is a temptation to be resisted." It notes his occasional "desire to be fair" to Jews, invokes his friendships with individual Jews, and quotes Katherine Anne Porter's 1950 statement in the *New York Times* that his "so-called anti-Semitism was . . . only equalled by his anti-Christianism," in an attempt to contextualize Pound's anti-Semitism and prevent it from "interfer[ing] with the appreciation his *oeuvre* deserves." Significantly, the article is illustrated with a reproduction of a manuscript, titled "Canto 120" at the bottom, signed by Pound. The reproduction gives no indication, however, that the signature, while Pound's, is a photocopy of his signature published on the seventh leaf of Gianfranco Ivancich's *Ezra Pound in Italy: From the Pisan Cantos*. It is added to the reproduction to give authority to a manuscript that in reality lacks it, for the manuscript was written by the art director of the review in 1986 to illustrate the article. Its successful emulation of Pound's handwriting, and its inclusion of his signature, erroneously confirm for the hopeful that Pound indeed authored the poem. It is no coincidence that "Canto 120" would be chosen to illustrate an article containing such a thesis, and though the act of copying may have been innocent enough, it clarifies how crucial it is to substantiate the authority behind this particular poem before invoking it as proof of Pound's remorse at the end of his life.

Thus the canto's line sequence and number may or may not be Pound's. I incline toward the latter possibility, for if they are his, why did he not submit the poem to Laughlin in 1969, or anytime in the next four years? Under whose authority was it reintroduced in 1981 within the "Notes for CXVII et seq." fragments?[15] If they are not Pound's, we then must notice how large the discrepancy between authorial and readerly desire can be, and how powerfully a reader's interpretation of the poem (and of its apparent relationship to its poet) can alter the text. If they are Pound's lines, his crucial refusal to put them in *The Cantos* or, considering their pseudonymous publication in *Anonym*, to have them attributed to him, must be recognized when encountering their ostensibly sanctioned inclusion (and culminating position) in the 1972 New Directions *Cantos*, and later seemingly authoritative appearance in the "Notes for CXVII et seq." fragments.[16]

Laughlin, whose motives have always been exemplary, had copyright as his foremost reason for including the poem in the 1972 text, but a lingering desire to see it there may have deflected him from pursuing less aesthetically invasive methods of obtaining copyright. In this case one might have been to publish the poem in some less crucial context than the end of

The Cantos; Laughlin published it in the *New York Times Book Review* after Pound's death, in fact. No copyright is recorded in the Library of Congress for "Canto CXX" in 1969, when the poem appeared in *Anonym,* or for 1972, when it appeared in the *New York Times.* Thus, although copyright under Pound's name was stated there, it in fact did not exist. The 1972 *Cantos* inclusion of "CXX" may have been an effort to redress that legality, making the text even more a victim of external, not aesthetic, circumstances.[17]

In 1966 Pound showed Laughlin what the "ending" was to be, the poem (now terminating the post-1979 New Directions and the 1987 Faber texts) dedicating *The Cantos* to Olga Rudge:

> That her acts
> Olga's acts
> of beauty
> be remembered.

> Her name was Courage
> & is written Olga

> These lines are for the
> ultimate CANTO

> whatever I may write
> in the interim.
>
> (24 August 1966)

It offers another clue to any interpretation of *The Cantos'* teleology: since Pound never sent it to Laughlin for inclusion in *Drafts & Fragments,* we are left to assume that even by 1968, when submitting the material and signing the proofs, he believed in the possibility of extending his long poem to a later paradisal conclusion in which the Olga Rudge canto would figure as the close, or at least as part of it.

It is difficult, and perhaps inappropriate, to speculate on the fate of these last poems had this piracy on the high seas of *Cantos* texts not occurred. At one extreme are the possibilities that Cantos 110 to 116 and the fragments would never have been included in the complete *Cantos* text, or that eventually they would have been included posthumously (taken from their magazine forms, which were often very different from their present ones), offered and read with the tentativeness such a gesture requests. At another extreme is the improbable vision of a text Pound arranged, named, worded, and sanctioned at greater leisure than the sudden response to the piracy required: a text, that is, devised and published in accordance with Pound's wishes. It is improbable because during the late 1960s that serendipitous combination of vigor, health, and time was not his. It is improbable for another, and I think more crucial, reason, too, which is related to Pound's rereading of *The Cantos* during the composition of the *Drafts & Fragments* poems, as I will discuss later.

Hence, we have been given, over twenty-two years, at least six extremely different versions of a volume entitled *Drafts & Fragments*.[18] Each incorporates varying editorial decisions concerning sequence and content. Each responds in its own way to what its editor(s) vainly hoped Pound intended, or to what they thought *The Cantos* requested in the absence of its author: some including a canto "CXX" and some not; one including two versions of a Canto 115 and excluding the "Notes for CXVII et seq." fragments; one rearranging these fragments in a sequence different from the others, placing the troublesome foster child "CXX" among the "Notes for CXVII et seq." family, putting the displaced Cantos 72 and 73 next, and then ending with the poem to Olga Rudge. The New Directions edition of 1989 maintains the changes of its immediate predecessor but restores the two displaced cantos to their numerically proper sites in the poem. (This latest restoration is, to me at least, extremely problematic, and indicative of just how delicately any editorial decisions about a sequentially ordered and historically composed text such as *The Cantos* must be made and implemented. Though the cantos' numbers invite the restoration, to grant that request retroactively drapes the illusion of calm over what was an extremely disrupted moment in the text's composition, in effect erasing its history.) The six versions of a *Drafts & Fragments* text merely represent the number of editions that actually contain different poems and sequences. That number does not include, for instance, the 1975 Faber *Cantos,* which refused entry to "CXX." Although it is identical to the New Directions 1970 edition, it is so as a result of deliberate policy, not external circumstance, and thus the two texts exist in extremely divergent "bibliographical environments"[19] of which the reader may be entirely unaware. Too, the number I have given of six versions scarcely begins to reflect the several, though less spectacular, differences in precise wording and spelling. If these were included, the number would be far higher.[20] Nor does it include the very different versions of individual cantos published in magazines and journals in the six years preceding publication in a volume.[21]

Because four of the six different volume versions (the exceptions are the pirated edition and the New Directions 1968 edition) have been part of a complete *Cantos* text over which we used to imagine Pound had exerted some editorial control, the assumed history (now in the process, hopefully, of being rewritten) of their predecessors has somewhat falsely sanctioned *Drafts & Fragments* for the reader. Although Pound maintained an evasive policy about his involvement in *The Cantos'* editing (writing in 1938 that he did "not care a hoot how much I am *edited*. I am not touchy about the elimination of a phrase"), the ironic fact is that *The Cantos* and its terminal *Drafts & Fragments* have frequently been read until recently with an unconscious belief, or at least conditioned hope, in the "monolithic authority" behind the text that simply is not present.[22] Ultimately *Drafts & Fragments* reveals, perhaps most clearly of all *The Cantos'* volumes, a textual instability that is characteristic of each of them; its production underlines how *The Cantos* was never innocently subordinate to the dictates of its poet, but a product of the combined and interpretive "readings" of its readers and editors as well. In the case of *Drafts & Fragments*, readers and editors have resuscitated a volume whose maker may otherwise have let it collapse before it achieved the satisfaction of intact sequential numbering, a 120th canto, or the courtesy of closure.

Besides the instabilities of title, sequence and choice of material, and hostaged publication, there is yet another problem, intrinsic to *Drafts & Fragments*, that magnifies the importance of its textual status. As the last volume of *The Cantos*, empowered by the magnitude of that imposing text to which it now belongs, it can be regarded as Pound's intended close to the poem. Since the structure of *The Cantos* itself has been described so variously, it is not surprising that its final volume has attracted similarly divergent responses. *Drafts & Fragments* has been interpreted as an indication of "Pound's refusal to provide a coherent ending,"[23] but also as the "open-ended and relaxed finale that [*The Cantos*] needs."[24] It ends Pound's long poem in "an appropriately indirect, but rather pathetic manner," writes another reader;[25] yet another, though, sees among its "unforgettable words and images" a direct reference to Canto 1, and hence a circular structure, in which the final canto fragments of that reader's edition, "Notes for CXVII et seq.," do not communicate pathos but a "hopeful warning to . . . fellow human beings."[26] Retroactively, through a multitude of *Drafts & Fragments* versions (all the progeny of a pirated text, itself a reader's response to Pound's reluctance by 1967 to publish a horizon to the poem), *The Cantos* has been read as incomplete, closed, failed, and successful.

Thus the *Drafts & Fragments* volume's contents and interpretation necessarily involve and implicate the long poem to which it is appended and help situate *The Cantos* in a judgmental debate over the nature of its achievement. It is partly for these reasons that it has been made to bear the weight of such editorial resurrection and reconstruction. A reading based upon the 1972 New Directions edition of *The Cantos* that includes "CXX" will differ from one based on the New Directions 1970 edition (and its 1971 printing) and the 1976 Faber edition, which do not. A reading based on New Directions' 1989 edition and Faber's 1987 edition will generate a third set of possibilities, for their camouflage of the "CXX" lines as the third fragment of "Notes for CXVII et seq." is presumably to release the last line—"To be men not destroyers"—into the poem's culminating position. The reading that believes the itinerant "CXX" to be the end will sympathetically regard "the last words of the entire epic [as] a gentle, almost muted prayer for forgiveness . . . a startling ending."[27] A consequence of placing "Notes for CXVII et seq." at the end is the response that, mentioned earlier, sees *Drafts & Fragments* lending *The Cantos* "the open-ended and relaxed finale it needs," and that regards it as, somewhat mystically, "look[ing] beyond the poem" (as Hesse had predicted it would). Yet, if we are to believe his statement concerning the Olga Rudge poem, Pound did not intend the fragments to end *The Cantos* either (which unintentionally validates the claim that they "look beyond the poem," since they were not to close it). A third possibility, which, as we have seen, is not ignored by readers, is that Canto 116 (whose final lines are "A little light like a rushlight / To lead back to splendour") ends *The Cantos*. This reading desires a conciliatory ending, in which the last lines ("Pound's final statement") longingly recall an earlier Pound, and possibly an earlier prefascist part of *The Cantos* too, for "splendour" refers not only to a crucial line about coherence in Pound's translation *Women of Trachis*, but also to Hermes of Canto 17.[28] None of these responses is wrong, for there is nostalgia in Canto 116 and self-disparagement in "CXX." The point is that if these and future responses are to be valid, they must be made in accordance with a sufficient understanding of the historical dynamics and interwoven authority—Pound's, his editors', his readers', and even *The Cantos'* itself—that has generated a text capable of so many definitive, but divergent, assumptions concerning its very provisional contents and significance. Otherwise, any *Cantos* text that includes the *Drafts & Fragments* volume will continue implicitly to sanction not only its version of the poem's ending, but consequently its reading of the whole poem, and obscure the fact of what turns out to be Pound's extremely uneasy feelings about it.

"CXX" was introduced into editions of *The Cantos* because Pound had relinquished control over his long poem to a degree unprecedented both for him and for the kind of poem *The Cantos* seemed to be. This loss of control was apparently manifested only in isolated incidents such as these—in other words, it seemed to involve merely the practical sphere of publication and editing of cantos written after *Thrones de los Cantares*. It seemed, too, that such a phenomenon was neither unusual nor unexpected, for Pound's health declined after the publication of that 1959 volume; his personal life and repeated geographical dislocations increasingly became an impediment to the laborious care such control demands. Yet he effectively abandoned the composition of what were to become the poems of *Drafts & Fragments* in 1960, twelve years before he died, twelve years during which, if compromised by ill health, he was nevertheless active in the literary field. He gave public readings, traveled to the United States for an honorary degree, sustained his correspondence, attended the funeral of T. S. Eliot in London. The silence on *The Cantos'* front is notable, therefore, because it cannot entirely be explained by these external impediments. The answer to it, I think, lies with Pound's developing response to his life and *The Cantos* as much as with extenuating circumstance.

The publishing history of *Drafts & Fragments* is certainly tangled, but it may do more than caution us against definitive interpretations of it and its larger context, *The Cantos;* in the wake of its unceremonious textual journey we may also recognize the current of Pound's own disenchantment with the poem, and specifically with the paradise he had been trying to fashion for it all along. His loss of control over these late cantos is not simply reflective of an inability to handle the practicalities of publication, therefore: the resistance he encountered in trying to write what was to be the paradise to his long poem forced him to recognize that its own dynamics had eluded his control, that the poem had ceased to remain compliant, and had instead become adversarial. Indeed, *Drafts & Fragments* frequently ruminates upon how his vision of consolidating *The Can-*

tos' project to write paradise is compromised, making it the self-absorbed palinode to *The Cantos* that we now read more by accident than by Pound's design. The volume is as much a product of readerly and editorial intervention as it is of Pound's intention: yet even the intentions that are fulfilled in *Drafts & Fragments* are merely a fragment of the paradise that Pound envisioned for it.

Pound's problems with writing the paradisal close he still envisioned for the poem as late as 1958 seem to have inaugurated his reconsideration of *The Cantos,* and very possibly, as a response to that failure to "make it cohere," his own silence. The many people who knew Pound and wrote of his deliberate "silence" after 1961, and particularly of his later admissions that *The Cantos* was a "botch," a "mess," "gibberish," "stupidity and ignorance all the way through,"[29] all declared a puzzled disbelief in Pound's opinion and implied that a kind of geriatric depression occasioned his pessimistic view of his poem and life. But Pound's physical and emotional distress, and eventual silence during the last decade of his life, were not the only cause of *The Cantos'* fragmented close—if anything, the reverse is equally true. The typescripts of what would become the *Drafts & Fragments* poems reveal a remarkably tortured and difficult composition, possibly caused by his reassessment of *The Cantos'* political and racial ideologies. By November 1959, immediately after writing the early versions of Cantos 110 to 116, his earlier political views are suppressed, for he writes Laughlin then that he "has forgotten what or which politics he ever had. Certainly has none now."[30] *Drafts & Fragments* is the trace of that very crucial point in *The Cantos* where political and racial certainty is exchanged for recalculation and denial, themselves later to evolve into tentative admission and regret. It is significant that the ensuing absence of any *Cantos* composition occurs alongside Pound's spoken confession in the 1960s of his earlier racial and political errors.

Keeping in mind that the impetus for the volume's publication did not come from Pound, then, we should do him the justice of exploring more options than the extenuating circumstances of old age and depression for the hyperfragmentary form of *Drafts & Fragments* and entertain the notion that he had some additional reasons of a poetic and ideological nature for not publishing its lines until his hand was forced. In a sense, the *Drafts & Fragments* poems present an extreme version of the situation Ron Bush uncovers in *The Pisan Cantos,* where the poems are "set in motion under the auspices of one set of poetic values" and then significantly changed during their revisions as circumstances and personal attitudes intervene. Pound had always hoped for a close to his *Cantos* that would consolidate the paradise he had tried to write into it almost from the beginning; by the late 1950s, however, he had begun to reconsider the foundations of that paradise, thus imperiling the termination the poem earlier seemed to request. The "spasm of defensiveness" that finally shapes *The Pisan Cantos* is replaced in *Drafts & Fragments,* I think, by a deep reflectiveness that, while frequently serene, is at times profoundly discomforting for him.

A small clue to this lies in his different predictions for *The Cantos'* close between 1944 and the crucial year of 1958 when composition of the final cantos began. In 1944 he was confident it would comply with the loosely Dantean structure the poem had already begun to establish: "[*The Cantos* is] an epic poem which begins 'In the Dark Forest,' crosses the Purgatory of human error, and ends in the light," he wrote in *An Introduction to the Economic Nature of the United States.* His views in 1958, though, were less certain; he seemed to be shifting now between a vision of the poem's stability, which would occasion a paradisal close, and its growing inadequacy—between a defensive and a critical reading of it. In the spring of 1958, immediately prior to composing Canto 110 and beyond, he remarked confidently to Charlotte Kohler of the *Virginia Quarterly* that his characters "have . . . passed through Hell and Purgatory and are somewhere in Paradise. When you paint on a big canvas . . . you have to start colors down here . . . but it all ties in, it all ties in."[31] Yet he also wrote to Norman Holmes Pearson later in the same year, after writing (but not yet revising) much of the *Drafts & Fragments* poetry, that he foresaw a close not in such structural terms but as more provisionally guided by his own shifting response to the poem: "Cantos won't be finished until my demise, shd always reserve possibility of death-bed swan."[32] Within this dilemma of reading, that is, he began composing the last poems. One might speculate that the Pound of that time and later had begun to reconsider *The Cantos'* earlier politics and racial assertions and ultimately regretted them as improper reflections of his truer beliefs.[33] Because this wiser rereading could not permit the political and social paradise for which *The Cantos* had always searched, yet which he had not entirely discarded, the composition of the final poems became an enterprise beset by paradox and compromise, and as a result he did not pursue their publication too vigorously.

"It makes a great difference," Jerome McGann writes, "if, for example, an author writes but does not print a poem; it also makes a difference whether such a poem is circulated by the author or not, just as it makes a very great difference indeed when (or if) such a poem is printed, and where, and by whom."[34] These differences, so great in the history of text production of *Drafts & Fragments,* alert us to the spectacle of Pound reading Pound, and of his eventual disenchantment with at least some dimensions of *The Cantos.* His concept of "ending," in this respect, is really of revelation, the apocalyptic moment of "see[ing] again," as he puts it in Canto 116, what much of the poem has contained all along. The troubled composition of the last poems and Pound's withdrawal from the usual process of their publication illustrate both their new and difficult status for him and his acknowledgment that *The Cantos'* structural finality, so dependent upon ideological stability, is now inevitably to be placed "beyond the poem's horizon."[35] They also illustrate for us that any textual finality is Canto 113's "hall of mirrors," a mirage more reflective of our "dream of the whole poem" (as Williams would say in *Paterson*'s book 4) than of *The Cantos* itself.

 Drafts & Fragments is a vivid display of the historical dimension of text production and its consequences for interpretation. It is also the site where Pound acknowledges, contrary to the desires of some of his readers, that his poem, in keeping with its mandate to include history, must not avoid its own reconsideration and reinterpretation. The composition and publication history suggests, crucially, that he may never have felt comfortable with the intentions of closure that a published last volume for *The Cantos* might imply. The poems of *Drafts & Fragments* cannot, therefore, be read outside the context of their textual production, a history that is intrinsic to the volume's gestures of incompletion and self-interrogation (including the multiple identities, poetic and personal, that "self-" fitfully merges here). No matter how successfully any edition of *Drafts & Fragments* delineates the composite authorities that fashioned the poems, it can never communicate through the text itself how its mere existence is so historically determined by the occurrence of the pirated edition—a situation that removes the *Drafts & Fragments* volume from the company of its 109 forerunners, whose inclusion (though not necessarily textual precision) in *The Cantos,* no matter how complex and multiply authored their texts, is at least fully generated by Pound himself.

NOTES

1. Letter from Donald Hall to Ezra Pound, 21 May 1960, Box 18, Folder 700. NHBY, PA.
2. Hall kept the top copies and returned the carbons to Pound. The decision to make the copies is understandable; Pound had asked Hall for his opinion of the five cantos shown to him in Rome, and Hall felt that he had an interest in, and responsibility toward, nurturing them. As he wrote to Laughlin in 1982, when recalling the situation: "I was (gladly, gladly) being his secretary for a brief time there" (copy in Hall's possession).
3. Tom Clark, letter to the author, 26 Oct. 1982.
4. Sanders misread Pound's longhand "Alma Patrona" (nourishing or bounteous female guardian) in the first line of the Hall typescript as "Alma Pulnuoa." Massimo Bacigalupo, in *The Formed Trace: The Later Poetry of Ezra Pound* (New York: Columbia University Press, 1980), 461–62 accepts Sanders's error and thus sees Pound's invocation of a white goddess.
5. James Laughlin, letter to Robert Gales, 9 Sept. 1968, New Directions archive, Norfolk.
6. A case in point is Pound's response to Laughlin's query concerning the ideograms in Canto 112 beneath "as Jade stream." (Laughlin, in a letter of 26 June 1968 to Pound, asked a number of textual questions about the *Drafts & Fragments* typescripts. Pound, needing to conserve his energy by this point, wrote his answers in the margins of the letter itself and returned it to Laughlin.) Beside Laughlin's question about the ideograms, Pound paradoxically draws in the ideograms and writes the word "delete." Laughlin, writing to the printer of the first authorized edition, Kim Merker, advises him to "put everything in" (Laughlin, letter to Kim Merker, 27 June 1968, New Directions archive, Norfolk).
7. Ezra Pound, letter to James Laughlin, June (?) 1968, New Directions archive, Norfolk.
8. Another example of this enormous conviction involves Pound's line "Mozart, Linnaeus, Sulmona" in Canto 115. Hesse wrote to Laughlin that "Sulmona (place name) is an obvious error. The line should certainly read: Mozart, Linnaeus, *Agassiz*—the same three men whom Ezra places in Paradise in fragment CXII in the line: Mozart, Agassiz and Linnaeus." Laughlin wrote Pound that "Another didakt worries because it says here 'Mozart, Linnaeus, Sulmona' when somewhere earlier there is a line 'Mozart, Linnaeus, Agassiz.' Jas does not see why you have to say the same thing every time, but passes this along for what it may be worth. 'Sulmona' is, I believe, a hamlet in the Abruzzi, with which EP may well have associations" (James Laughlin, letter to Ezra Pound, 26 June 1968, New Directions archive, Norfolk). It is also the birthplace of Ovid and thus releases a constellation of significances, one of which is a reminder of the ur-cantos and Canto 2, where *Metamorphoses* figured prominently; as such, it suggests how the writing of *The Cantos'* last poems recalled for Pound the arduous process of writing the first.

9. James Laughlin, letter to Kim Merker, 27 June 1968, New Directions archive, Norfolk.

10. James Laughlin, letter to Ezra Pound, 26 June 1968, New Directions archive, Norfolk. Pound wrote his "yes" response in the margin beside Laughlin's question.

11. James Laughlin, letter to Kim Merker, 27 June 1968, New Directions archive, Norfolk.

12. James Laughlin letter to Douglas D. Paige, 16 August 1968, New Directions archive, Norfolk.

13. "Fragment from Canto 115," *Threshold* 17 ([spring? 1962]): 20. The *Anonym* version, entitled "Canto 120," is authored by "The Fox," *Anonym* 4 ([summer?] 1969): 1, and reprinted in the *New York Times*, 26 November 1972, 42.

14. See Charles Norman, *Ezra Pound: A Biography* (London: Macdonald, 1969), 465.

15. Laughlin has no record of when or how he first saw a Canto 120, and the decision to resituate it in the "Notes for CXVII et seq." fragments for the 1986 *Cantos* was based on "what seemed appropriate" at the time. James Laughlin, letter to the author, 30 January 1989.

16. Peter du Sautoy, chairman of Faber and Faber at the time, declined to print the poem in their 1975 edition of *The Cantos*, writing in the *Times Literary Supplement* in 1976 that "the new edition of *The Cantos* which we have recently published consists of sheets of the American edition . . . published by New Directions. There is one small difference: the sheets we have used do not contain the 'Canto 120' that appears in the New Directions edition as we did not feel certain that these lines were what Pound intended to come at the end of his long poem. We hope that it is a convenience to scholars that apart from this minor difference the two texts are now identical.

   As for Cantos 72 and 73, we shall include them if and when they are offered to us by Pound's literary trustees." *Times Literary Supplement*, 20 August 1976, 1032.

17. See Christine Froula, *To Write Paradise: Style and Error in Pound's Cantos* (New Haven: Yale University Press, 1984), 175 for her research on the copyright attributed to "Canto 120."

18. These six are the 1967 pirated edition, the 1968 New Directions edition (identical to the 1969 limited edition printed by Stone Wall Press), and the 1970, 1972, 1986, and 1989 editions in the New Directions *Cantos*.

19. Jerome J. McGann, *The Beauty of Inflections: Literary Investigations in Historical Method and Theory* (Oxford: Clarendon Press, 1985), 85.

20. See Barbara Eastman, *Ezra Pound's Cantos: The Story of the Text, 1948–1975* (Orono, Maine: National Poetry Foundation, 1979), 129–41 for a detailed account of these changes.

21. Hall had sent a copy of the poems he received from Pound to Laughlin in June 1960, and Laughlin wrote to Pound saying that "there is some really marvellous stuff in this new material" (James Laughlin, letter to Ezra Pound,

9 June 1960, New Directions archive, Norfolk). In 1965, after directing the magazine publication of some of the material, Laughlin suggested the idea of a post-*Thrones* volume to Pound, but Pound's response was merely conciliatory: "I will try to look into the question of draft of cantos. I haven't much here. Please let me have a list of what has been printed where, as far as you can" (Ezra Pound, letter to James Laughlin, 12 February [1965?], New Directions archive, Norfolk).

22. Barbara Eastman's *Ezra Pound's Cantos* was the first study to concentrate on the provisionality of the text's state. Froula extends the findings through an intensive examination of Canto 4, and writes that the "editorial difficulties have to do not only with the technical problems posed by the poem's highly complex textual history but, more important, with a perhaps unprecedented divergence between the author's intentions regarding his text and those which the policies of his editors have tended to project upon it" (*To Write Paradise*, 6). "Monolithic authority" is her term.

23. Michael André Bernstein, *The Tale of the Tribe: Ezra Pound and the Modern Verse Epic* (Princeton: Princeton University Press, 1980), 125.

24. Bacigalupo, *The Forméd Trace*, 489

25. Leon Surette, *A Light from Eleusis: A Study of Ezra Pound's Cantos* (London: Oxford University Press), 260.

26. James J. Wilhelm, *The Later Cantos of Ezra Pound* (New York: Walker and Co., 1977), 168.

27. Bernstein, *Tale of the Tribe*, 124.

28. In Sophocles' *Trachiniae*, Herakles realizes the ironic truth of the Dodonian oracle while he is in mortal agony; he had interpreted it earlier as a prediction not of his death but of a comfortable old age. Pound, in a footnote to his translation, calls this the "key phrase" of the play:

> Time lives and it's going on now.
> I am released from trouble.
> I thought it meant life in comfort.
> It doesn't. It means I die.
> For amid the dead there is no work in service.
> Come at it that way, my boy, what
> SPLENDOUR,
> IT ALL COHERES.

Ezra Pound, trans., *Women of Trachis* (New York: New Directions, 1957), 49–50. In Canto 17: "Splendour, as the splendour of Hermes."

29. Michael Reck, "A Conversation between Ezra Pound and Allen Ginsberg," *Evergreen Review* 55 (June 1968): 29. That poor health, political exile, and emotional suffering complicated Pound's writing of paradise and assisted *The Cantos'* termination is an inescapable fact. Yet if they elucidate local passages of *Drafts & Fragments,* they also write Pound into a Dantescan narrative of exile caused by public and political misinterpretation, a narrative that hinted

that the poem's failing close was a consequence of external, not intrinsic, conditions and permitted him on the occasion of the Hall interview to cast himself in the heroic capacity of "the last American living the tragedy of Europe."

30. Ezra Pound, letter to James Laughlin, 24 November 1959, New Directions archive, Norfolk.
31. Quoted in Harry Meacham, *The Caged Panther* (New York: Twayne, 1967), 141.
32. From an unpublished letter, 5 December 1958, in the Norman Holmes Pearson Papers, Beinecke Library.
33. For a very thorough investigation of the roots of Pound's anti-Semitism and fascism, which suggests that they were inherited attitudes later to dismay him, see Wendy Stallard Flory, *The American Ezra Pound* (New Haven: Yale University Press, 1989), particularly chap. 6.
34. Jerome J. McGann, "Keats and the Historical Method in Literary Criticism," *MLN* 94 (1979): 993.
35. Balachandra Rajan, *The Form of the Unfinished: English Poetics from Spenser to Pound* (Princeton: Princeton University Press, 1985), 295.

Prospects

9

The History and State of the Texts

Richard Taylor

Whereas an earlier essay emphasized the interplay of personalities and often conflicting values or goals that affected the text of *The Cantos,* not much attention was given to a systematic or chronological review that would account for the many variant readings that have come into existence, nor to the ways in which particular texts actually evolved. In coming to terms with the state of the present texts, it is important to review the historical process and to concentrate on major problem areas, even at the risk of returning to some of the points made earlier, although using different approaches and documentation.

Our general understanding of textual criticism, its aims and procedures, has changed rather dramatically over the past twenty years or so, and it is no longer possible to consider the texts of *The Cantos,* or of any other major modernist work, without first rehearsing, at least in outline form, relevant perspectives. We no longer think of authors as being isolated or unified individuals, constant in their values and decisions, but rather as being in every-day interaction with other sensibilities, events, and literary tradition. The two possible models for creative writing still hold good, however, and choosing between them in the case of *The Cantos* is fundamental to any further step in the direction of textual criticism. The first contends that the most important moment in the creative process is the initial flash of inspiration and that subsequent rewriting, the working out of an idea into final form, compromises the tension that gave birth to the work by moving further and further away from it, perhaps even censoring or repressing it. The other model holds that the original conception is little more than a rough sketch that must be elaborated upon, filled out, even reshaped in a more clear-headed, craftsmanlike way, perhaps even by persons other than the originator. In both cases attention is focused on the process, the development and transmission of the text, rather than the end product or work that either first or finally finds its way into print.

The process of publication is always one of socialization, and any number of outside influences directly affect the text as originally submitted. The degree to which this happens in *The Cantos* over time has a very important bearing on our perception of the work. As they either develop or decline, authors also change their worldview as well as their aesthetic values, and there is also the possibility of unauthorized publication, either pirated by unscrupulous editors or sanctioned by advisers and copyright holders. Works or versions that an author wished to suppress might even be republished, or drafts that had been rejected and abandoned in the course of writing (not to mention work in progress that in the author's judgment was not yet ready for publication), do find their way into print.

In the absence of a retrospective edition prepared by the author, or in cases where either the creative power or health of an author is in decline, scholarly editors might then choose what they believe to be an "authoritative" version as copy text for a critical edition and then free the work from unauthorized alteration as well as accidental error. The greatest problem, of course, is in determining "final intentions," not to mention unraveling the social interaction of actual book production and making decisions based on literary interpretations where necessary. Critical editions of this type tend to eclecticism, and they rely on the literary taste of the editor who is free to choose readings from differing versions, conflating them into a new whole, a text in which every word had actually been written by the author at one time or another, but had never appeared together in that particular combination or form. In this case the role of the editor is to recover the "work," a hypothetical entity to which all known versions contribute.

> In this sense, the work may be the form traditionally imputed to an archetype; it may be a form seen as immanent in each of the versions but not fully realized in any one of them; or it may be conceived of as always potential, like that of a play, where the text is open and generates new meanings according to new needs in a perpetual deferral of closure.[1]

The current view is that texts are inherently incomplete: open, unstable, and subject to endless remaking. The question inevitably arises as to whether the text exists at all apart from the reader's creative act of interpretation, and editors now entertain renewed respect for the historicity of each individual version.

> In *Scholarly Editing in the Computer Age* [Peter Shillingsburg] sketches four main orientations towards literary forms: historical, which emphasizes the accurate presentation of documents as they existed historically or might ideally have existed; aesthetic, which relies finally on the editor's taste; authorial, which emphasizes authorial versions of a text over nonauthorial ones; and sociological, which emphasizes the social nature of text production and does not grant complete authority to the author alone.[2]

The orientations listed are undoubtedly important, but the exact weight and balance given them in any particular case depends very much on knowing something about the nature of the text at hand, and, more particularly, the course of its development and transmission. *The Cantos,* for example, are necessarily subject to indeterminacy and instability both because of the great size and complexity of the surviving body of textual witnesses and the checkered history of attempts to revise and correct the text, as well as vexing questions of nonauthorial interventions which have arisen over the years. Not only are they fragmentary in style, but they also contain innumerable quotations from both reliable and unreliable sources, as well as references to a great many historical persons and events. Pound himself was not always interested in factual accuracy nor in consistency of presentation, and the process of creation extends from at least 1915 to 1968. Many of the cantos were published in periodicals before being gathered into separate volumes, and it hardly matters here which of those publications were limited deluxe editions. One should note, however, that *Cantos LXXII & LXXIII* as published in book form has no relevance to dates of composition or first printing (1945). The following outline provides a scheme of major gatherings into individual volume form, but does not account for the occasional change of title:

A Draft of XVI Cantos (Paris, 1925)
A Draft of the Cantos 17–27 (London, 1928)
A Draft of XXX Cantos (Paris 1930; New York, 1933, 1940; London, 1933)
Eleven New Cantos, XXXI–XLI (New York, 1934; London, 1935)

The Fifth Decad of Cantos (London, 1937; New York, 1937)
Cantos LII–LXXI (London, 1940; New York, 1940)
The Pisan Cantos (New York, 1948; London, 1949)
Section: Rock-Drill (Milano, 1955; New York, 1956; London, 1957)
Thrones (Milano, 1959; New York, 1959; London, 1960)
Drafts & Fragments (Iowa City, 1968; New York, 1969; London, 1970)
Cantos LXXII & LXXIII (Washington, DC, and Toronto, 1973; Milano, 1983)

Collected vs. Variorum Editions

As early as 5 August 1939, Pound had suggested that Faber and Faber might bring out a collection of cantos to be entitled either "Septuagint" or "Seventy One,"[3] but the war intervened, and then there was the sensation of the treason trial followed by the uproar over the Bollinger Prize for the *Pisan Cantos*. Pound reminded T. S. Eliot that he had made the same suggestion in 1935 when *A Draft of Cantos XXXI–XLI* was in press: "If no plates of XXX exist/ I probably shd/ consider revisions in that part/ IF plates exist, the revisions can wait till 1950 or whenever D/v. etc."[4] Eliot acknowledged Pound's proposal of a collected edition on 19 October 1945 when considering the publication of cantos written at Pisa.[5] The overview of subsequent publication history which follows distinguishes between volumes of *The Cantos* in which the text was either altered significantly or enlarged, and reprintings of an already established text. The New York editions were published by New Directions and the London volumes by Faber and Faber. The contents of each is given by canto number in Arabic numerals within parentheses.

New Directions	Faber and Faber
1948 (1–71, 74–84), rpt. 1951 [2 states], 1956, 1958 [with errata sheet], 1960, 1964	1950 (1–71) [pages numbered consecutively]
	1954 (1–71, 74–84) [with errata sheet], rpt. 1957
1965 (85–95 added), rpt. 1966	
1970 (96–117 added), rpt. 1971 [titles romanized, pages numbered consecutively]	1964 (85–109 added), rpt. 1968

1972 (120 added), rpt. 1973, 1975,   1975 [1976] (120 excluded)
  1977, 1979, 1981, 1983   [ND sheets]

1986 (120 untitled and included   1981 (120 included) [ND sheets]
  in 117; 72, 73 and Fragment
  1966 added at end)

1989 (72 and 73 in numerical   1989 [ND sheets]
  order, full repagination)

Since corrections were entered silently at various stages and by various hands, ranging from one or two changes to one hundred and thirty-eight in the New Directions edition of 1970, for example,[6] it cannot yet be assumed that texts listed as reprints of a given edition are identical to that of the first publication or, for that matter, to any other text in the same series. The situation has been rendered even more complex by the fact that two very different versions of the poem were in circulation from 1950 to 1975; at which point, and for purely economic reasons, Faber and Faber decided to take unbound sheets from New Directions and abandoned their own edition.

The differences between the American and British versions are easily explained and there is a good deal more to the story than the imposition of a publisher's house style or rigor of copy editing. Publishing schedules at New Directions were usually under great pressure because it was difficult to estimate future sales with any accuracy, and printings were very often rushed affairs. In the 1950s and 1960s print-runs were also kept to a minimum because it was believed that a "definitive" edition would soon be to hand.

British sales were not so extensive, but they were much steadier, and prior planning was possible. London also had the advantage of printing the first collected edition (1950) by the offset method (photoreproduction), which allowed immediate changes to be made by stripping in the new word(s) or line(s) and photographing the corrected page, not to mention the introduction of consecutive page numbers. New Directions was still using the original metal plates that could not be easily altered. More important, however, Faber and Faber were nearly two years behind in getting out a collected edition, one that contained only the first seventy-one cantos. It wasn't until 1954 that the *Pisan Cantos,* which was selling slowly although steadily, could be included. The time lag gave Pound ample opportunity to reread his text, correct, rethink, and revise. With the demise of the Faber edition we have lost important aspects of the histori-cal text, and this should make us aware of how important it is to read *The Cantos* in a wider perspective, to engage in a radical reading that does not adhere to the linearity and specificity of a particular document, but includes the multiplicity of variant readings over longer periods of time. Fortunately, readers now respond to the different discursive acts of various texts and especially to their more hidden implications. However private the discourse, the text is not so much a "material thing" as it is an event or set of events in which certain communicative interchanges are experi-enced.[7]

A variorum edition, rather than a reading text, is the ideal vehicle for a serious reader of *The Cantos;* an edition based on the present collected edition and including all variant readings, line by line, from setting copy for the first (possibly periodical) publication of each canto to the latest printing. Such a compendium is being prepared, using the 1975 New Directions publication as a base text, but completion of the project is still some years away. No privilege will be given to any particular reading, and the authenticity of variants will be documented by quotations from letters between author, literary agents, lawyers, publishers, editors, printers, friends, and family.

Ultimately all texts are collaborative events, but some authors par-ticipate more willingly than others in the process. A text may well evolve in ways that the author could not have foreseen, let alone "intended." One must distinguish between what might be considered a single, inte-gral work (the 1975 New Directions edition, for example) and an extended series of historical documents presenting very different ver-sions, for the most part authorized by the poet although authority and sometimes even authorization might have been shared among a larger number of people.

Selected Poems

The publication history of those cantos that were printed in selected edi-tions, either in New York or London, offers yet another striking example in the process of socialization undergone by modernist texts. More read-ers make their acquaintance with Pound's cantos via selections than via a complete text. The following outline gives an overview of major editions and reprintings.

New Directions	Faber and Faber
	A Selection of Poems (1, 2, and 45), 1940, rpt. 1942, 1945, 1946, 1950.
Selected Poems (from 1–84), 1949, rpt. 1950.	

—— (from 1–94), 1957; rpt.
  1959, 1960, 1962, 1963,
  1965, 1966, 1967, 1968,
  1969, 1970, 1972, 1974,
  1976, 1977, 1979, 1980,
  1983, 1985, 1986.
	Selected Poems (from 1–94), 1975.
	  —— (from 1–117), 1977.

Selected Cantos (from 1–117),
  1970; rpt. 1971, 1972,
  1973, 1975, 1977, 1979,
  1981, 1983, 1986.
	Selected Cantos (from 1–109)
	  1967; rpt. 1969, 1974.
	  —— (from 1–109) 1987 [type reset].

From an unpublished letter written by T. S. Eliot to Ann Ridler it is obvious that neither he nor Pound was wholly responsible for *A Selection of Poems*. "Thank you very much for your Ezra Pound selection in which seems to me very satisfactory and has saved me a great deal of trouble. I have made a few alterations . . . Finally I have added *Cantos 1* and *45* which Pound said he wanted and *Canto 2* to please myself."[8]

In the same way the choice of material to be included in the New Directions edition of *Selected Poems* was very much a collaborative affair. Laughlin wanted to offer the public good poetry at a bargain price ($1.00), and the selection was made by the American poet John Berryman. Pound was not particularly happy with the result and protested more than once about the length and arbitrariness of excerpts from the *Pisan Cantos*. He advocated using a sixteen, rather than a thirty-two pages sheet, and reducing the selections accordingly.

Of course to make half the book Cantos. is flagrant violation of the agreement: and E.P. is not in the least pleased by that fact. It also, etc. wd/ be improved by cutting at least three galleys from the Pisan lot. But not if it means delay. NO the hash made of Pisans is too filthy to

pass. I acceded to request to put in a FEW bits of cantos/ you have
the thing HALF cantos/ BUT the PISAN chunk is just a mess of
snippets/ and CANNOT stand as is. Better omit the whole of it. at
any rate it is not in scale with the rest. and to print it with invisible
dots for breaks is LOW. I haven't energy to do selecting. but the
ONLY possible alternative to TOTAL and preferable omission is to
put in one or two coherent bits. Not a lot of breaks in the sense.[9]

On 28 March 1949 Laughlin responded

Many thanks for fixing up the proofs of the SELECTED volume, and
your comments have been suitably digested. Let me explain how it
came about that so much CANTOS material was included in the
selection. We had originally planned that the CANTOS would only
occupy 20% or 25% of the book at the most, and Berryman was aware
of that. However, as he got into the selection, he told me that he kept
finding passages that were so marvelous that he simply couldn't leave
them out. Thus by the time the selection reached me, it was almost
30% CANTOS already. But when I looked through it myself, I noted
that he had given no representation at all to certain very important
themes, such as the Italian, the Chinese and the Old Yankee. So I felt
that suitable chunks of these epochs had to be added to give a
rounded picture. Then when I looked over what he had chosen from
the Pisan Cantos, I found that it was nothing but a tiny little collec-
tion of snippets. If you think it is snippity now, you ought to have
seen what it was like when Berryman turned it in. In many instances
he had picked out single lines from here or there or little short para-
graphs that had no connection with nothing at all. These were, it is
true, very beautiful lines, but by themselves they were awfully lonely.
I then set about trying to give them some fat on the sides of their
bones, with the results that you have seen. I agree with you that the
volume, as it now stands, is overweighted with CANTOS, and I have
asked the printer to give me a page count of how the thing is going
to form up when he pages it, and after I have this, I will see what can
be done about cutting down the representation for the CANTOS.[10]

Pound later objected to at least one passage, which was omitted, but
approved the inclusion of China and Adams material and found the
strength to correct page proofs. The volume was reprinted in 1950, and

soon after, preparations were under way for a serious revision. Most of the work was done by Hugh Kenner, who not only culled misprints but also made suggestions as to rectifying what he considered to be unfortunate cuts.[11] Not all of the suggestions he outlined in a letter to Robert Mac-Gregor of New Directions (15 January 1957) were actually carried out, however:

> What you should include from ROCKDRILL is 91 down to the bottom of page 73: "So hath Sibile a broken isette." Much more immediate appeal than 92. After all you're not committed to a whole canto. Second choice, 93, beginning near top of p. 88 ("The autumn leaves blow from my hand") to end of page 92. Third choice. 90 intact; and 92 would be my fourth choice. If it were a case of leaving out, I'd leave out XV–XVI, pages 118–123 of Selected Poems, on ground that componants there exhibited were represented elsewhere.[12]

MacGregor wrote to Pound on 21 January 1957:

> We would also like your permission to include some short passages from SECTION: ROCKDRILL. We suggest Canto 91, from the beginning down to the bottom of page 73: "So hath Sibele a broken isette." If we have room we would like also to include from Canto 93, beginning near the top of page 88 with, "The autumn leaves blow over my hand," to the end of page 92.[13]

Hayden Carruth, a free-lance author and editor who was also working on the volume, participated in the decisions, but the final compromise was largely determined by practical factors, as MacGregor informed Kenner on 20 March 1957: "it turned out that we couldn't add pages to the book without making it another kind of a project and much more expensive. . . . We took slightly different parts from SECTION: ROCKDRILL than you first suggested, mainly because they would fit as far as space was concerned."[14] In the end, Cantos 15 and 16 were omitted and selections from Canots 74, 76, and 80 altered, while passages from Cantos 91 and 92 were added, and an acknowledgment to both Kenner and Carruth was included on the back of the title page. Later, when the edition was taken over by Faber and Faber (1975), the shape of selections from *The Cantos* underwent still further changes. The London edition of 1977 was extended by including selections from Cantos 98, 107, 110, and 116 and all of Canto 115 from *Drafts & Fragments* (1969), but the changes followed New Directions' policy in their edition of *Selected Cantos.*

Selected Cantos

The history of *Selected Cantos* is even more problematical than that of *Selected Poems* in that there was a marked difference between the two editions from the very beginning. The story opens in a visit to Pound made by J. Laughlin and reported to Eva Hesse in a letter of 14 September 1964. Peter du Sautoy of Faber and Faber was also convinced of the need for a new selection from the whole poem (1–109) to be made by the author himself. A marked-up copy of the Faber edition indicating the poet's choices and including a few minor corrections reached London in 1965 and was published two years later exactly as outlined by the author. In 1970 New Directions brought out its own edition which was based on Pound's list of selections to be included, a list that was identical with that supplied to Faber and Faber. No authorial corrections were stipulated, however, as New Directions intended to set up type from their own collected edition which already differed in a great many individual readings from the London text. Faber, of course, was using offset methods of reproduction and so could include corrections while avoiding the introduction of typographical error. Twenty-eight lines from Canto 16 (19–46) were inadvertently omitted from the first New York edition and they were not reinstated until the fourth reprinting in 1975. The text of the American edition differed in other significant ways from that of Faber and Faber, not merely because of the many variations in wording, punctuation, and so on.

Because of the compressed setting, a few extra pages were available to New Directions, and Pound's selection was extended by the addition of the final seventy-eight lines of Canto 52, which was originally represented by lines fifty through seventy-nine. The first hundred and seven lines of Canto 83 were also added although that canto had not been included by the author, nor had Cantos 115 and 116, which were also printed. These last two cantos had not yet been authorized for publication when Pound made the selection in 1965, although he undoubtedly endorsed the later publication as well as actively participated in the project. *Drafts & Fragments of Cantos CX–CXVII* (1969), however, came into being in order to protect copyright.

In 1967 a pirated version of work in progress had been mimeographed and stapled together in New York City; a number of copies were actually sold before the "edition" was suppressed, but the intervention of outside legal and economic factors played as great a role in the history of publication at this point as did the commercial and aesthetic judgment of publishers and editors. By 1970, however, Pound was so withdrawn and indifferent to the world of affairs that New Directions acted unilaterally with regard to the contents of the *Selected Cantos*. On 10 April 1970 Laughlin wrote to Hesse, who had long been much involved, along with others, in gathering possible corrections for a "corrected" edition of *Cantos:*

> I also enclose a copy of the little publisher's Note which I have writ-ten to explain our additions to the Faber text of "Selected Cantos." I did not think it was honest not to mention our additions in some way. But, as you requested, I have not mentioned you by name as the source of them. Nor have I referred to the fact that we have made cer-tain corrections to the Faber text, I think that is just too complicated to explain, and few people except the experts will notice it.[15]

Once again, however, practical considerations forced a change in their earlier decision. On 14 July 1970 Laughlin wrote:

> In paging up the "repros" for the "Selected Cantos," from Marder-steig's handsome composition I discovered that I had "goofed" in my calculations, and we were a page long. Accordingly, the best thing to do seemed to be to eliminate the "Cthonian" passage which you had added from Canto 82. I'm sorry about this, as I thought it was an excellent suggestion, but it proved to be the easiest out to make, both for length, and coming late in the book, so that there were fewer folios to repaste.[16]

As we can see from Laughlin's reply to du Sautoy, Faber and Faber were not altogether pleased by editorial interference with the original text, but they obviously did use the precedent as rationale for extending their 1977 edition of *Selected Poems* to include even more material from *Drafts & Fragments*.

> I think you are quite right to chide me a little for having made addi-tions to Ezra's basic selection for our "Selected Cantos," I may have

overstepped the proper licence of a publisher. But I felt there were good reasons for doing so, at least as far as we were concerned. First of all, there are such lovely bits in the "Drafts and Fragments," and, on top of that, with our new Mardersteig composition for the book, we had a few blank pages, but I just couldn't see leaving them blank. So far I have had no "blast" from Ezra for doing what I did, since I put in the little note in the front of the book explaining exactly what I added to his basic selection.[17]

However well-intentioned, the addition of two hundred and eighty lines does change both the shape and tenor of the work, and the result can hardly be acknowledged as the author's original intention. We cannot know whether he might have agreed to the additions as he hadn't the opportunity to make the decision. Indeed, that particular text underwent changes that he could not have imagined, and we are again forcibly reminded that the particular document we have in hand does make a great difference in our apprehension of and response to the poem.

Even though the London *Selected Cantos* is obviously preferable to the New York edition, both are more faithful to the author's reading of the epic than the choices made by Berryman (as modified by Laughlin, Pound, Kenner, and Carruth) for *Selected Poems*. In any case none of the selected editions contains texts that fall within a direct line of descent for any particular canto, nor do they always carry the authority of collected editions that continued to evolve and change. In order to prove the point, and before going on to consider efforts to "correct" the text in greater detail, it might be helpful to give a stemma of development for Canto 1. One must always bear in mind that a number of corrections, emendations, and errors were introduced into various texts of the selected editions that had little or no effect on subsequent reprintings of collected editions.

Ur-I (originally entitled **III**)

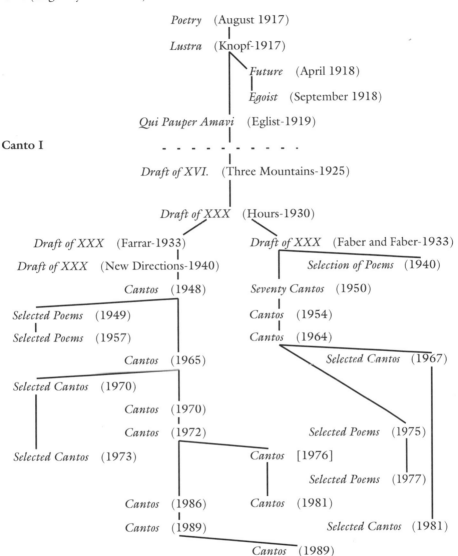

Poetry   (August 1917)

Lustra   (Knopf-1917)

Future   (April 1918)

Egoist   (September 1918)

Qui Pauper Amavi   (Eglist-1919)

Canto I

Draft of XVI.   (Three Mountains-1925)

Draft of XXX   (Hours-1930)

Draft of XXX   (Farrar-1933)   Draft of XXX   (Faber and Faber-1933)

Draft of XXX   (New Directions-1940)   Selection of Poems   (1940)

Cantos   (1948)   Seventy Cantos   (1950)

Selected Poems   (1949)   Cantos   (1954)

Selected Poems   (1957)   Cantos   (1964)

Cantos   (1965)   Selected Cantos   (1967)

Selected Cantos   (1970)

Cantos   (1970)

Cantos   (1972)   Selected Poems   (1975)

Selected Cantos   (1973)   Cantos   [1976]

Selected Poems   (1977)

Cantos   (1986)   Cantos   (1981)

Cantos   (1989)   Selected Cantos   (1981)

Cantos   (1989)

Corrections and Emendations

Probably the most operative event in the publishing history of *The Cantos* is the ongoing effort to accommodate revisions and corrections. The story begins with Faber's decision to publish a collected edition and to reset the text. On 11 May 1949 Laurence Pollinger, Pound's literary agent in London, wrote to Dorothy Pound: "About three weeks ago Faber wrote that they would like to publish a collected edition of Ezra's CANTOS up to but excluding PISAN CANTOS. . . . They have no standing type of the CANTOS so this is really a new book."[18] Pound wrote in the margin: "O.K. as new set up let us correct errors." By 11 June the collected cantos were ready for the press and on the sixteenth Pollinger reported to Dorothy Pound: "The corrected copy of SEVENTY CANTOS is just here and is being handed to Eliot."[19] Production difficulties ensued which seriously delayed publication, and a number of people suggested further emendations, notably John Drummond (friend and translator) and Peter Russell (poet and critic). Realizing that extensive revision would be an expensive proposition, the production department at Faber and Faber advocated limiting the number and incorporating them in an errata sheet. Pound, on the other hand, began to worry that unimportant refinements would further delay publication as they had in 1946 when Dorothy Pound wrote to Laughlin (31 July): "yesterday E. said to photograph his pencilled-in ideograms if it would hurry up the printers of the last cantos—it would at least add an interest anyway."[20] A good many changes were made in that Faber edition, including the addition of Chinese ideograms in blank spaces at the end of several cantos. Laughlin was equally interested in correcting the New York edition, and Pound wrote to him in July 1950:

> Yes send on the "battered copy", I will keep corrections down to one or two main points, and as many outrages to the greek as I can spot or remember. and add the DAWG ideogram, and one other correct. Can yu foto them from the debased Faber edtn/ of Pisans? . . . There were also EIGHT large and handsome ids/ to fill in spaces at end of the 52/61 Chinkese cantos BEEyewteefully done and soup-lied to Faber fer their new ed/ wot they keep DEElaying. . . . . the new ids/ EmPHAsise the main points of the doctrine an Jas/ MaZwell Embellish with 'em[.] The other change is in p/ 15 yr/ edtn/ Canto IV. taking the Catullus back to HarryStopHerKnees [Aristophanes],

whaar Cat[ullus]/ mebbe got it, anyhow the greek shows the real way Cat/ wd/ hv/ tookd it fer graunted the Epithalamium wd/ be sung. Recon the choon stayed thaaar right down into the middle ages.[21]

The corrections were set up in type, at least those that could be stripped in, and Pound saw proof sheets, but somehow they were misplaced in the print shop. He wrote to Laughlin in February 1951:

> Yes. but yr GOS DAMND printer has NOT included the corrections/ or at least the one important one on p/ 15 [IV: 86–87]. Had been holding off on yr/ specialist in SAMPLE pages and thought restraint rewarded, AS new Cantos seem to be on rather better paper and better ink/ BUT the omission of p/ 15 emend AFTER all the proofs yu had sent/ gives yu good grounds for murdering the damn printer. also only one of the tail piece idiograms has been putt in [LII: 158]. at least yu can make the BUGGAR print an erata slip at his own dirty expense. in civilized conditions yu cd/ throw the whole edtn back on him. what the HELL if all the plates had been corrected as they must hv/ been to make the proofs?>?>?[22]

Pound was also anxious that the notes for Cantos 52–71, which had been misplaced in Faber's first collected edition, should precede the section in forthcoming reprints, but type was never reset. He did agree, however, to prepare an errata sheet for the 1954 printing. Other hands were also at work, and David Bland, Production Manager of Faber and Faber, wrote to Russell on 21 January 1954:

> Thank you very much indeed for your help in this matter and for identifying "Wemyss". We had suspected that there might be many other mistakes, and in fact we are altering the transposed pages which you mention. Pound himself has supplied a short list of errata, but this does not include either of the two major corrections which you mention. I think it might be a good plan to add these to the slip, but I suppose we ought to refer the matter to Pound himself before doing this.[23]

Pound was not only interested in revising the text, but also in providing a useful and scholarly apparatus. On 14 July [1954] he wrote to Norman Holmes Pearson, who was coordinating corrections to the text, and he included an oft-repeated *cri de coeur:*

Of course if some frosh/ wanted to be USEFUL, he cd/ make an INDEX of proper names (and even subjects) in the Cantos. save gramp/ making memos on back leaf. Question of what edition/ Fabers new 84 has some corrections/ and a eroter list/ (emended by office punk, to take life out of it. But it is such a lousy firm, they prob/ wdn't add the index, so better stick to Nude Erections (chordee rather) paging. Faber STILL got the rays ideogram, and notes on China Adams section in wrong place/ despite request.[24]

It would be futile to contend that one or the other of the collected editions was superior. Each had its own advantages as well as failings. The independent Faber text has unfortunately been discontinued, however, and its authoritative readings are not represented in the present version. Over the years much has been made of the general superiority of the London editions, but when preparing the *Selected Cantos* in 1965, Pound wrote to Laughlin (1 September), "For your information more misprints in Faber, than in N.D."[25] As late as 21 December 1971 Laughlin shared some of his doubts with Kenner:

> As you say, Faber did go pretty far in changing things in their resetting of the later sections. I'm glad that we made the decision to photograph the Mardersteig settings, which presumably followed Ezra's own instructions, even though the type doesn't exactly match. But I still feel that in these pages there are certain words or phrases which are "runovers," that is, dropped below the line where they belong at the right side, rather than meaningful placements in terms of a visual pattern.[26]

A considered judgment on such issues awaits careful collation of published versions with the actual setting copy, not to mention proof sheets and correspondence with publishers, editors, printers, and so on.

Yet another question that arises when considering the authority and "correctness" of the text has to do with stylistic uniformity and the accuracy of quotations and historical detail. Throughout his working life Pound's approach to the problem was fairly consistent. Laughlin, for example, wrote the following to Achilles Fang, on 19 July 1950:

> Very tactfully I enquired of Ezra whether he would like to have you suggest certain changes for the new printing of the Cantos, with

respect to the spelling and date errors in the Chinese Cantos. Here is his response, which I quote to you verbatim: "No need to correct chinese Cantos—they are not philology, all the funny spellings indicate tradition, how the snooz got to your-up [;] some latin, some by Portergoose, some by frog . . . when it comes to tradition—yes, thank Fang for any precisions, but, there is also another point, even where diagrames (romanj) fer Ez himself to study, and work on theory that changes of dialect, etc.—do not affect melodic coherence—this not dogma, it is conjecture."[27]

A few years later [spring 1953 or 1954] Pound mentioned the subject to Laughlin again: "Fang ain't to make changes in TEXT, but if he deigns, he can supply a lot of pretty IDEOgrams fer the margin. . . . all for the disTANT future, not fer the present emission."[28] Writing to his son-in-law, Boris de Rachewiltz, on 16 August [1954], he reiterates the point: "I do not think Spelling of chinese names of ANY importance/ No spelling will ever content everyone/ so shd/ leave 'em as in orig/ wop edtns/."[29]

The poet's preoccupation with page design, typography, and uniformity are reflected in his correspondence with Vanni Scheiwiller who published first editions of both *Section: Rock-Drill* and *Thrones* in Milan. On 25 November 1954 Pound wrote:

Cantos 90–95, the difference in spacing between the lines has an importance for placing of the text on the page perhaps TWICE that which is the only possiblity on a typewriter/ ought to be reduced to 1 1/2. NOT as here, twice that. Hudson exaggerated in the first proofs of 85. I think that the Arabic numbers 85 without *CANTO* 85 would be preferable to the Roman numerals LXXXV/ when one reaches LXXXVIII/ too much. but I leave it to Mardersteig . . . in every case I want to see proofs in final form, or nearly final/ . . . For clarity I have written the Greek quotations very big/ they needn't be so large when printed/ font size as used by Faber in 84 Cantos. don't be upset that Leocothoe is written in two ways/ Leucothoe. It's OK. Kádmon's daughter, all the same. I amuse myself with the BIG Greek dictionary the accents occur in so many different ways that not even a fusspot would dare pontificate about the choice. . . . 90/5 musicality etc/ indicated by typography. therefore disposition of verses etc. more complicated . . . whether the 88 should be centered or on right/? etc/ how would a great printer manage it, let's hear HIS opinion/ . . . Later/ because of the large ideogram LING, Canto 85 and the Egyptian verse/ I think that the numbers would be better at the left than in the middle.[30]

Apart from the fanciful spelling and grammar of Pound's Italian, it is interesting to note how impervious he was to questions of formality and accuracy as well as how ready he was to leave certain decisions for others to make. A letter to Scheiwiller dated 21 June 1955 confirms the point with even greater emphasis:

> Proofs arrived/ many thanks for assiduous care/ especially where you have found errors. but in some places QUOTATIONS are not gram-matical exercises. Donna che VOLGO (quoted from a Canzoni). later "Tolg*o*"/. "Volge" falsifies/ other points of minor importance the latin words should keep their relationship with an absent context/. Canz/ dell fortuna/ Io son la donna che VOLGO. Fixed spelling belongs to certain periods not to others. Certain cases are not worth changing type already set. etc. But very many thanks for the correc-tion of errors, Hudson, for example, was on the verge of spoiling a line by abandoning the dialect of the original. I hope they will keep my corrections. and not insist on dictionary spelling. . . . Where I have nothing against it, I have left your emendations or corrections. Thanking you, Variation Leocothoe, Leucothea/ done intentionally. do as you like/ but as far as I'm concerned it is not worth bothering Mardersteig in order to make Riccardus and Richardus uniform, etc. because in the Middle Ages such uniformity was NOT observed. The concepts of the poets from early centuries are a bit falsified when the texts are Renaissanced etc.. But I am not fanatical in asking for this diversity in each case. do as YOU like, except in cases where I have inked in preferences.[31]

Fortunately, almost every decision and alteration in the text can and will be documented objectively by existing evidence, as well as revisions of prior decisions such as can be seen in Laughlin's letter to Hesse of 9 May 1966:

> Our latest printing of the "Cantos" still has the Arabic numerals for 85 to 95, but this is only because this is a temporary printing, in which we are offsetting from "Rock Drill," and I know that Ezra

wants them to be Roman numerals throughout, because he told me so the last time I saw him. We will get them all that way eventually when we make a proper revision and resetting of the text.[32]

Pound not only changed his mind from time to time about page design and typography, not to mention variant readings, but he often revised quotations to fit in with his metrical scheme. Kenner reported to Laughlin in a letter of 27 October 1955: "When I asked Ez in May 1950 why he used the spelling 'brododaktulos' he said he could not recall any reason except that it sounded better."[33] In the same way the preparation of each new publication encouraged revision as he confirmed in a letter of 23 April [1955] to Ingrid Davies: "One ALWAYS improves ANYthing if forced to retype. Gtly annoyed at NOT having spare carbon of Cantos 88/9. BUT did improve paragraphing when forced to prepare same for Hud/"[34] He wrote again on 7 November:

Literary item, Canto 96 sweated into let us hope correct form and transmitted. Must have added 46 or thereabouts commas, faked two gk. accents, no longer having text of whatever they were quoted from/ and the suffering reader may console herself with the thought that the blasted author will HAVE to look up some of the gk/ himself in future, BUT then it is all stuff he wd/ like to look up if there is *NO* other way of recalling wot the HELL it refers to.[35]

Although he was well aware of his own deficiencies ("I am the WORST proof-reader natr/ ever let liv. so loathe the physical action of reading I do NOT see anything if I know it is supposed to be there."[36]), he did want a "Definitive Cantares" reset by Mardersteig, although he left the actual work to others. For example, he wrote the following to Pearson (24 January 1957): "What wd/ be useful is an index saying what canto and what line something appears in. . . . Of course a good text, lines numbered by 10/s/ with Fang's proper chinese names in margin/ that I wd/ look at."[37] Unfortunately, a reset and thoroughly revised edition was never published, but the corrected text brought out by New Directions in 1970 incorporated many of Pound's desired corrections as governed by views outlined by Kenner in a letter to Laughlin of 15 October 1968:

My opinion is that one should leave Ezra's text alone unless one is *quite* sure his intention does not surpass one's perception. He frequently feeds one language through another, as in the Jap spellings in *Cathay*, to indicate a chain of transmission. Which is to say that while I have no special knowledge of the details you mention in 113, I should be inclined to back your inclination to tell *New Yorker* to leave 'em alone. Better the author's error, if errors they be, than someone else's.[38]

In a letter to Laughlin, Hesse later concurred, and in a long, detailed examination of problems arising from her translation of *Drafts & Fragments* that outlines a number of possible errors and traces them through earlier cantos (18 June 1975), she concludes: "These many small slips should I think be considered as reflecting the element of human error in the *Cantos* as a dimension of the poem; nothing much is gained by correcting them."[39]

Involvement in Correction Procedures

Concerted efforts toward correcting the text had been going on for some long time, however. Fang had offered to work on the Chinese Cantos, and Pearson sent on queries based on annotations collected by his graduate students, with the common goal of a "definitive" edition. Pound welcomed the idea in a letter of 11 March [1953], so long as he was free to accept or reject suggested changes.[40] He even outlined a methodology for gathering possible corrections at Yale and proposed a committee to Kenner who reported the names to Laughlin on 20 December 1953: "[Hugh] Kenner, [Roy Harvey] Pearce, [Norman Holmes] Pearson, [Clark] Emery, [D. D.] Paige, [Guy] Davenport, OP [Omar Pound], [Achilles] Fang, [John] Idlet."[41] After the publication of *Section: Rock-Drill* (1955) Hesse became increasingly involved, and Mary de Rachewiltz, Pound's daughter, contributed lists to the common pool that derived from translation exercises with her father. Robert Mayo, editor of *The Analyst* (1953), and John Edwards, who edited the *Annotated Index* (1959), were consulted, and Reno Odlin sent in a number of queries and suggestions. E.P. himself dictated a very long list of corrections to Olga Rudge which is dated 10 December 1963. Views differed, however, as to which existing texts were the most accurate, not to mention ongoing conflicts between concepts of historical accuracy and creative revision as well as those concerning uniformity of presentation and the acknowledgment of variable traditions. Fortunately, there was a consensus of opinion that many of the corrections offered were doubtful and all queries should ultimately be referred to the author.

There can be no doubt that Pound long wanted a corrected and copper-bottomed text. On 28 December 1955 Laughlin wrote to Eliot:

> He told me lots of fascinating things about the structure of the Cantos which I had never known before. He says now that there will be between 100 and 120 of them, probably 112, and there is every indication that he is working hard on them. At some point, he wants us to do a completely new edition of them because there are so many variations and errors in our present texts.[42]

On 29 January [1956] Pound complained to Pearson:

> Some urge toward a correct edtn/ of Cantares/ WITH Fang's ideog/s in margin of Chink Canters, still keep on finin errors/ Faber qt/ gk/ Canto 39 p. 202 three errors. Damn all I cant spend my time readin what I HAVE writ/ got to pay some attention to the FURTHER devilUPment of the poEM.[43]

Efforts to complete the project continued into 1963, but had already peaked around 1958 when the new edition seemed imminent. Throughout this period New Directions had been limiting their print-run and only corrected the most obvious errors. More problems arose than had been solved, however, and the successful completion of the project seemed further off than ever. Even Pound's enthusiasm sometimes waned, and on 17 June 1958 MacGregor wrote to Fang:

> J. Laughlin is just back from Washington and reports that Pound seems quite exhausted with the decisions of life, and he thinks it would be a mistake for me to send [E.P.] questions about the revisions in the new printing. I am going ahead, therefore, and getting a few changes in hand, as well as the errata list and then I will just tell him what I am doing.[44]

On 9 September [1959] the poet was again ready to tackle the problems and wrote to Pearson:

> everyone I suggest to do work seems disqualified to receive practical support. My last suggestion was fellowship to do thesis on actual articulation of at least some of the sources of canto facts ANDH/ not

as retrospect but as FIELD for further clarification of history/ such as in Rouvere on Medici Bank. Would there be any chance of a grant or fellowship for ME, to sort out such books as Memorie Istoriche, La Zecca e la Moneta di RIMINI. Bologna 1789. Salmasius, etc. The, I suppose unique, greek with latin translations, of Martial done for Lorenzo dei Medici in 1480. etc.[45]

No grant was forthcoming, nor was an application for support from the Bollinger Foundation for a scholarly project to establish a corrected text of *The Cantos* pursued (1963). It was, of course, rather late in the day to coordinate the disparate researches and studies that had already taken place, or even to settle on a single base text to which all other versions might be compared. From the correspondence now available Pearson seems to be the only scholar who specifically mentions the need to go back to setting copy. On 19 November 1963 he wrote to Laughlin:

Hugh's suggestion of a formal committee and a grant is a sound one—given at least three contingencies: (1) that Ezwroh really assist (there[,] even a little help is better than none, and he does seem to be in an amiable mood; (2) that Mary [de Rachewiltz] would assist, for the mss are left to her; (3) that the mss of the Cantos at Brunnenburg would be made available at some point or other. Nothing can be more important than the establishment of the text of the cantos, which was my aim when I thought I had Ez keen on it. He agreed to answer queries, but soon lost interest, & was often quixotic. We agreed also to designate the lineage in terms of true lines versus run-overs because of the size of the page, so that a definitive lineation could be determined. but he never did get to this; and I admired his determination to plan ahead rather than to contemplate and revise. The problem of correcting actual factual mistakes is a difficult one. The problem of correcting his frequent Greek and Chinese characters seems more pedantic to him than to others. Gradually I came to rely on Mary [de Rachewiltz] and the excuse of her translations to solve the problems with him as she came to them. These problems will probably always remain, but need be no bar. I am happy to help in any way that seems best suited to the goals and the tactics of arriving at them. I am happy to go to Ezra, but would have no confidence in complete and definitive results.[46]

In the end Pearson silently withdrew from the project, and Kenner's views as outlined to Laughlin in a letter of 17 December 1963 emphasize its basic unfeasibility:

> no one seems to realize how far your fifth printing and the Faber Seventy Cantos can have crept apart. I'm pretty sure, for instance, though I can't be certain without access to Faber copies, that the English text of the Lerici has been set from one of the Faber versions, whereas Mary [de Rachewiltz] made her translation from a New Directions copy! The sheets of EP's corrections which you sent me as from Olga [Rudge] illustrate another kind of lost labor; Ezra was going through your second printing, though at least some of those errors were caught midway through your second printing. . . . Mary got rid of a lot of [errors] in Lerici by simply going back to the sources, and prevailing upon EP to accept her findings. I take it Eva [Hesse] has been doing work of this kind, too. And lots of other people have, also. I should follow the principle that many of the errors are just plain errors: for instance the unpronounceable Greek word on the first page of XXII (corrected in Lerici), where the printer has mistaken a capital Upsilon for a gamma. But there are lots and lots of borderline cases that should be referred to EP.[47]

Earlier, Laughlin had written to Hesse (30 October 1963):

> I guess Ezra has never really cared about such details. Perhaps this is because in old manuscripts and texts things are spelled so many different ways, and he feels that if the general meaning gets through, that is enough. Nevertheless, I do feel that we must do our best to try to make things right for him. I think that it is a very good idea that you should "vet" the final corrections list, even after Kenner has been over it, careful as he is. I wish there were some way that we could all get together, the whole "correction committee," and then send a delegate to Ezra to work out the final answers to problems.[48]

Different lists of problematical readings that had been accumulated from various sources over so long a time were finally conflated by Laughlin and entered into a copy of the New Directions collected edition. The "committee" never met, but Laughlin visited Pound in Venice and later reported to Jay Martin (15 November 1965):

The Task of getting things corrected has advanced not at all because Ezra just cannot concentrate on the corrrections suggested by various experts. I tried to get answers when I saw him in Venice last January, and it was painful. He would stare at the page where the correction was marked for a long time, without answering and then just start turning pages aimlessly.[49]

Progress toward a "definitive" edition had been undermined from the beginning by contradictory intentions and inconsistent methods; it was ultimately doomed, however, by Pound's indifference. The plan failed, but the process of emending the text continued, and according to Barbara Eastman, some two hundred and thirty-six changes were incorporated in the printings from 1970 to 1975.[50] The majority of them, however, can be traced to corrections authorized by the poet himself. There are, of course, a number of changes that were introduced at that point, as well as later, that are obviously problematical, not to mention questions that have arisen over the authorization of *Drafts & Fragments* (1968).

Authorization of *Drafts & Fragments*

Both Peter Stoicheff and Ronald Bush take the view that Pound was, perhaps, something of a pawn in the effort to publish the last gathering of cantos,[51] and there can be no doubt that the publication was spurred on by a pirated edition of work in progress (*Cantos 110–116*. New York: FUCK YOU/ Press, 1967). The story has already been rehearsed in great detail, but the shifting pattern of Pound's intentions certainly deserves more documentation. Up to the point of his release from St Elizabeths he had been in a highly creative phase and on 5 December [1958] wrote to Pearson: "Cantos won't be finished until my demise, shd/ always reserve possibility of death-bed swan."[52] He seems to have been preoccupied very much with work in progress and wrote to Eliot on 12 January [1959]:

> There are some fragments of Cantos 110–116, that I wd/ like you to guard from destruction if necessity arises. one line at least that: Wyndham accepted blindness rather than risk having his mind stop. I DO need a few months to work in. An amiable photographer so relieved to hear that the Cantos are a failure, and that they or A canto hadn't a form that I cd/ define at that particular moment in state of exhaustion. Of course that will go out as authorized, timeless, universal. You

might at least note that there are at least elements of form, progress, design.[53]

From a letter written to Laughlin on 24 November [1959] it is clear that Pound had not altogether set his mind against publishing: "Nor shd/ later Cantos be released until Thrones has had time to operate."[54] As early as 31 December 1959 Kenner commented to Laughlin: "I heard a rumor a while back that Canto the last was to be 117, on which reckoning one more volume should do it."[55] Long before the 1967 piracy that led to the publication of *Drafts & Fragments,* a number of periodical publications from work in progress had been authorized by Pound himself:

Periodical	**Canto**
Threshold ([Spring?] 1962)	CXV
Paris Review (Summer/Fall 1962)	From CXV, CXVI
Agenda (March/April 1963)	Notes for CXI
National Review (10 September 1963)	*From* CX, *From* From CXII, *From* CXIV, *From* From CXV, Notes for CXVII et seq. [a]
Agenda (December/January 1963/1964)	[Reprinted from *N.A.*]
Agenda October/November 1965)	From CXV

Different versions of the variously named poems were also published as well as selections therefrom, but they were all released by Pound himself, or at least with his blessing. Note that the poet specifically authorized the publications of Canto 115 as revised (1965). Elsewhere I have asserted that the *Threshold* version of Canto 115 (1962) was selected from among Pound's papers by his daughter and sent for publication while he was undergoing treatment at a private clinic in Merano,[56] but it now appears that Pound himself had given a copy of that text to Desmond O'Grady who had been commissioned to pass it on to Professor Roger McHugh of University College, Dublin, then guest editor of *Threshold.* Laughlin had suspected all along that O'Grady had functioned as intermediary and so held the lines taken from that text and later entitled Canto 120 as published in *Anonym* (Spring? 1969) to be authoritative. From the specific comment in his letter to Eliot [12 January 1959], and the fact that different versions or excerpts were published, Pound's active engagement in the creative process cannot be doubted.

Interim, there were also a number of unauthorized periodical publications:

Periodical	Canto
Poetry (October/November 1962)	CXIII
Niagara Frontier Review (Fall 1965/Spring 1966)	CX, CXVI
Anonym (1969)	CXX

Laughlin, for example, supplied *Poetry* with a text for their fiftieth anniversary issue,[57] but the history of the other two publications remains something of a mystery. The pirated pamphlet, *Cantos 110–116* (1967), falls between the *Niagara Frontier* and *Anonym* printings, yet only the former periodical publication could have had an effect on the decision to authorize *Drafts & Fragments* (1968).

On 1 March 1968 Laughlin wrote formally to du Sautoy:

> The cable above mentioned had chiefly to do with the possibility of a book of "Canto fragments." I had written Ezra about the piracy here, and pointed out that if we could do an official book, even a limited edition, it might help stop more of that sort of thing. His reply indicates that he sees some merit in this plan, and now he has asked me to send him copies of all the texts of the fragments which I have, so that he can look them over, and I have done so.[58]

A few days later (6 March 1968) he wrote more spontaneously to Kenner:

> Ezra seems to be a little bit more peppy lately. I've had several notes from him, and I believe he is actually bestirring himself to try to put the "Canto Fragments" in shape for a temporary book, hopefully to head off any more piracies like the disgusting ED Sanders mimeographed effort, did you see that? A shameful business.[59]

The effective relationship between publisher and text, however, is made clear in a Laughlin letter to J. P. Lippincott and Co. of 7 May 1968:

> As you know, ever since that miserable Sanders piracy of Pound's "Canto Fragments." I have been pushing Ezra to try to get the material that he has completed so far in shape so that we can publish a

proper book here and get some decent copyright protection for it. I
now hear from him in Venice that the work is proceeding, though it
is slow, because his eyes are in bad shape. It sounds as though what
we will get will be about twenty to thirty pages of the portions of
Cantos 110 to 117 which he has completed. So I think we will have
to have some title such as "A Draft of Cantos 110 to 117." There is
precedence for this title as the first 30, when they were first done here,
were titled "A Draft of Thirty Cantos." Were it not for the acute
copyright problem, I would say that a limited edition was indicated
for this, but I feel it is important to get the book out widely so as to
stop more piracies. So I guess I will have a very small book and David
will just have to figure out some way to make it "bulk." It could be
suggested that this material could simply be added at the back of the
big "Cantos" volume, the way we will be doing with "Thrones." now
that that is out of stock as a separate book, but this could not happen
quickly enough, for our copyright purposes, since we have nearly a
two year supply of the big "Cantos" in hand, and also it would not
get the special edition that we want to head off piracy. I couldn't
really put it into this catalogue anyway because I wouldn't know how
to describe it till I see what I get. Sorry I didn't know about this the
other day, when we had our meeting, so that we could discuss the
problem. I just learned this morning that he was actually working on
getting the stuff in shape, pursuant to my request. I hope this won't
make too many complications for you all down there, please let me
know if you think of a better way to handle it.[60]

At the same time and with Pound's participation, Laughlin was
attempting to place revised or uncopyrighted texts in various periodicals.
Most noteworthy, perhaps, is the revision of the pirated Canto 116 and
the first periodical publication of "Notes for CXVII et seq." The autho-
rized version of Canto 116 was not merely a function of a literary-award
reprint, but also involved Pound's active interest in correcting the *Nia-
gara Frontier* text that had been set from an unrevised draft.

Publication	Canto
American Literary Anthology. New York, 1968	CXVI
Stony Brook (Fall 1968)	CXIV

New Yorker (30 November 1968)   *From* CXIII
Sumac (Winter 1969)   Notes for CXI, Notes for CXVII
                                                       et seq. [c]

Pound himself submitted setting copy for *Drafts & Fragments,* answered editorial queries, and corrected proof sheets. He even agreed to add an earlier fragment under a title suggested by Laughlin, "Addendum for C," although he originally wanted it incorporated into Canto C. Explaining the problem to Kimberly Merker, who was editing the Stone Wall Press limited edition, Laughlin lamented (27 June 1968): "If he wants now to attach it to Canto 100, that gives us a bit of a problem with our title. I hope we can persuade him just to have it at the back, among the fragments, with some indication that it eventually belongs with Canto 100[.][61] When *Drafts & Fragments* was added to the collected edition in 1970, the last line of the text as authorized by the poet was "To be men not destroyers."

From the evidence at hand it would appear that the author had always been reasonably in control of the text, even in the case of *Drafts & Fragments.* It is true that he had been seriously unwell for sustained periods after his release from St Elizabeths, but it is equally true that there were other periods of creative activity such as was prompted by the encounter with Donald Hall in 1960, or spurred on by the Ed Saunders piracy in 1967. Indeed, there were a number of different versions or drafts of those poems published under the title *Drafts & Fragments,* but such had always been the case. The manuscript archive at the Beinecke Library contains hundreds of pages of rejected drafts (Pound called them "inedits"), and he had always been in the habit of mining that material and reworking selected lines or passages into later poems. The ups and downs of his declining health do give occasion for a good deal of speculation, but there is no concrete evidence that the poet acted against his will. In fact, he had been at some pains to publish various versions of work in progress before as well as after the various piracies. Whether his creative and critical faculties at that time were impaired is quite another matter, and one that must be left to the aesthetic judgment of the reader.

Textual criticism, on the other hand, must necessarily deal with the actual witnesses on hand and the historical facts as we know them. In *The Cantos* we have a text in which the initial creativity and composition is neither compromised nor diminished by a long and careful process of relatively minor revision and correction. The present edition (ND, 1989), however, does not represent the ideal text its author had in mind, but rather suffers from printing error, editorial oversight as well as interference, and the loss or omission of corrections/revisions actually stipulated by Pound himself. Written evidence of authorial intention as well as of editorial interference abounds. The decisions to be made in creating a new reading text need not be subjective, and, even in those few cases where documentation is not available, enough precedent exists to guide necessary choices in a coherent and consistent manner. Even though the present edition is nothing so corrupt as has often been suspected, a revised reading text could eliminate error and unauthorized emendation, as well as restore last revisions and corrections. Once a variorum edition, containing all variant readings and relevant documentation, is available, that final step can be taken.

NOTES

1. D. F. McKenzie, *Bibliography and the Sociology of Texts* (London: The British Library, 1986), 29.
2. Michael Groden, "Contemporary Textual and Literary Theory," *Representing Modernist Texts, Editing as Interpretation,* ed. George Bornstein (Ann Arbor: University of Michigan Press, 1991), 271.
3. Unpublished letter, Faber and Faber, London.
4. Unpublished letter, Faber and Faber, London.
5. Unpublished letter, Lilly Library, Bloomington: Pound, II.
6. See Barbara Eastman, *Ezra Pound's CANTOS: The Story of the Text, 1948–1975* (Orono, ME: National Poetry Foundation, 1979), 35.
7. See Jerome McGann, *The Textual Condition* (Princeton, NJ: Princeton University Press, 1991), 21.
8. Unpublished letter, R. A. Gekoski.
9. Unpublished letter, James Laughlin.
10. Unpublished letter, James Laughlin.
11. See unpublished letters of 24 March and 3 April 1953, Lilly Library, Bloomington: Pound, II.
12. Unpublished letter, New Directions, New York.
13. Unpublished letter, Beinecke Library, New Haven: Pound, I.
14. Unpublished letter, New Directions, New York.
15. Unpublished letter, James Laughlin.
16. Unpublished letter, James Laughlin.
17. Unpublished letter, James Laughlin.
18. Unpublished letter, Lilly Library, Bloomington: Pound, II.
19. Unpublished letter, Lilly Library, Bloomington: Pound, II.
20. Unpublished letter, James Laughlin.

21. Unpublished letter, James Laughlin.
22. Unpublished letter, Beinecke: Pound, I.
23. Unpublished letter, Faber and Faber, London.
24. Unpublished letter, Beinecke Library, New Haven: Pearson, Pound.
25. Unpublished letter, James Laughlin.
26. Unpublished letter, New Directions, Norfolk.
27. Unpublished letter, James Laughlin.
28. Unpublished letter, James Laughlin.
29. Unpublished letter, New York Public Library: Berg, Pound.
30. Unpublished letter, Vanni Scheiwiller. "Canti 90–95, per la disposizione del righe teste sulla pagina la differenza di spazio fra le righe ha un importanza forse lo DOPPIO che è lo solo possibile sulla machina da scrivere/ dev' essere ridotto a 1 1/2. NON cosi, lo doppio. Hudson esaggerava colle prime bozze del 85. Credo che numeri arabici 85 senza *CANTO* 85 sarebbe preferibile ai numeri ROMANI LXXXV/ quando ci arriva a LXXXVIII/ troppo. Ma questo lascio al gusto del Mardersteig . . . in ogni caso bisogno che io vedo bozze in forma finale, o quasi . . . non preoccupare che Leocothoe, sta scritta in due modi/ Leucothoe. sta bene. Kádmon Thugater, lo stesso. Mi diverte col GRANDE dizionario greco/ gli accenti stanno in tanti modi, che nemmeno un pignolo osarebbe pontificare sulla scelta. . . . 90/5 qualità musicale etc/ indicata tipograficamente. quindi disposizione dei versi etc. piu complicata . . . se il 88 deve essere nel centro, o a sinistra/? etc/ come avete un gran tipografo, sentiamo il SUO opinione . . . piu tarde/ a cause del grande ideogramma LING, Canto 85 e il verso eqiziano/ credo che i numeri staranno meglio a sinistra, che nel mezzo."
31. Unpublished letter, Vanni Scheiwiller. " Bozze arrivate/ tante grazie per assidue cure/ specialmente dove hai trovato errori. Ma in alcuni punti CITAZIONI non sono esercizii grammaticali. Donna che VOLGO (citazione d'un Canzoni) più tarde "Tolg*o*"/. "volge" falsifica/ altri punti minor importanza le parole latine devano mantenere raporti con un contesto non presentato/. Canz/ della fortuna/ Io son la donna che VOLGO. L'ortografia FISSA appartienne a certe epoche non ad altri. Certi casi non volgono la penna di cambiare il metallo già composto. etc. Ma ti ringrazio da cuore per correzioni degli errori, il Hudson per essempio stava per rovinare un verso abandonando il dialetto della citazione. Spero che lasciarano la mia correzione. e non insisteranno sull'ortografia del lessicone. . . . Dove non ho niente contrario io ho lasciato i tuoi emendementi o correzioni. Ringraziandovi, Variazione Leucothoe, Leucothea/ fatto con intenzione. Fa come ti piace/ ma per me non vale la penna di incommodare Mardersteig per uniformare Riccardus et Richardus, etc. perchè nel Meedioaevo NON si osserrava questa uniformità. L'idea dei poeti dei prima secoli è un po falsificato quando i testi sono cinquecentizzati etc. Ma io non sono fanatico nel domandare questa diversità in ogni punto. Fai come TI piache, salvo nei casi dove io fattto indicazione in inchiostro."
32. Unpublished letter, New Directions, Norfolk.

33. Unpublished letter, Beinecke Library, New Haven, Pound, I.
34. Unpublished letter, Harry Ransom Center, Austin: Pound Correspondence.
35. Unpublished letter, Harry Ransom Center, Austin: Pound Correspondence.
36. Unpublished letter of 9 February [?1955], Beinecke Library, New Haven: Pearson, Pound.
37. Unpublished letter, Beinecke Library, New Haven: Pearson, Pound.
38. Unpublished letter, New Directions, Norfolk.
39. Unpublished letter, New Directions, Norfolk.
40. Unpublished letter, Beinecke Library, New Haven: Pearson, Pound.
41. Unpublished letter, Beinecke Library, New Haven: Pound, I.
42. Unpublished letter, James Laughlin.
43. Unpublished letter, Beinecke Library, New Haven: Pearson, Pound.
44. Unpublished letter, New Directions, New York.
45. Unpublished letter, Beinecke Library, New Haven: Pound, I.
46. Unpublished letter, Beinecke Library, New Haven: Pearson, Pound.
47. Unpublished letter, New Directions, New York.
48. Unpublished letter, New Directions, Norfolk.
49. Unpublished letter, New Directions, Norfolk.
50. See Eastman, *Ezra Pound's CANTOS*, 35–36.
51. See Stoicheff, "The Composition and Publishing History of Ezra Pound's DRAFTS AND FRAGMENTS," *Twentieth Century Literature* 32, 1 (Spring 1986), 78–94 and Bush, "'Unstill, ever turning' The Composition of Ezra Pound's DRAFTS & FRAGMENTS," *Ezra Pound and Europe,* ed. R. Taylor and C. Melchior (Amsterdam: Rodopi, forthcoming).
52. Unpublished letter, Beinecke Library, New Haven: Pearson, Pound.
53. Unpublished letter, Faber and Faber, London.
54. Unpublished letter, James Laughlin.
55. Unpublished letter, New Directions, Norfolk.
56. See "Reconstructing Ezra Pound's CANTOS," *Ezra Pound and America,* ed. Jacqueline Kaye (London: Macmillan, 1992), 143.
57. See Taylor, "Towards a Textual Biography of THE CANTOS."
58. Unpublished letter, New Directions, New York.
59. Unpublished letter, New Directions, Norfolk.
60. Unpublished letter, New Directions, New York.
61. Unpublished letter, New Directions, Norfolk.

10

Afterword: *Ubi Cantos Ibi America*

Mary de Rachewiltz

Some questions that seemed important to me before and during the 1989 conference "A Poem Including History: *The Cantos* of Ezra Pound," which was sponsored by Yale University, have in the meantime become obsolete or been satisfactorily addressed by the papers and in conversations at the time.

A few mea culpas might be in order. For instance, the fetish of the first draft, the first printing, has sometimes led me into error. Thus for the text of Canto 72 in the 1983 limited edition printed by Mardersteig, I decided upon *s'affascia*. It made sense. It had several strata of meanings and echoes. I was called to task. Impressed with the "new" theory that what counts is the ur-text, I changed it for the 1985 Mondadori edition, substituting *s'affasca*, a word that doesn't exist in the Italian language—or at any rate I've been unable to discover it in any dictionary or author. There's no reason why poets shouldn't invent words, and it sounds okay. But it's wrong.[1]

Later I saw a notebook, previously unknown to me, that seems to contain the first handwritten draft of Cantos 72 and 73 as well as the famous unfinished translation into English by the poet himself. One surprise in the translation is the awkward phrase "unlids itself." For an Italian who knows the hymn "Fratelli d'Italia" (Brothers of Italy), written in 1847 by Goffredo Mameli, it echoes his line "Si scopron le tombe, si levan i morti" [The tombs are uncovered, the dead are rising]. For such a reader "unlids" makes sense, though I don't see that it adds anything to the English, nor that it relates to *s'affascia*. Not that future generations, or even today's younger one, will care about either the subtleties of the verb *fasciare* of the Fascist fascio, or its agrarian links. They'll *far d'ogni erba un fascio* (indiscriminately bundle weeds with wheat). Perhaps the technical terms referring to radio waves will survive: *onde affasciate, onde a fascio.* But the important points are these: *(a)* that Pound wrote Cantos 72 and 73 in Italian and the connections that resonate for him would occur only to someone who does *not* think in Italian, and *(b),* that these two cantos belong in their proper sequence before *The Pisan Cantos.*

A similar problem is the baker/barber boy in Canto 62. In his first version—"erroneous version"—Pound had conflated the Italian *Risorgimento* with the American "revolution." In the one case it was a baker's boy who threw the first stone at the oppressors. In John Adams's text, it was a barber's boy. Pound eventually gave in to scholars and in later printings, out of boredom perhaps, he amended it to read:

> and in this case was a
> barber's boy ragging the sentinel.

The weight of the historical fusion into a poetic image now rests exclusively on the phrase "in this case," implying that there were other cases. These may be minor details. But when, in *Drafts & Fragments,* the word *anthesis* replaces *antithesis,* there is a world of ethical difference.

Whenever I have tried to emend contradictions, I have discovered that Pound had been aware of them all along, that the "fault" was in me, and not in the author who was merely trying to work out his poem in public. This proclivity applies to his texts, to his political and economic theories, and to his private life. It was "a poem written in public," as Hugh Kenner has said. My primary concern is that nothing be lost, nothing distorted: a matter of imagination, rather than philology.

A variorum edition would be a help and in fact is needed. Yet we must keep and extend a "persistent awareness." Richard Taylor's argument that "a critical edition must be based on a scholarly reconstruction of the poem's chronological development as well as on a careful consideration of both its inherent nature and its relationship to social context" is reassuring, but the right angle may be missing:[2]

> Acquit of evil intention
> > or inclination to perseverance in error
> to correct it with cheerfulness
> > particularly as to the motives of actions
> of the great nations of Europe.

> (Canto 62)

I do not intend or expect to convert anyone, but Pound's motives, I believe, can be seen more clearly if we curb a tendency to chop and change and cut down to worm size. In other words, I invoke "magnanimity," even from philologists who may not see eye to eye with the poet's record of what *he* saw and heard and felt. Ronald Bush's reading of *The Pisan Cantos,* based on a careful textual history of their genetic development, is an example of openness and largesse of interpretation that emerges from a sustained act of philological attention.

Let me turn directly to the subject raised by my title, which might be translated: "Wherever we find *The Cantos,* there we find America." It is intended as a protest against, or rather an exhortation to, those who have misread and rejected *The Cantos* as America's epic. In 1946, after his second visit to St. Elizabeths Hospital, Charles Olson wrote to me: " 'Tell Mary,' he said as I was leaving, biting a smile, 'I am not repulsive.' " Yet students still ask me: why does Pound have such a bad reputation? Why are *The Cantos* not read more widely? Because of the multilingualism? Because of the ideology? Or is it simply because we do not yet know how to read them and how to teach them, although we know how vital, how enriching, the interaction of languages and races can be?

Perhaps one should address the "economic" virtue of *The Cantos.* I mean that intangible something that can be called *sovereignty,* even, if a pun may be allowed, *pontification.* More seriously, I mean the holiness of a poem's sacrificial function. Whether the etymology of this word is *pons* (a bridge) or *puntis* (a sacrifice), Pound fits both: "not the priest, but the victim" (Canto 74, Canto 78). From the beginning he had set out to build a bridge over *worlds.* When his mother prodded him into writing an "Ode to the West," he resented and resisted the idea. And yet the *West,* the hugeness of its spaces asking to be cultivated, was always there. He fled to Europe and in fact never traveled very far into the vastness of America. Nevertheless, America grew inside him, and he enriched it—just as Adams and Jefferson and Otis enriched New England and Virginia with European rice and vines and law codes and Greek types.

But let us stick to economics, another kind of economics. The Ezra Pound archive came to Yale thanks to the generosity of an anonymous donor and the moral and financial support of a few enlightened friends. Donald Gallup has told the story in *Pigeons on the Granite.* Yet I have the impression that, although the Pound archive is constantly on demand, it does not serve its purpose as well as it should; the "Center" did not hold (i.e., the Center for the Study of Ezra Pound and His Contemporaries), and the material reality of the manuscripts of *The Cantos* is often neglected.[3]

For years I was under pressure about the "Pisan Notebooks," repeatedly told that *The Cantos* could not be read or understood if these manuscripts were not instantly made available to scholars. James Laughlin, to whom they had been entrusted, had to exert great caution and patience with me. When he finally relinquished them, I immediately deposited them in the Beinecke Library, and shortly afterward they were made available to scholars. But when I came to see them again, they no longer looked like the material I had handed in. They had undergone radical preservation—please do not think for a moment that I don't realize the need for conservation—they had lost their aura of frailness and tragedy. A facsimile edition of them in their original state had never been printed, and in fact they have been almost forgotten by researchers who had previously claimed they were the most important and even, in financial terms, the most valuable manuscripts of the century.

Now if the National Endowment for the Humanities or the like were to fund a comprehensive textual edition of *The Cantos,* including facsimiles, we might do for Pound what the recent Frankfurt edition has done for Hölderlin. If *The Cantos* had a wider circulation, and were more widely taught in schools, students would be better educated. Pound himself would have insisted on a good reading text: large pages, space that allows for slow reading and the accumulation of notes, something affordable to students, perhaps one that does not differ greatly from what we have grown up with.

In using the expression "Ubi Cantos Ibi America," I do not mean to suggest that the poem is fixed in geographic space or in time. We can learn a lesson from Lorenzo Valla's original phrase, which appears in the preface to his *Elegantiae* (circa 1455), "Magnum ergo Latini sermonis sacramentum est . . . ubicumque Romana lingua dominatur" [The great sacrament of the Latin tongue . . . is found wherever the Roman language continues to dominate], a phrase that Pound had already condensed in ur-canto III and quoted in the *Literary Essays* (220). Not only has the Roman Empire crumbled, but even the Latin tongue has now gone out of use.

Thus it may be precisely the multilingualism of *The Cantos* that sustains America. It is my firm conviction that Dante has done more for Italy than the various emperors, Garibaldis, or Mussolinis.

As for Canto 73, I am not afraid to get blown up by the mines laid, in this case, by brothers, the pedants who love neither Pound nor poets in general. What Pound has Cavalcanti's ghost say about Italy in 1945, I say of America today. Our image abroad must be redressed, and only a work as monumental and solid as *The Cantos* can withstand the monumental arms racket and obfuscation of history and culture.

Though we should not neglect the serious task of research and emendations of Ez-mendments, we also need a more fundamental spadework by expert scholars working in harmony. There's a need to correct the imago of the poet, the bad press, the irrelevant biographical information given in anthologies, the misinformation found in *The Companion to the Cantos*, as well as in my own notes to the bilingual edition, not to mention the mistranslations—these are all problems of transmission.

Above all, we need good teachers, people such as Professor Levy in Freiburg as portrayed in Canto 20, teachers who will puzzle over the meaning of a single word such as *noigandres*. For my part I have only questions, and rhetorical questions at that. I think it can be safely assumed that the last spontaneous "corrections" made by Pound himself were in *Thrones*, Canto 103. But in two copies at Brunnenburg his own handwritten corrections differ. He insisted that an "erratum" slip be enclosed, yet, in the later editions, the lines, in Canto 103, after "France after Talleyrand started" are still unclear.

It had been a distressing day when the first copy of *Thrones* arrived. At that time there was no telephone in the house, and, like a furious bull with a beehived head, Pound charged up the steep path to send a telegram, or make a phone call—I forget which—to Scheiwiller and Laughlin, the publishers.

Note 24 to Canto 103 in *The Companion* is unsatisfactory. The fact is that Pound himself was confused and realized he was confused, but passionately wanted to get it right. He knew he was not remembering details, had no time to reread all the history books he had underscored, and recheck his notebooks, the notebooks of *The Cantos*. I dwell on this incident to correct the impression that he was careless. I myself have contributed to the image by saying that he paid little attention to what edition he was using when we first worked together. But the point of emphasis was different then. In the early 1940s he was not concerned with revising his "drafts," but with teaching me how to translate them from English *and* to experience their sound in Italian.

By 1959–60, when Scheiwiller and I pestered him to adopt certain "corrections" in Cantos 1–30, he put up incredible resistance when faced with the Italian texts we placed before his eyes. Here were the very books he himself had used as sources! (One feels so self-righteous when young, even if one's motives are pure.) The wrangle over Canto 21! Yet the line

"And the Sultan sent him his brother's assassin" did have his full approval.

The list of errors that Eva Hesse compiled should not have been mechanically incorporated by New Directions. It was meant to be submitted to Pound for verification. Similar lists had been compiled by others, among them John Drummond, Achilles Fang, and Norman Holmes Pearson. Hers, like theirs, was meant to call attention to specific questions, to be submitted to the poet himself—but after 1959–60 it was too late.

Something had happened: first freedom had proved fictitious; then had come illness and the loss of "youth," which had equally proved a mirage. In the sudden solitude, he saw through his crystal *umbilicus* that "other" Pound whom he did not like. "Outis," or Odysseus, was no longer "üper moron," beyond destiny. He was no longer master of his property, of his own work, and he no longer recognized *The Cantos*. *The Cantos* had achieved their independence, gone their own way, and no longer had need of him. He repeated, "A nuisance to have outlived one's own utility." One can't help hearing an echo of the youthful, "Go my songs . . ."

Silence remained his strength when the wave of physical and metaphysical fatigue came over him. He even said that he had not "chosen" silence, but that silence had taken possession of him. Is it therefore in silence that this poem should end? "Let the wind speak—that is paradise." Or: "To be men not destroyers." Or again: "To lead back to splendour." Who is to decide? A computer? The only thing that is quite obvious is that none of the "proposed endings" is an ending, neither the Chinese ideograms, nor the paean to courage. The latter, of course, must be retained.

Technically, the text of *The Cantos* up to *Drafts & Fragments* is one problem; *Drafts & Fragments,* as Stoicheff admirably shows in his essay (see pp. 213–31), is another. Yet a third problem comprises the various lines that may still be floating around. Indeed, even in 1958, when he was still vigorous and read the entire *Cantos* out loud, with gusto, with pride, without a trace of regret or intention to change anything, he found the desperate effort at mnemonics too strenuous, too painful, when faced with details, and the extreme condensation of Cantos 98 and 99. He used to repeat that he felt the wheels in his brain were missing a cog, and he even made drawings on the backs of envelopes and the like to illustrate his point. This I do not call madness or senility—simply fatigue. Wieland

Schmied called it *Erschöpfung* (exhaustion), and there is no appropriate English word for it.

The poem, as I said, had left him. The poem had left him when he realized that in the strict legal sense it no longer actually belonged to him. The action of the U.S. courts in judging Pound mentally incompetent—and thus legally no longer a responsible agent or entity—effectively stripped Pound of his will. And I mean this in several senses, not the least of which involves Pound's will and testament, in which he sought to transmit his literary property (and/or heritage) to his natural heir. The question of textual transmission is much in the forefront of the essays included in this volume, but the crucial issue of legal and *genealogical* transmission is perhaps an even more vexing question—at least to me. I mention it not out of personal bitterness (although I still grieve at the shattering effect it had on Pound), but simply to call attention to the effect it has had on the availability and archival disposition of materials that are directly relevant to the questions of textual criticism that have been raised. Some of this material still remains in private hands—fragments, as it were, "shelved (shored)" (Canto 8) against Pound's legal ruin. The poem, of course, belongs to the readers—in their mind indestructible. And its authority lies within the poem *itself. It* coheres all right: *read it.* And let's present the world with a readable, comprehensible, and comprehensive text.

EDITOR'S NOTES

1. Another variant in Pound's hand is "si fascia."
2. Quoted from an early ts. Cp. *Ezra Pound and Europe,* ed. J. Kaye (London: Macmillan, 1992), 145.
3. The author is referring to the Center for the Study of Ezra Pound and His Contemporaries, a group of scholars that hoped to design and execute a systematic program of research into the works and life of Ezra Pound. Its principal members included Donald Gallup, then curator of American Literature at the Beinecke Rare Book and Manuscript Library of Yale University, and Professor Louis Martz, then in the Department of English at Yale and Director of BRBL. The center was never formally incorporated nor disbanded; it was active from about 1975 to 1984.

11

A Statement from New Directions

New Directions Publishing Corporation

Because Griselda Ohannessian could not come to New Haven, she asked me to pass on a few remarks. With all due respect for your endeavors, she thinks it should be said that James Laughlin feels strongly—indeed very strongly and by association so do those working at New Directions—that Ezra Pound himself would not have wanted a quote-unquote corrected text to be established for his *Cantos*. The ND opinion, though we know it is not shared by some of you here, is that the intrinsic character of the work is constituted in part by the very things—the so-called mistakes and inconsistencies—that a scholarly editing of the text would alter. So, as a matter of principle and conviction, we intend to maintain the text as it now stands.

When and if a corrected text has been completed, New Directions would naturally give consideration to subleasing the rights for a cloth-bound scholarly edition or for computer discs, or even perhaps some other proposed format. Let us just repeat for the record: we differ with those scholars proposing a corrected text and believe such an edition to be contrary to what Pound personally would approve and that it would compromise the integrity of the *Cantos* as presently published under our imprint.

Peter Glassgold
October 20, 1989